LAST CHANCE
FOR VICTORY

Jubal Early's 1864 Maryland Invasion

by
Brett W. Spaulding

For my girls
Mary, Hannah and Kate

Contents

List of Illustrations

List of Maps

Acknowledgements

The concept of this book was prompted by frequent questions from visitors at Monocacy National Battlefield. Inquiries about small details or events that occurred during the campaign often required a good deal of research time. In order to quickly and accurately address these inquiries I decided to compile research papers covering the military campaign. Before long the papers began to multiply and as you might imagine the research project grew into the book that you are now holding. This experience was both enlightening and enjoyable, and enabled me to learn a great deal more about the campaign.

While researching and writing this book I received assistance from a number of people that I would like to recognize. I would like to thank the dedicated interpretive and volunteer staff of Monocacy National Battlefield, specifically Cathy Beeler, Chief of Resource Education and Visitor Services, Park Rangers Tracy Shives and Barbara Justice, Seasonal Park Ranger Mike Clarke and Volunteers Alan Duke and Mary Ann Heddleson. With their assistance I was able to locate valuable information and find the time to research and write the book. I would also like to thank Louise King for editing the material, which was by no means an easy task.

I would also like to extend a special thanks to Archeologist Tom Gwaltney who volunteered his time and expertise to create the maps. Without Tom's diligent work and patience it would not have been possible for the reader to visualize the events of the campaign.

I owe my greatest debt of gratitude to Gail Stephens. Gail is a valued member of the Volunteer-In-Parks program at Monocacy National Battlefield and a published author. Her insight, guidance and assistance enabled me to clarify details and made the entire project run smoothly. Without her help I would have truly been lost.

I would especially like to thank my wife, Mary, as well as my parents for their support and encouragement. This provided me with motivation throughout the entirety of the project.

This project was made possible in part by a grant from the National Park Service Capital Training Center and the National Park Foundation, the national charitable partner of America's National Parks.

LAST CHANCE

FOR VICTORY

Jubal Early's 1864 Maryland Invasion

CHAPTER ONE

SECURE THE VALLEY

In May of 1864, Union Lieutenant General Ulysses S. Grant launched a campaign in an attempt to destroy Confederate General Robert E. Lee's army. Grant practiced unrelenting warfare. He believed by continuously attacking and pursuing the Confederate army he would demoralize and physically defeat them while they exhausted their resources. This would, in turn, result in the defeat of Lee's army and end the rebellion of the southern states.

One part of the plan focused on the Shenandoah Valley in Virginia. In 1864 the Valley was one of the most important sources of supply for the Confederate army. Grant gave command of the West Virginia Department to Major General Franz Sigel. With an army of about 18,000 troops, Sigel was ordered to eliminate Confederate opposition in the Valley and cut if off from the Confederacy.

If successful, the Union would effectively cut off a major source of food and other supplies to Lee's army located near Richmond, Va. Although the productivity of the Shenandoah Valley had been greatly reduced by the constant presence of both Northern and Southern troops during the three years prior to 1864, it was still an important food source. Likewise, southwestern Virginia was a critical source of salt, iron and lead. Union occupation of the Valley would further reduce the resources that were extremely important to the war effort. Finally, taking control of the Shenandoah Valley would eliminate access to the Virginia & Tennessee (V&T) Railroad. This line was used to move men and supplies from southwestern Virginia to the Valley and from Tennessee to Richmond.

Sigel sent a portion of his army to southwestern Virginia to destroy the V&T Railroad at the New River Bridge and the salt works at Saltville, Va. At the same time, he moved up the Valley Turnpike to confront the forces of Confederate Major General John C. Breckinridge, former vice president of the United States, who commanded the Department of Southwest Virginia and was responsible for defending the Valley against Union forces. On May 15, 1864, Breckinridge defeated Sigel at the Battle of New Market. Sigel's defeated army fell back to Cedar Creek and the force sent into southwestern Virginia

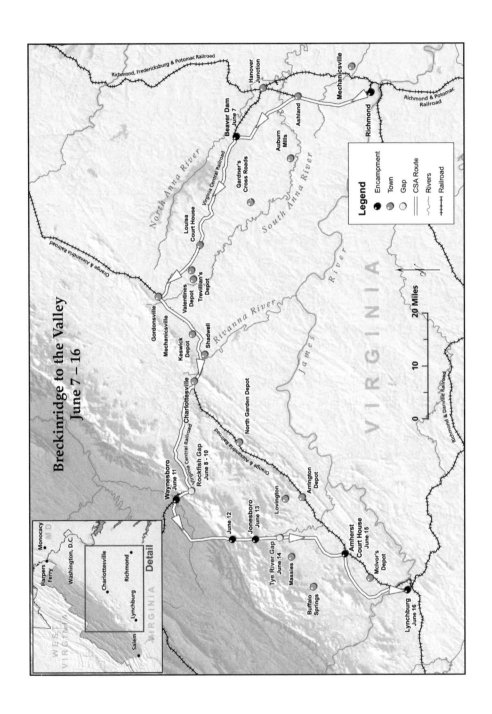

Breckinridge to the Valley
June 7 – 16

Legend
- Encampment
- Town
- Gap
- CSA Route
- Rivers
- Railroad

VIRGINIA

Detail

0 10 20 Miles

Mechanicsville
Richmond
Richmond & Potomac Railroad
Hanover Junction
Richmond, Fredericksburg & Potomac Railroad
Beaver Dam June 7
Ashland
Auburn Mills
Gardner's Cross Roads
North Anna River
South Anna River
Virginia Central Railroad
Louisa Court House
Orange & Alexandria Railroad
Gordonsville
Valentines Depot
Trevillian's Depot
Mechanicsville
Keswick Depot
Shadwell
Rivanna River
Charlottesville
James River
Rockfish Gap June 8 - 10
Virginia Central Railroad
North Garden Depot
Orange & Alexandria Railroad
Waynesboro June 11
June 12
Jonesboro June 13
Lovington
Arrington Depot
Tye River Gap June 14
Massies
Amherst Court House June 15
McIvor's Depot
Buffalo Springs
Lynchburg June 16
Richmond & Danville Railroad

Monocacy
MD
Harpers Ferry
Washington, D.C.
WEST VIRGINIA
Charlottesville
Richmond
Lynchburg
Salem
VIRGINIA

2

failed to do significant damage and retreated into West Virginia. With the Union army contained, Lee moved Breckinridge and most of his Valley troops to Richmond, where they joined the Army of Northern Virginia and strengthened the defensive lines. Breckinridge's army boarded railroad cars on May 19 and left the Valley defended by inexperienced and poorly armed troops under the command of Brigadier General William E. "Grumble" Jones.[1]

After Sigel's defeat, command was given to Major General David Hunter on May 19. Hunter began to move up the Valley on May 26 with orders to take Lynchburg and Charlottesville, Va., and destroy all supply lines. Lynchburg was an extremely important city to the south. It was a major manufacturing and hospital center, the key quartermaster and commissary area east of Knoxville, Tenn., and a major railroad terminus for the Orange and Alexandria (O&A) and the V&T railroads. On June 5, Hunter defeated Jones at the Battle of Piedmont. Jones' army was primarily comprised of cavalry, with very little infantry. During the engagement Jones was struck in the head by a bullet and killed instantly. The out-gunned and out-manned Confederates retreated up the Valley to Waynesboro, Va. Breckinridge, who was entrenched at Chickahominy, east of Mechanicsville, Va., received orders from Lee on the evening of June 6 to return to the Valley.[2]

Breckinridge to the Valley

After midnight on June 7, Breckinridge, who was disabled and unable to ride after a fall from his horse at Cold Harbor on June 3, marched his army from Chickahominy to the Confederate capitol, arriving in Richmond around 9:00 a.m. Here the army boarded trains and moved northward until they were forced to disembark at South Anna Bridge, which had been burned. From here they marched northwest to Beaver Dam Station and camped for the evening.[3]

---

1 Richard R. Duncan, *Lee's Endangered Left: The Civil War In Western Virginia Spring of 1864* (Louisiana State University Press, 1998), p. 74, 134-135; Joseph Judge, *Season of Fire: The Confederate Strike on Washington* (Berryville, Virginia: Rockbridge, 1994), p. 59

2 Jubal Early, *Narrative of the War Between the States* (Wilmington, North Carolina: Broadfoot, 1989), p. 370; Duncan, p. 259-260

3 R.A. Brock, ed. *Southern Historical Society Papers* Vol. XXII (Richmond, Virginia: The Society, 1894; Reprint, New York: Kraus Reprint Company, 1977), p. 295; Duncan, p. 250; U.S. War Department, *The War of the Rebellion: A Compilation of the Official Records of the Union and Confederate Armies* (Washington, 1880-1901), Vol. 51, Series 1, Part 2, p. 982-983, 1020 (hereinafter cited as *OR* with references to volume, series, part and page)

Maj. Gen. John C. Breckinridge

The following day (June 8), trains were once again boarded and the movement resumed by rail. Breckinridge's army passed through Charlottesville and arrived in the Blue Ridge Mountains at the Blue Ridge Tunnel in Rockfish Gap. Hunter's army was located nearby in Staunton, Va. On June 9, the army remained in camp, and the next day Breckinridge moved his command about a half mile, ordered earth works dug for defense, and formed a battle line. He expected Hunter to attack as he moved on Charlottesville, but no attack was made.

Learning of Hunter's plan to march south on June 10, he believed that Lynchburg—not Charlottesville—was Hunter's objective. On June 11, Breckinridge moved his army to the west side of Waynesboro and camped around 11:00 a.m. At sunrise on the 12th, Breckinridge marched for Lynchburg. The army covered about 23 miles and bivouacked in a gap along the Blue Ridge Mountains. Early on the 13th the army marched some 20-odd miles until they bivouacked at Jonesboro, Va. They marched a couple of miles to the Tye River and camped for the night on the 14th. Another long march was undertaken on the 15th when the army marched roughly 20 miles. They passed the town of Glasgow and made camp a few miles from Amherst Court House.[4]

Breckinridge reached Lynchburg about 10:00 a.m. on June 16 after marching about 14 miles. The army passed through the city and camped west of the fairgrounds. In Lynchburg, Virginia Military Institute cadets, local militia and an invalid corps were added to Breckinridge's army. Since May the cadets had taken part in the Battle

---

4   George S. Morris, *Lynchburg in the Civil War* (Lynchburg Virginia: H.E. Howard, 1984), p. 41; CPT Rufus J. Woolwine, 51st VA, Diary, June 12-15, 1864, Woolwine Papers, Virginia Historical Society (VHS); 51st Virginia Regiment Record Book , Echols Division, June 12-15, 1864, VHS

of New Market, ordered to Richmond, then back to Lexington, driven out of that city by Hunter, and finally ordered to help defend Lynchburg. Breckinridge's army and new additions were placed in a line of battle covering roads leading from the southwest; during the next two days the army made preparations to defend the city.[5]

Reinforce the Valley

Major General Braxton Bragg, military advisor to Confederate President Jefferson Davis, contacted Davis on June 10 and stressed the importance of expelling the Union force from the Valley. Bragg sent a message to Davis saying, "If it could be crushed, Washington would be open to the few we might then employ." Lee acknowledged the advantage of defeating the Union army in the Valley and removing the threat, but he was reluctant because the effort would require an entire corps and he did not wish to commit at least 25 percent of his army to the operation. Additionally, he feared that by detaching such a large force, he would leave the defenses of Richmond too weak to withstand an assault by Grant.[6]

Unwilling to yield the Valley, Bragg contacted Davis again on June 12. He wrote, "The dispatches from western Virginia induce me to invite your attention again to the inadequacy of our forces in that section." Breckinridge's army had taken considerable losses at the Battle of Cold Harbor. When he arrived in the Valley and united with Jones' troops, his army only consisted of about 5,000 infantry and 4,000 cavalry troops.[7]

Lee changed his mind late on June 12 and called for Confederate Lieutenant General Jubal Early, commander of the II Corps, who had replaced Lieutenant General Richard S. Ewell on May 28. (Ewell retired from active field duty on that date due to failing health. Early was promoted to lieutenant general on May 31.) Lee ordered Early to join forces with Breckinridge, strike Hunter's army in the rear and, if possible, destroy it. Early would have to decide if it was feasible to move down the Valley, and, if possible, capture Washington. Early was directed to immediately return to Richmond if this could not be accomplished. The capture of Lexington and burning of former Vir-

---

5   Woolwine, Diary, June 16, 1864, VHS; 51st VA Record Book, June 16, 1864, VHS; Absalom J. Burrum, Thomas' Legion, Diary, June 16, 1864, East Tennessee Historical Society (ETHS); *OR*, 37, s. 1, pt. 1, p. 91

6   *OR*, 51, s. 1, pt. 2, p. 1003; Clifford Dowdey and Louis H. Manarin, *The Wartime Papers of Robert E. Lee* (Boston: Da Capo Press, 1961), p.775

7   *OR*, 37, s. 1, pt. 1, p. 758; *OR*, 51, s. 1, pt. 2, p. 1002

ginia Governor John Letcher's home and the Virginia Military Institute on June 12 probably hastened Lee's decision to reinforce the Valley. Ultimately, Lee sent Early due to the threat of Hunter capturing Lynchburg.[8]

Hunter to Lynchburg

The day after the Battle of Piedmont (June 5), Hunter moved his army about 10 miles on a very slow and cautious march to Staunton, entering the city around 1:00 p.m. Hunter waited for about 10,000 reinforcements from the armies under Union Brigadier Generals George Crook and William W. Averell. They had been operating in southwestern Virginia against the V&T Railroad and the salt works. They arrived in Staunton on June 8. This provided Hunter with an army of about 18,000 troops. While in the city, the Union army captured and paroled about 400 sick and wounded Confederates. The commissary and ordinance stores were distributed among the troops or destroyed. The wagon shops, storehouses, depot, woolen factory, government stables, steam mill, railroad tracks, telegraph and a bridge were all burned. The time it took Hunter to march to Staunton and bivouac allowed the Confederates to evacuate their stock, destroy bridges and block the roads.[9]

LOC

Maj. Gen. David Hunter

On June 10, the Union army broke camp and marched for Lexington with two infantry divisions (Generals Jeremiah C. Sullivan and Crook), two cavalry divisions (Generals Alfred Duffie and Averell),

8 Early, p. 371
9 Charles R. Williams, *The Life of Rutherford Birchard Hayes* (New York: De Capo, 1971), p. 223; LTC Charles G. Halpine, Diary, June 6-7, 1864, Folder 191, Halpine Collection, Huntington Library, San Marino, CA (HL); *OR*, 37, s. 1, pt. 1, p. 95-96, 153

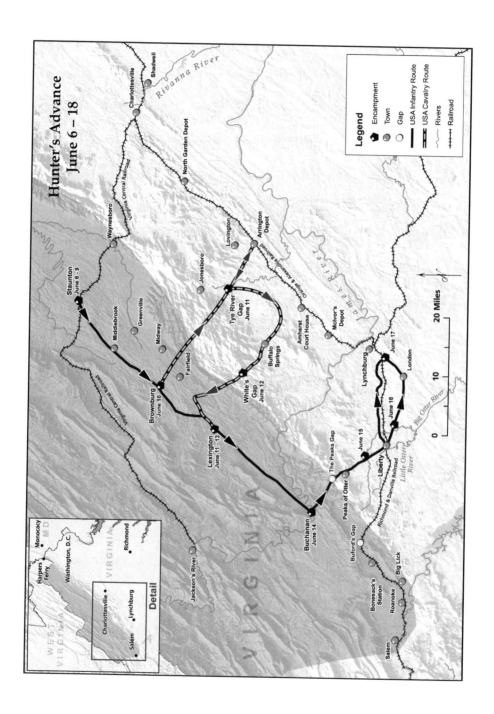

Hunter's Advance
June 6 – 18

Legend
- Encampment
- ● Town
- ○ Gap
- ━━ USA Infantry Route
- ┅┅ USA Cavalry Route
- ～～ Rivers
- ┽┽┽ Railroad

Shadwell

Rivanna River

Charlottesville

North Garden Depot

Virginia Central Railroad

Waynesboro

Lovington

Jonesboro

Arrington Depot

Staunton
June 6 – 9

Middlebrook

Greenville

Midway

Fairfield

Tye River Gap
June 11

Buffalo Springs

Orange & Alexandria Railroad

Amherst Court House

McIvor's Depot

Virginia Central Railroad

Brownburg
June 10

White's Gap
June 12

Lexington
June 11 – 13

Lynchburg

London

June 17

June 16

June 15

Liberty

The Peaks Gap

Buchanan
June 14

Peaks of Otter

Jackson's River

VIRGINIA

Richmond & Danville Railroad

Little Otter River

Big Otter River

Buford's Gap

Big Lick

Bonesack's Station

Roanoke

Salem

20 Miles

0   10   20

Detail

WEST VIRGINIA

MD

Harpers Ferry

Monocacy

Washington, D.C.

VIRGINIA

Richmond

Charlottesville

Lynchburg

Salem

7

and eight batteries consisting of four guns each for a total of 32 artillery pieces. With such a large force, Hunter split his army and ordered Sullivan to take one route while Crook and Averell took another, paralleling each other in a southerly direction. The march covered 25 miles on the pikes, with Crook and Averell skirmishing nearly the entire way. Hunter accompanied Sullivan's division, which was unopposed as they passed through the towns of Middlebrook and Brownsburg, Va., and camped for the night near the latter. Confederate Brigadier General John McCausland, with a brigade of cavalry, slowed Hunter's advance to Lynchburg by burning bridges, blocking roads with stones and felled trees, as well as attacking and harassing the army.[10]

As Hunter's army proceeded south, Duffie was ordered east over the Blue Ridge Mountains to attack the Charlottesville-to-Lynchburg railroad. This would isolate Lynchburg from Charlottesville and delay any reinforcement's en route from Richmond. On June 11, they crossed the Tye River Gap and encountered a Confederate wagon train full of supplies. Six wagon loads of food stuffs were taken, while the remaining wagons containing stores, Confederate bonds, currency and other documents were burned. Later in the afternoon a detachment of 11 men was sent to destroy Arrington Depot. The depot was burned and four small bridges and about five miles of track were destroyed. It took the Confederates two days to repair the railroad. The next day the division intended to destroy Amherst Court House, but while en route they received orders to meet the army at Lexington. They proceeded up Piney River and encountered about 300 Confederate cavalrymen. A brief engagement ensued, with a number of Confederate prisoners taken. Duffie's command continued the movement, passing through Buffalo Springs, and after bivouacking at White's Gap, arrived in Lexington on the 13th. The damage to the railroad by Duffie accomplished very little, and the line was repaired within a few days.[11]

On June11, Hunter's army reached Lexington after a 15-mile march. They found the Confederates well posted in defensive positions and supported by artillery. While they engaged the Confederates, Averell led a brigade of cavalrymen, joined by an infantry brigade

10 George W. Baggs, 36th OH, Journal, June 10, 1864, Charles Goddard Papers, VHS; Halpine, Diary, June 15, 1864, HL; R.A. Brock, ed. *Southern Historical Society Papers* Vol. XXX (Richmond, Virginia: The Society, 1902; Reprint, New York: Kraus Reprint Company, 1977), p. 280; Judge, *Season of Fire: The Confederate Strike on Washington*, p. 79; *OR*, 37, s. 1, pt. 1, p. 96, 120; Duncan, p. 234
11 Duncan, p. 231-232; Judge, p. 79, 88-89; Morris, *Lynchburg in the Civil War*, p. 39-40; *OR*, 37, s. 1, pt. 1, p. 97, 140-141

commanded by a Colonel Carr B. White, on a flanking movement to the west of the city across the North River. As soon as the Confederates discovered the flanking movement, they retreated from the area. This left Lexington open to the Union army's depredations.

The next day (June 12), Hunter ordered the home of former Virginia Governor John Letcher burned. Letcher had issued a proclamation that urged civilians to rise up and wage war against the Union. Hunter's aide-de-camp, Lieutenant Colonel Charles Halpine, wrote, "How I felt on seeing Gov. Letcher's family sitting out on the lawn on their trunks and furniture while their house was on fire beside them." Washington College was looted and the Virginia Military Institute also was burned, although the decision to do so was not backed by all the officers. Halpine wrote, "No seat of learning should be destroyed."[12]

Hunter was now about 40 miles away from his objective, Lynchburg. He moved with extreme caution and rested his troops for long periods while in the cities of Staunton and Lexington. He sent Averell to Buchanan, Va., on June 12, and the main body of troops left Lexington on the morning of June 14. They marched 24 miles and arrived at Buchanan around 6:30 p.m. On the 15th the army was delayed for most of the day when McCausland burned the bridge over the James River. The fire burned out of control and inadvertently destroyed a number of private residences.

After building a bridge for the artillery and wagons, they managed to cross the Blue Ridge Mountains at Peaks of Otter and bivouacked near Otter Creek after covering roughly 15 miles. On June 16, Hunter sent Duffie down Forest Road toward Lynchburg, while Crook destroyed the tracks of the V&T Railroad near Liberty and burned a few bridges. Averell continued to engage McCausland on the Salem Turnpike (also known as the Bedford Turnpike) and Sullivan followed in support. A distance of about 11 miles was covered before they camped near Big Otter River on the Forest Road.[13]

Early to Lynchburg

On the morning of June 13, Early's army, consisting of three divisions and two artillery battalions totaling about 9,000 men, left the defenses near Mechanicsville about 2:00 a.m. The army marched roughly 25 miles through the town and proceeded up the Brook Turn-

---

12 Halpine, Diary, June 11, 1864, HL; Baggs, Journal, June 11-12, 1864, VHS; Williams, *The Life of Rutherford Birchard Hayes*, p. 223; *OR*, 37, s. 1, pt. 1, p. 97, 120

13 Halpine, Diary, June 14-16, 1864, HL; Baggs, Journal, June 14-16, 1864, VHS; Williams, p. 224; Judge, p. 93; *OR*, 37, s. 1, pt. 1, p. 98-99, 111, 120, 132, 134

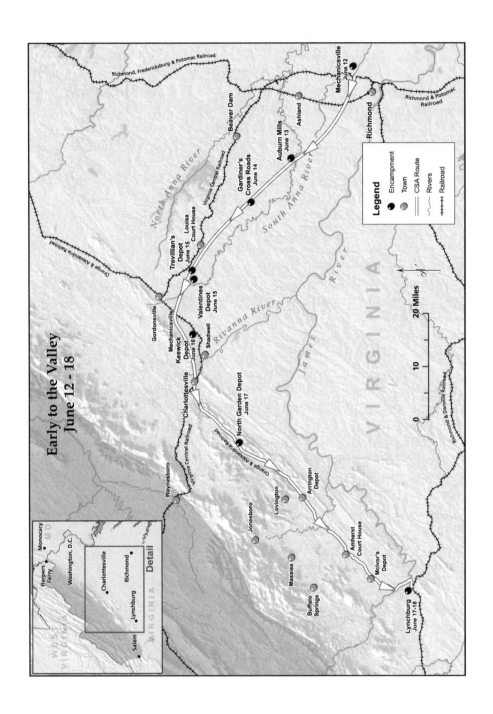

Early to the Valley
June 12 - 18

Legend
● Encampment
● Town
━━ CSA Route
〰️ Rivers
┼┼┼┼ Railroad

Mechanicsville
June 12

Richmond, Fredericksburg & Potomac Railroad

Richmond & Potomac Railroad

Richmond

Beaver Dam

Ashland

Auburn Mills
June 13

Gardiner's
Cross Roads
June 14

North Anna River

South Anna River

Virginia Central Railroad

Louisa
Court House

Trevillian's
Depot
June 15

Orange & Alexandria Railroad

Valentines
Depot
June 15

Gordonsville

Mechanicsville

Keswick
Depot
June 16

Shadwell

Rivanna River

James River

Charlottesville

North Garden Depot
June 17

Virginia Central Railroad

Orange & Alexandria Railroad

Waynesboro

Jonesboro

Lovington

Arrington
Depot

Massies

Buffalo
Springs

Amherst
Court House

McIvor's
Depot

Lynchburg
June 17-18

V I R G I N I A

Richmond & Danville Railroad

0   10   20 Miles

N

Detail

WEST
VIRGINIA

MD

Monocacy

Harpers
Ferry

Washington, D.C.

Charlottesville

Richmond

Lynchburg

Salem

VIRGINIA

pike through Yellow Tavern and Ground Squirrel Church, arriving at Auburn Mills on the South Anna River. The march resumed on the 14th, with Major General Stephen D. Ramseur's division in the lead, followed by the divisions of Major Generals John B. Gordon and Robert Rodes. The march covered roughly 20 miles and stopped near Gardner's Crossroads. The following day (June 15) Gordon's division led the army, followed by Rodes and Ramseur. It was another hard and long march, with the army covering some 25 miles, passing Louisa Courthouse to Valentines and Trevilian's Depot, where they bivouacked. On the 16th, the

LOC

Lt. Gen. Jubal Early

army took the Mechanicsville Road, and after a 22-mile march, stopped at Keswick Depot on the O&A Railroad. Each day's march was physically demanding, and the extreme heat, dust and distance broke many of the men down and forced others to ride in the ambulances.[14]

Breckinridge received a message from Early on June 16 at 11:40 p.m. instructing him to send all engines and cars of the O&A Railroad to Charlottesville, his army's destination that day. As soon as the cars arrived, troops would be loaded and sent to reinforce him at Lynchburg. When the cars arrived early in the morning on the 17th, they were boarded by Ramseur's division and one brigade and part of another from Gordon's division. After some delay the first of the troops set off after 8:00 a.m. and arrived in Lynchburg around 1:00 p.m.

---

14 *OR*, 51, s. 1, pt. 2, p. 974-975, 1012; CPT William Old, Early's Adjutant, Diary, June 13-16, 1864, Manuscript Division, Library of Congress (LOC); SGT Aaron L. DeArmond, 30th NC, Diary, June 3-16, 1864, Civil War Miscellaneous Collection, U.S. Army Military History Institute (USAMHI); J. William Jones, *Southern Historical Society Papers* Vol. 1 (Richmond, Va.: 1876), p. 373; CPT Cary Whitaker, 43rd NC, Diary, June 13-15, 1864, BR 662, Brock Collection, HL; CPT Buckner M. Randolph, 49th VA, Diary, June 13-16, 1864, Randolph Sec. 10, VHS; Henry Beverige, 25th VA, Diary, June 13-16, 1864, Duke University Library (DUL)

Mechanical problems delayed the arrival of the army. One engine broke down and a car from another train came off the tracks. The rest of Early's army, including Rodes' division, Nelson's and Braxton's batteries, and the remainder of the brigade and a half from Gordon's division, marched south along the railroad until they reached North Garden Depot and bivouacked for the night. The cars returned the next morning and the remaining infantry set off around 10:00 a.m. They arrived in Lynchburg between 3:00 and 4:00 p.m. on the 18th. The artillery and caissons were loaded on the cars while the empty carriages were hauled to Lynchburg.[15]

Battle of Lynchburg

Hunter's slow movement on Lynchburg allowed Breckinridge time to prepare a defense and gave Early time to reach the city. Hunter's army outnumbered Breckinridge's two-to-one. When Early's reinforcements arrived, the opposing forces were more equal, but Hunter still believed he was grossly outnumbered. Thus, Hunter's slow pace ultimately destroyed his best chance to take Lynchburg.

On June 17, Hunter's army was delayed for three or four hours at Big Otter River while a bridge was constructed to allow the artillery and wagons to cross. After overcoming this obstacle, Confederate Brigadier General John D. Imboden's cavalry brigade was engaged around 4:00 p.m. at Diamond Hill, about five miles from Lynchburg on the Salem Turnpike, and McCausland's cavalry brigade was likewise engaged with Duffie on Forest Road.

During a delaying action lasting about three hours, the Confederate cavalry was slowly driven back about two miles. One piece of artillery, a few caissons and a number of prisoners were captured by the Union in this engagement. As darkness fell and visibility deteriorated, fighting ceased. Hunter's army camped on the outskirts of Lynchburg in close proximity to Breckinridge's army.[16]

---

15 *OR*, 37, s. 1, pt. 1, p. 762-763; Old, Diary, June 17-18, 1864, LOC; Vernon Crow, *Storm In The Mountains* (Cary, NC: Cherokee, 1982) p. 80; Duncan, p. 266; Brock, ed. *SHSP* Vol. XXII, p. 295; William Beavans, 43rd NC, Diary, June 17-18, 1864, No. 3244, Manuscript Department, UNC; Whitaker, Diary, June 17-18, 1864, HL; SGM Joseph McMurran, 4th VA, Diary, July 17-18, 1864, Microfilm Reel Miscellaneous Nr 1316, Library of Virginia; Terry L. Jones, ed. *Campbell Brown's Civil War: With Ewell and the Army of Northern Virginia* (Louisiana University Press, 2001), p. 261

16 Baggs, Journal, June 17, 1864, VHS; CPT J. McEntee to Colonel (Sharpe), July 1, 1864, RG 393, E3980, AoP Miscellaneous Letters and Reports Received, NARA, Washington D.C.; Williams, p. 224; Halpine, Diary, June 16, 1864, HL; Judge, p. 96, 99; Brock, ed. *SHSP*, Vol. XXX, p. 289; *OR*, 37, s. 1, pt. 1, p. 99

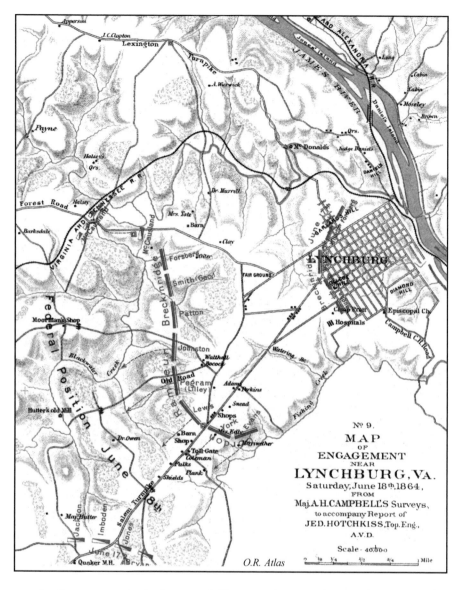

No. 9.
MAP
OF
ENGAGEMENT
NEAR
LYNCHBURG, VA.
Saturday, June 18th, 1864,
FROM
Maj. A.H. CAMPBELL'S Surveys,
to accompany Report of
JED. HOTCHKISS, Top. Eng.,
A.V.D.

Scale - 40600

O.R. Atlas

As the men rested, they could hear trains coming and going in the city. Early had devised a plan to use a switch engine to move train cars out of town and back again. Every time the train returned, Hunter's men heard citizens cheering, bands playing, bugles calling and drums beating in celebration of the arrival of imaginary reinforcements. The show led Hunter to believe the city had been heavily reinforced throughout the night of June 17.[17]

17 Judge, p. 101; Williams, p. 224; Morris, p. 46; *OR*, 37, s. 1, pt. 1, p. 99

As the Confederate cavalry was conducting its delaying action, Early arrived on June 17 and assumed command of the forces at Lynchburg. He found that defenses were constructed too close to the city and he ordered new defenses built about one and a half miles to the west. Early feared Union artillery and small arms fire would damage the town and hurt civilians. As Early's reinforcements entered the city, they were marched out past the fairgrounds and formed a battle line covering the routes of Hunter's advance. The brigade and a half of men from Gordon's division that came in on the first train were posted on the left of the Salem Turnpike. Ramseur's division was to the right of the turnpike, in the center of Early's line. Breckinridge's division (commanded by Major General John Elzey) was on the extreme right of the line near Forest Road, while the cavalry protected the flanks.[18]

Heavy skirmishing and cannon fire commenced on the morning of June 18. Hunter placed his cavalry on his flanks and the artillery between his two infantry divisions. After reconnoitering the area and receiving word that the Confederates had been reinforced, Hunter decided to attack the opposition's flanks. General Duffie was ordered to attack the Confederates near Forest Road with a cavalry division and two infantry regiments. Duffie engaged McCausland's forces on the right flank around 12:30 p.m. and successfully pushed them back to their defenses. Two additional charges were attempted to dislodge the Confederates without success. Duffie believed that he faced a superior force and held his position until he received further orders.[19]

Crook was sent to the right with orders to attack Gordon on the left flank, but this was found to be impracticable as there were no roads to their front and the undergrowth hampered the movement. Worse yet, the artillery could not be used and a very steep hill made it impossible to move farther to the right. The Confederates held a strong defensive position. Crook returned around 1:00 p.m. and was placed on the left of the Union line.[20]

Just then, the Confederates mounted an attack down the Salem Turnpike with hopes of turning the Union battle line on the right flank, where Crook had previously been positioned. The Union sharpshooters were driven back to the main line, but Sullivan's division was able

18 Crow, Storm In The Mountains, p. 80; Duncan, p. 271; *OR*, 37, s. 1, pt. 1, p. 765

19 Halpine, Diary, June 18, 1864, HL; McEntee to Colonel (Sharpe), July 1, 1864, NARA; *OR*, 37, s. 1, pt. 1, p. 99

20 Brock, ed. *Southern Historical Society Papers*, Vol. XXII, p. 296-297; McEntee to Colonel (Sharpe), July 1, 1864, NARA; Baggs, Journal, June 17, 1864, VHS; *OR*, 37, s. 1, pt. 1, p. 121, 130

to fend off the Confederates until Crook reinforced his position. Sullivan counter-attacked and pursued the retreating Confederates back to their entrenchments. Finding the entrenchments too strong and exposed to artillery and rifle fire, Sullivan's forces were compelled to fall back to a new line, where they remained until they received further orders.[21]

Hunter's Retreat

Hunter learned from captured Confederate soldiers that Early's corps was in Lynchburg. This information led Hunter to decide to retreat toward Salem, Va., around 4:00 p.m. on June 18. From Salem he would continue into West Virginia, abandoning the Shenandoah Valley entirely. He wrote in his official report:[22]

> It had now become sufficiently evident that the enemy had concentrated a force of at least double the numerical strength of mine, and what added to the gravity of the situation was the fact that my troops had scarcely enough of ammunition left to sustain another well-contested battle.[23]

Though Hunter was not outnumbered, he clearly believed his ammunition was running low. This, despite the fact that while in Lexington on the 11th, his army was overtaken by 200 wagons from Martinsburg, W.Va., containing commissary stores, clothing and ammunition. Hunter ordered the baggage and supply train to immediately prepare to fall back by way of the Salem Turnpike. With about five hours of daylight left, he decided to maintain a firm front and continue to press the line at all points. Darkness would mask the army's movement and hopefully provide a few hours head start before the Confederates would know they were gone. As darkness fell, the army began to quietly fall back, with the exception of a line of pickets that were ordered to hold their position until midnight, then follow the army.[24]

The order was executed without a problem; however, during the retreat roughly 85 wounded soldiers were mistakenly left behind in a

---

21 Baggs, Journal, June 18, 1864, VHS; Judge, p. 102; Halpine, Diary, June 18, 1864, HL; *OR*, 37, s. 1, pt. 1, p.112, 125

22 Halpine, Diary, June 18, 1864, HL; COL David H. Strather, Hunter's Chief of Staff, Report of Operations May 21-August 9, 1864, RG 94, Serial 70, Box NR 72A, Union Battle Reports, NARA

23 *OR*, 37, s. 1, pt. 1, p. 100

24 Williams, p. 225; Brock, ed. *Southern Historical Society Papers*, Vol. XXX, p. 290; Strather, Report of Operations May 21-August 9, 1864, NARA

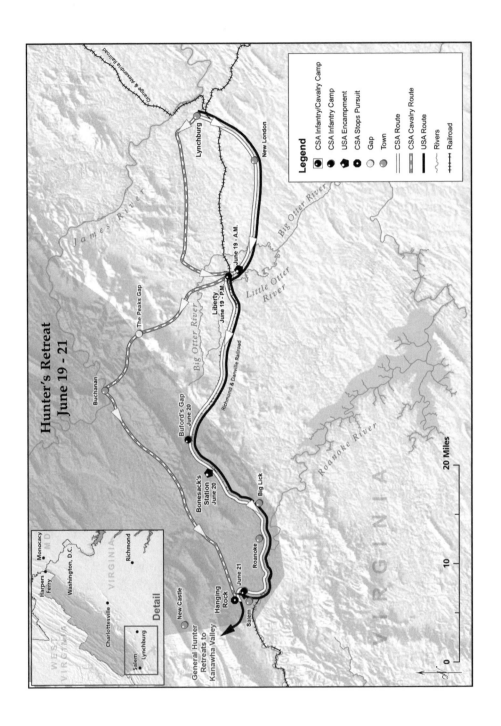

Hunter's Retreat
June 19 - 21

Legend

◉	CSA Infantry/Cavalry Camp
●	CSA Infantry Camp
♦	USA Encampment
◉	CSA Stops Pursuit
○	Gap
◉	Town
‖	CSA Route
▥	CSA Cavalry Route
—	USA Route
∿	Rivers
+++	Railroad

Lynchburg

New London

Orange & Alexandria Railroad

James River

Big Otter River

June 19 - A.M.

Little Otter River

Liberty
June 19 - P.M.

The Peaks Gap

Big Otter River

Buchanan

Richmond & Danville Railroad

Buford's Gap
June 20

Bonesack's Station
June 20

Big Lick

Roanoke River

Roanoke

June 21

Hanging Rock

Salem

General Hunter
Retreats to
Kanawha Valley

New Castle

VIRGINIA

Detail

WEST VIRGINIA

MD

Harpers Ferry

Monocacy

Washington, D.C.

Richmond

VIRGINIA

Charlottesville

Salem

Lynchburg

Salem
Lynchburg

20 Miles

0   10   20

N

temporary field hospital at Major George C. Hutter's barn. (Hutter was a former U.S. paymaster who resigned his commission when Virginia seceded, but did not join the Confederate army due to advanced age.) Early was informed that the Union army was in motion, but he did not know if they were retreating or planning an attack. His entire army was now in Lynchburg and he had planned to attack at first light. Now he would have to wait for further information before making a decision. At roughly 2:00 a.m., Hunter's army bivouacked about nine miles from Liberty after marching about 16 miles.[25]

Hunter's army remained in Liberty until about 2:00 p.m. on June 19 when the army resumed the march with Averell's cavalry left behind as the rear guard. Early was informed that Hunter had retreated in the early hours; at roughly 4:00 a.m. he ordered an immediate pursuit. Ramseur's division was the advance guard and started down the Salem Turnpike. After a 25-mile march, they reached Liberty around sunset. Skirmishers were sent forward and a brigade was deployed. After a brief engagement, Averell's cavalry withdrew through the town. Meanwhile, Hunter prepared the infantry for a Confederate attack about one mile west of town, but none came. Because of the late hour and long march, the Confederates bivouacked near the Little Otter River on the east side of Liberty.[26]

Around midnight the Union army left their battle line and resumed the march to Buford's Gap. They bivouacked about three miles west of the gap at Bonsack's Station on the morning of June 20. Early's army left Liberty at dawn and after covering 20 miles there was a skirmish with Hunter's rear guard that lasted through the afternoon until night. The Confederates bivouacked at the railroad near Buford's Gap. Later that evening, Bonsack's woolen factory and several other buildings were burned by Hunter's men, who marched through the night and arrived in Salem about sunrise on the 21st. The Confederates began moving out at about 4:00 a.m., with Rodes' division leading the army. After marching 17 miles, they bivouacked on the Lexington Turnpike. The entire march from Liberty to Salem along the V&T Railroad was marked by devastation, with bridges, water tanks, depot building, tracks and homes destroyed along the route.

25 Morris, p. 44; Baggs, Journal, June 18, 1864, VHS; Halpine, Diary, June 18, 1864, HL; OR, 37, s. 1, pt. 1, p. 160
26 Morris, p. 48; Baggs, Journal, June 19, 1864, VHS; Randolph, Diary, June 19, 1864, VHS; OR, 37, s. 1, pt. 1, p. 100-101; Walbrook D. Swank, ed. Stonewall Jackson's Foot Cavalry: Company A, 13th Virginia Infantry (Shippensburg, Pa.: Burd Street Press, 2000), p. 68; COL Thomas Toon, 20th NC, Diary, June 19, 1864, Thomas Toon Papers, North Carolina State Archives (NCSA); Woolwine, Diary, June 19, 1864, VHS

What items the Union soldiers could not carry off were destroyed, especially food. Other than some skirmishing with the rear guard, Early's army was unable to catch up with Hunter.[27]

Battle of Hanging Rock

When Hunter retired from Lynchburg on June 19, McCausland's cavalry was sent down the Lexington Turnpike to pursue him. They made their way to Liberty and arrived after dark, missing the engagement there. The following morning they were ordered to cross the Blue Ridge Mountains and proceed to Buchanan, which they reached about 4:00 p.m. There they would block Hunter's expected route of retreat down the Shenandoah Valley toward Martinsburg, W.Va., and force him to fight his way to safety. Hunter, however, was marching to Salem, making his way toward West Virginia. McCausland was out of position, and about 7:00 p.m. began to ride down the Buchanan Road to intercept the Union army.[28]

The cavalrymen rode through the night and came upon Union pickets three miles east of Salem on June 21. They drove the pickets back to the main body of Hunter's army and continued to engage the rear and flanks. Union baggage wagons and artillery were sent ahead on the New Castle Road to safety, but were inadvertently sent off without guards. McCausland took advantage of this mistake, and when the wagon train reached the entrance of Mason's Cove at Hanging Rock, he unleashed his troops and hit the rear of the train.[29]

Two batteries were attacked and 10 guns and caissons were damaged. The Confederates cut the harnesses to pieces, drove off or shot the horses, and damaged the wheels to the guns, limbers and caissons. There were also a number of casualties in the engagement before the Union cavalry arrived and drove the Confederates off. The carriages of two of the guns were repaired, but the remaining eight guns and their limbers and caissons could not be fixed. Before the Confederates could regroup for a second attack there was a huge explosion. Hunter's men blew up three of the caissons and threw the

27 Halpine, Diary, June 20, 1864, HL; Swank, p. 69; Randolph, Diary, June 20-21, 1864, VHS; Baggs, Journal, June 20, 1864, VHS; *OR*, 37, s. 1, pt. 1, p. 101; Strather, Report of Operations May 21-August 9, 1864, NARA; Judge, p. 107; Old, Diary, June 19, 1864, LOC; Jones, p. 265; Beverige, Diary, June 21, 1864, DUL; *OR*, 37, s. 1, pt. 1, p. 766
28 Jones, p. 265; J. Kelly Bennette, 8th VA Cavalry, Diary, June 19-20, 1864, Collection 886, UNC
29 McEntee to Colonel (Sharpe), July 1, 1864, NARA; MG David Hunter, Report of Operations June 8-July 14, 1864, Union Battle Reports, NARA; Jones, p. 265; Bennette, Diary, June 21, 1864, UNC

ammunition of the others into the river. The remaining eight guns were spiked and abandoned to prevent them from being used by the Confederates.[30]

Unable to close the gap between themselves and Hunter's army, the Confederates broke off the pursuit. Early felt that he would hamper his army's effectiveness for further operations if he continued to pursue Hunter, who was moving into the mountains. The tired and weary soldiers bivouacked after sunset about six miles north of Salem on the macadamized road to Lexington. The march from Lynchburg had been excessively hot and fatiguing. The army had also left Lynchburg with less than one day's rations. Early needed time to supply his army and prepare to execute his next objective after successfully defending Lynchburg and driving Hunter from the Valley. [31]

After the attack at Hanging Rock, Hunter continued to retreat toward the Kanawha River in West Virginia. He planned to make his way to the Ohio River and take steam ships to the railhead at Parkersburg, where he would use the Baltimore and Ohio (B&O) Railroad to move his army back to the northern end of the Valley at Martinsburg. Hunter's movement left the Shenandoah Valley virtually undefended, with only a few thousand Union troops located at Martinsburg and Harpers Ferry. Early would take advantage of this and invade the north. Hunter lost valuable time reorganizing, refitting and waiting for steamers to transport his army. A long drought had also lowered the water level on the Ohio River and created additional delays in moving the army back to Martinsburg. Hunter's army would not arrive back in the Valley until after Early had moved on Washington and crossed the Potomac River back into Virginia.[32]

In December of 1864, Hunter sent a message to Grant, and for unexplained reasons he blamed one person for his failure to take Lynchburg. Part of the message read:

> ...so I dashed on toward Lynchburg, and should certainly have taken it, if it had not been for the stupidity and conceit of that fellow Averell, who unfortunately joined me at Staunton, and of whom I unfortunately had at the time a very high opinion, and trusted him when I should not have done so.[33]

---

30 Duncan, p. 297-298; McEntee to Colonel (Sharpe), July 1, 1864, NARA; *OR*, 37, s. 1, pt. 1, p. 101; Bennette, Diary, June 21, 1864, UNC

31 Jones, p. 265; Woolwine, Diary, June 21, 1864, VHS; Randolph, Diary, June 13-16, 1864, VHS; Richard W. Waldrop, 21st VA, Diary, June 21, 1864, Manuscript Dept., UNC

32 *OR*, 37, s. 1, pt. 1, p. 102; Strather, Report of Operations May 21-August 9, 1864, NARA

33 *OR*, 37, s. 1, pt. 2, p. 366-367

Chapter Two

EARLY STRIKES NORTH

At Salem, Va., Confederate Lieutenant General Jubal Early broke off the pursuit of Union Major General David Hunter's army and on June 22 moved his headquarters to Botetourt Springs. Ramseur's division marched about four miles to the springs and bivouacked for the remainder of the day, while the rest of the army remained in their camps north of Salem. This was the first opportunity the army had to rest since leaving the Richmond area on June 13. During this time the soldiers drew about two days' rations, cooked, washed clothes and bathed while they waited for the wagons and artillery to catch up. Officers also attended a dance at Hollins Institute (a female seminary).

Early made the decision to proceed down the Valley and carry out the plan that Confederate General Robert E. Lee had devised to invade Maryland and attack Washington. Lee believed the capital was lightly defended due to Lieutenant General Ulysses S. Grant's removal of Union veterans from the defenses to the Richmond area. By attacking Washington, Lee hoped Grant would weaken himself by either moving troops north, opening himself to attack by Lee, or attacking with results that Lee believed would resemble Cold Harbor on June 3.[34]

While the army rested, the cavalry was sent to Fincastle, Va., to watch for Hunter's army. Early wanted to make sure that Hunter did not swing around and move back into the Valley north of his army at Lexington or Staunton. The cavalry troops reconnoitered the area

---

34 Jubal Early, *Narrative of the War Between the States* (Wilmington, N.C.: Broadfoot, 1989), p. 379; Charles C. Osborne, *Jubal: The Life and Times of General Jubal A. Early, CSA* (Chapel Hill, N.C.: Algonquin Books, 1992), p. 261; CPT William Old, Early's Adjutant, Diary, June 22, 1864, Manuscript Division, Library of Congress (LOC); Buckner M. Randolph, 49th VA, Diary, June 22, 1864, Randolph Sec. 10, Virginia Historical Society (VHS); William Beavans, 43rd NC, Diary, June 22, 1864, No. 3244, Manuscript Department, University of North Carolina (UNC); *U.S. War Department, The War of the Rebellion: A Compilation of the Official Records of the Union and Confederate Armies* (Washington, 1880-1901), 37, Series 1, pt. 1, p. 769 (hereinafter cited as *OR* with references to volume, series, part and page)

and reported that there was no indication the Union army was making its way back into the Valley.[35]

The army was up at daylight on June 23 and began marching at sunrise on the macadamized road toward Buchanan. Ramseur's division led the army, followed by the divisions of Gordon, Rodes and Breckinridge (whose division was commanded by Confederate Major General Arnold Elzey). The day was excessively hot and the terrain was very hilly, rocky and otherwise fatiguing. The army traveled about 20 miles before bivouacking a few miles southwest of Buchanan. Unable to use the bridge over the James River, which had been burned by Confederate Brigadier General John McCausland on June 15 to delay Hunter's advance on Lynchburg, Ramseur's division crossed the river and camped a few miles north of Buchanan.[36]

On June 24, the march to Lexington was resumed at about 3:00 a.m. The remaining divisions crossed the James River and a number of soldiers made a detour to see the Natural Bridge; a 90-foot-high rock formation spanning a 265-foot gorge. After the short sightseeing trip and a march of approximately 20 miles, Early's men arrived just south of Lexington and bivouacked for the night. Sergeant Richard Waldrop, 21st Virginia Infantry Regiment, described the day as "one of the hottest days I ever felt and as a natural consequence a good many men gave out on the way."[37]

On June 25, at about 3:00 a.m., Early's army passed through Lexington. While in the city, they paid their respects to Confederate Lieutenant General Thomas "Stonewall" Jackson. The men formed two ranks, the officers dismounted, and arms were reversed. As they passed Jackson's grave, they removed their hats and showed admiration for a beloved hero. J. Kelly Bennette, the assistant surgeon of the 8th Virginia Cavalry Regiment, described the sight of Jackson's grave in his diary, stating:

35 J. Kelly Bennette, 8th VA Cavalry, Diary, June 22, 1864, Collection 886, UNC; Achilles J. Tynes, 8th VA Cavalry, Letter, June 22, 1864, Accession #27936, Library of Virginia (LOV)

36 Richard W. Waldrop, 21st VA, Diary, June 23, 1864, Manuscript Division, UNC; CPT Cary Whitaker, 43rd NC, Diary, June 23, 1864, BR 662, Brock Collection, Huntington Library, San Marino, CA (HL); Henry Beverige, 25th VA, Diary, June 23, 1864, Duke University Library (DUL); Beavans, Diary, June 23, 1864, UNC; Randolph, Diary, June 23, 1864, VHS; CPT Rufus J. Woolwine, 51st VA, Diary, June 23, 1864, Woolwine Papers, VHS; OR, 37, s. 1, pt. 1, p. 766

37 Joseph Judge, Season of Fire: The Confederate Strike on Washington (Berryville, Va.: Rockbridge, 1994) p. 113; Randolph, Diary, June 24, 1864, VHS; Waldrop, Diary, June 24, 1864, UNC; Woolwine, Diary, June 24, 1864, VHS

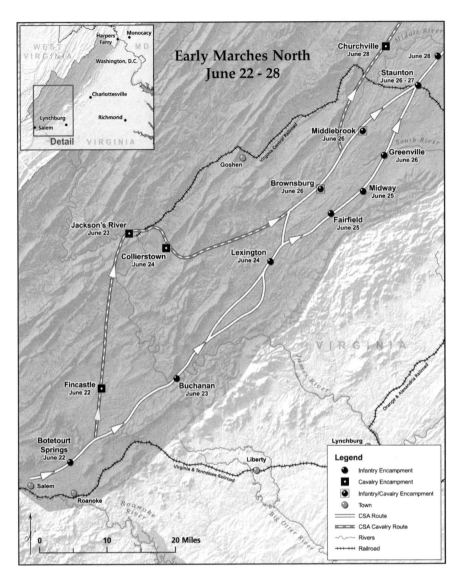

Early Marches North
June 22 - 28

Legend

- Infantry Encampment
- Cavalry Encampment
- Infantry/Cavalry Encampment
- Town
- CSA Route
- CSA Cavalry Route
- Rivers
- Railroad

[The] Yankees treat the grave of 'Stonewall' with a profound respect almost amounting to fanaticism. They did not touch the grave but they entirely destroyed the head and foot boards and nearly cut down the flag pole for mementos.[38]

When Hunter occupied the city (June 12-13), a guard was posted at Jackson's grave to ensure that no one desecrated it; however, souvenirs were taken from practically everything else.[39]

---

38 Bennette, Diary, June 25, 1864, UNC
39 Whitaker, Diary, June 25, 1864, HL; Randolph, Diary, June 25, 1864, VHS

After paying their respects to Jackson, the army resumed its march northward. Early split his force: Ramseur's and Gordon's divisions took one road, while Rodes' and Breckinridge's divisions took a parallel road. The march covered about 18 miles and ended in the evening, when Ramseur and Gordon bivouacked near the town of Fairfield. Rodes' and Breckinridge's divisions bivouacked near Brownsburg. The headquarters was established near the town of Midway. It was another scorching day that played havoc with the soldiers on both roads, causing many to fall out. Elzey (who commanded Breckinridge's division) was relieved of duty, citing medical reasons. He was replaced by Confederate Brigadier General John C. Vaughn.[40]

The march was resumed on the 26th at about 3:00 a.m. Ramseur's and Gordon's divisions passed through the towns of Midway and Greenville before they bivouacked about two miles south of Staunton. Rodes' and Breckinridge's divisions also started around 3:00 a.m. and traveled about 15 miles. They passed through the towns of Brownsburg and Newport, and bivouacked near Middlebrook. Waldrop described the day's march, "It was furiously hot all morning but we had a little shower in the afternoon, which cooled the atmosphere and made it much more pleasant." Early continued into Staunton, where he established his headquarters.[41]

The cavalry continued to reconnoiter the area as they rode north from Fincastle, still finding no indication that Hunter was trying to swing around in front of them. To avoid congestion with the infantry on the turnpike, the cavalry rode along parallel roads to the west and camped near Jackson's River on June 23. The next day (June 24) they continued down the Valley and camped near Collierstown, arriving at Brownsburg on the 25th. A few of the brigades continued to Middlebrook on the 26th, and all the cavalry regiments remained in camp until the morning of the 28th.[42]

On June 27, Early received a message from Lee asking whether the movement down the Valley and across the Potomac should be abandoned. Lee wondered whether Early's total force was large enough to carry out the mission. Early, however, believed his force was sufficient and that he faced no threat from Hunter. His message to Lee read, in part:

40 Woolwine, Diary, June 25, 1864, VHS; Old, Diary, June 25, 1864, LOC; Beavans, Diary, June 25, 1864, UNC; Waldrop, Diary, June 25, 1864, UNC; Early, p. 381
41 Whitaker, Diary, June 26, 1864, HL; Beavans, Diary, June 26, 1864, UNC; Woolwine, Diary, June 26, 1864, VHS; Randolph, Diary, June 26, 1864, VHS; Waldrop, 21st VA, Diary, June 26, 1864, UNC; J. Hotchkiss, Diary, June 25, 1864, Manuscript Div., LOC
42 Hotchkiss, Diary, June 25, 1864, LOC; Bennette, Diary, June 25-28, 1864, UNC

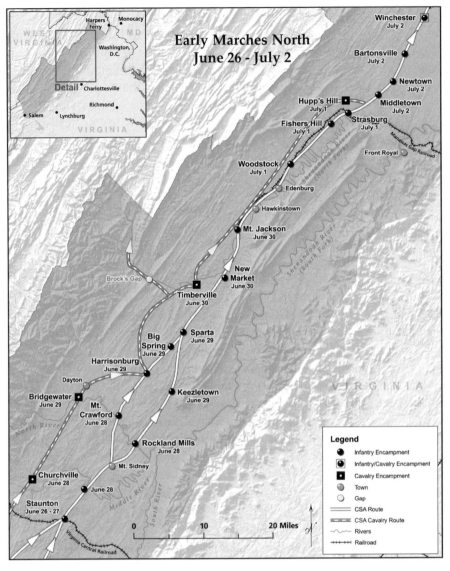

Early Marches North
June 26 - July 2

Legend
- Infantry Encampment
- Infantry/Cavalry Encampment
- Cavalry Encampment
- Town
- Gap
- CSA Route
- CSA Cavalry Route
- Rivers
- Railroad

[I have decided] to turn down the Valley and proceed according to your instructions to threaten Washington and if I find an opportunity – to take it. I think the circumstances form this movement. There is but a small force in the Lower Valley comprised almost entirely of 100 days men which is estimated roughly at from 1 or 2000 to 5000 men and I hear there is nothing at Washington but the same kind of men and not in large force.

Since Early felt he could continue, an addendum was made to the original plan. A select body of cavalry would be sent to cut the railroads between Washington and Baltimore, and between Baltimore and Philadelphia. This would slow reinforcements coming into Maryland. An effort would also be made by part of Early's cavalry to release Confederate prisoners from the Union prison at Point Lookout in southern Maryland.[43]

Rodes' and Breckinridge's divisions left Middlebrook at sunrise on June 27 and marched about 10 miles before they bivouacked about two miles southwest of Staunton. The army rested the rest of that day and made preparations to continue the march north. During this time, Early reorganized his force, reduced transportation and obtained provisions from Waynesboro that were sent by railroad.[44]

Early divided his army, giving Breckinridge a corps—consisting of his own division and Gordon's division—while Rodes' and Ramseur's divisions continued to report to Early. Breckinridge was also second in command of the army. Major General Robert Ransom commanded the four cavalry brigades and reported directly to Early. Confederate Colonel Bradley T. Johnson, who had arrived in Staunton with his battalion of Maryland cavalry, was put in command of the late Brigadier General William Jones' cavalry brigade and was promoted to brigadier general the following day (June 28). To expedite the movement, the wagon train was cut to a minimum, with Early's headquarters having one six-horse wagon and one four-horse wagon. Each division and brigade headquarters was permitted one four-horse wagon and one wagon for every 500 men to carry cooking utensils. The artillery had a number of cannons and horses unfit for the march that were left behind, so Early marched with three battalions of artillery.[45]

In addition to reorganizing his army, Early changed its name—from the II Corps, Army of Northern Virginia to the Army of the Valley District. The newly designated army was in desperate need of shoes, so before leaving Salem on June 23, Early ordered them, hoping they would arrive while he and his men were in Staunton. Unfortunately, the shoes had not arrived by the time the army resumed its march, so Early left wagons to transport these essential supplies.[46]

43 Early, p. 382; *OR*, 37, s. 1, pt. 1, p. 766-768; Jubal Early to Robert E. Lee, June 28, 1864, CW 100, HL

44 Randolph, Diary, June 27, 1864, VHS; Beavans, Diary, June 27, 1864, UNC; Whitaker, Diary, June 27, 1864, HL

45 Early, p. 381-382; J. William Jones, *Southern Historical Society Papers,* Vol. 1, (Richmond, Va.: 1876), p. 297; *OR*, 37, s. 1, pt. 1, p. 768; Old, Diary, June 27, 1864, LOC

46 Early, p. 381-382

After a much-needed but short rest, the army resumed its march on June 28. Gordon's division left about 4:00 a.m. and took the macadamized Valley Turnpike toward Harrisonburg. The remainder of the army did not leave until after 2:00 p.m. Breckinridge's division followed the route Gordon took, while Ramseur's division, followed by Rodes', turned off the turnpike at Mount Sidney and took the Keezletown Road, which paralleled the turnpike. After a march of about 18 miles, Gordon bivouacked near Mount Crawford. Breckinridge's men only made it a few miles out of Staunton before bivouacking near Middle River. Ramseur covered about 16 miles and bivouacked near Rockland Mills. Rodes' division camped about 7 miles north of Staunton on the Valley Turnpike. Imboden's cavalry brigade and a battery of artillery were ordered to go by way of Brock's Gap in the North Mountains to the Valley of the South Branch of the Potomac River. There they would destroy the B&O Railroad bridge and as many other bridges as possible between Cumberland, Md., and Martinsburg, W. Va. The remainder of Ransom's cavalry division passed through Brownsburg and Newport and bivouacked about one mile north of Churchville.[47]

The army was in motion again on June 29, another very warm day. Gordon started around 5:00 a.m. and marched about 18 miles, passing through Harrisonburg and bivouacking at Lacy's Spring (Big Spring). Breckinridge continued down the turnpike, covering roughly the same distance before stopping near Harrisonburg. Ramseur left around 4:00 a.m., covered about 16 miles, passed through of Keezletown, and camped at Carpenter's Hill near Sparta. Rodes' division also left around 4:00 a.m., turned off the turnpike down the Keezletown Road, and marched about 19 miles before they bivouacked beyond the town. Early had the headquarters camp established that night at Sparta. The cavalry proceeded from Churchville crossed North River and bivouacked north of Bridgewater.[48]

The final day of June was another warm and dusty day. Gordon's division led the order of march around 4:00 a.m., followed by

---

47 Randolph, Diary, June 28, 1864, VHS; Waldrop, Diary, June 28, 1864, UNC; Whitaker, Diary, June 28, 1864, HL; Beavans, Diary, June 28, 1864, UNC; Woolwine, Diary, June 28, 1864, VHS; Jones, *Southern Historical Society Papers*, Vol. 1, p. 375; 51st Virginia Regiment Record Book, June 28, 1864, VHS; SGM Joseph McMurran, 4th VA, Diary, June 28, 1864, Microfilm Room Misc. Nr 1316, LOV; Early, p. 382; Bennette, Diary, June 28, 1864, UNC

48 Hotchkiss, Diary, June 29, 1864, LOC; Randolph, Diary, June 29, 1864, VHS; Whitaker, Diary, June 29, 1864, HL; Waldrop, Diary, June 29, 1864, UNC; Woolwine, Diary, June 29, 1864, VHS; Bennette, Diary, June 29, 1864, UNC

Ramseur's division, which had returned to the Valley Pike. Gordon and Ramseur passed through New Market and camped north of Mount Jackson after traveling about 16 miles. Ramseur camped about a mile south of Gordon. Rodes' division also returned to the turnpike and bivouacked about a mile north of New Market. Breckinridge's division continued down the turnpike and bivouacked near New Market, while Early established his headquarters at Mount Airy, Va. Ransom's cavalry passed through Dayton, Harrisonburg and Timberville before they stopped for the night.[49]

By July 1, Early's infantry still had not encountered any opposition. It was another hot, dusty and tiring march. The divisions left their camps at Mount Jackson and New Market around daylight. Gordon led the march through Hawkinstown, Edenburg and Woodstock before establishing camp at Fisher's Hill, south of Strasburg. Ramseur camped about five miles south of Gordon's position. Both Rodes and Breckinridge passed through Mount Jackson on their way to Woodstock. Rodes camped about a mile south of the town and Breckinridge camped about a mile south of Rodes' position. Ransom rode through Woodstock and passed the infantry at Strasburg, bivouacking about two miles west of town on Hupp's Hill. The army traveled about 21 miles.[50]

July 2 was another furiously hot day. The heat and the length of the march—about 20 miles—resulted in lots of straggling. The army continued to press north and passed through the cities of Woodstock and Strasburg. Breckinridge bivouacked near Middletown, Rodes at Newtown, Ramseur at Bartonsville and Gordon near Winchester. The cavalry scouted ahead of the army and camped north of Winchester. When Early arrived at Winchester, he received a second message from Lee directing him to remain in the Valley until he was ready to cross the Potomac River and destroy the B&O Railroad and Chesapeake & Ohio (C&O) Canal to inhibit Hunter's return from West Virginia. Early had already taken measures to carry this out when Confederate Brigadier General John Imboden was detached on the 28th. During the evening McCausland was also ordered to take his brigade across North

---

49 McMurran, Diary, June 30, 1864, LOV; Beavans, Diary, June 30, 1864, UNC; Absalom J. Burrum, Thomas' Legion, Diary, June 30, 1864, East Tennessee Historical Society(ETHS); Hotchkiss, Diary, June 30, 1864, LOC; Randolph, Diary, June 30, 1864, VHS; Bennette, Diary, June 30, 1864, UNC

50 Randolph, Diary, July 1, 1864, VHS; Beavans, Diary, July 1, 1864, UNC; Burrum, Diary, July 1, 1864, ETHS; Woolwine, Diary, July 1, 1864, VHS; Waldrop, Diary, July 1, 1864, UNC; Bennette, Diary, July 1, 1864, UNC; Hotchkiss, Diary, July 1, 1864, LOC

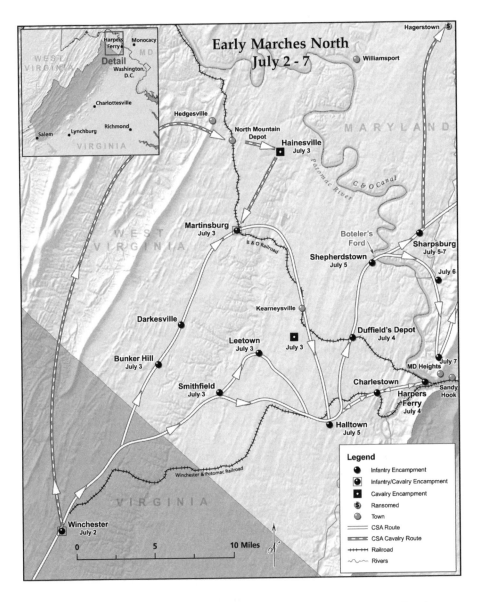

Early Marches North
July 2 - 7

Mountain, proceed down Back Creek, and burn the railroad bridge at the mouth of the creek before traveling from North Mountain Depot to Hainesville and continuing on the road from Williamsport to Martinsburg. Johnson's cavalry brigade was ordered to link up with McCausland at Hainesville.[51]

51 Waldrop, Diary, July 2, 1864, UNC; Woolwine, Diary, July 2, 1864, VHS; Randolph, Diary, July 2, 1864, VHS; Hotchkiss, Diary, July 2, 1864, LOC; Bennette, Diary, July 2, 1864, UNC; Early, p. 382-383

Union Situation

The veteran soldiers and artillerymen in the fort system around Washington had been sent to the Army of the Potomac to replace the enormous losses suffered by the Union army in the Overland Campaign. The campaign had left only invalids and inexperienced militia who were insufficiently trained to work the guns that protected the Union capital. The only Union force left in the Shenandoah Valley was the reserve division of former Valley commander Major General Franz Sigel. It consisted of a force of 100-days men—men who enlisted in the military for a term of 100 days—from the 135th Ohio, four companies of the 160th Ohio, and the 161st Ohio National Guard regiments, as well as a battery of six guns and 800 dismounted cavalry at Martinsburg. Sigel's command also included Colonel Mulligan with the 10th West Virginia Infantry Regiment; the 23rd Illinois Infantry Regiment; four artillery pieces, 700 dismounted cavalry and 600 cavalry at Leetown, W.Va.; Major General Julius Stahel with 600 cavalry on the Leetown Road near Darksville, W.Va.; and Brigadier General Max Weber with about 400 troops of the 5th New York Heavy Artillery Regiment at Harpers Ferry. The decision to remove the artillerymen from the capital had left Sigel in a vulnerable position. Should he need reinforcements, there would be few troops left in Washington.[52]

The Confederate movement had been reported to Sigel and Union authorities in Washington as early as June 28, but these accounts were dismissed. Confederate activity in the Valley was a common occurrence. On July 2, the severity of the situation was still unrecognized, but alarm began to rise. Sigel reported:

> There are strong indications of movement of the enemy in force down the Valley. Our cavalry met those of the enemy to-day at Winchester, and a number of refugees have arrived here who fled from that place, and say that Early with three divisions was moving toward Strasburg last night.

With continuous reports from refugees of 20,000 Confederates moving in his direction, Sigel chose to be cautious and sent a message in the evening to the President of the B&O Railroad, John Garrett, requesting 150 cars to evacuate the stores at Martinsburg. All available scouts and cavalry were sent to gather more information about the Confederate movement.[53]

---

52 *OR*, 37, s. 1, pt. 2, p. 4, 59; OR, 37, s. 1, pt. 1, p. 175; MAJ Theodore A. Meysenburg, Siegel's AAG, Journal, July 1, 1864, DUL
53 *OR*, 37, s. 1, pt. 1, p. 174-175; Meysenburg, Journal, July 3, 1864, DUL

There was still no alarm in Washington or Petersburg, despite the reports Sigel was sending. Union Lieutenant General Ulysses S. Grant ordered Hunter to send any troops he felt were unnecessary to hold the Kanawha Valley back to Martinsburg on the B&O Railroad, so they could operate from there to prevent a Confederate raid into Maryland. Hunter had already dispatched Brigadier General Jeremiah Sullivan's division, but they were not expected to arrive for another five or six days. Grant continued to believe Early had returned to Petersburg, but Breckinridge's location was a mystery.[54]

Maj. Gen. Franz Sigel

Martinsburg Evacuated

At roughly 11:00 p.m. on July 2, the Confederate cavalry with Early rode north. They passed through the towns of Middleway and Smithfield, W.Va. Shortly after sunrise, at about 5:00 a.m. on July 3, Johnson's cavalry brigade attacked the Union troops at Leetown while Confederate Major Harry Gilmor attacked the Union cavalry at Darksville. The plan was to have Johnson sweep around the east side of Martinsburg while Gilmor swept to the west. McCausland would ride along the road from the north. These combined actions were designed to cut off all lines of retreat for Sigel's army at Martinsburg.[55]

At Leetown, Mulligan was able to hold Johnson off until about 10:00 a.m., when they were severely pressed and forced to gradually fall back through the town to Kearneysville, W.Va. Gilmor drove the Union cavalry at Darksville back to Martinsburg, where

---

54 *OR*, 37, s. 1, pt. 2, p. 5, 8-9

55 Bennette, Diary, July 3, 1864, UNC; Meysenburg, Journal, July 3, 1864, DUL; *OR*, 37, s. 1, pt. 2, p. 20; Harry Gilmor, *Four Years In The Saddle* (New York: Harpers & Brothers, 1866), p. 186; Early to Lee, July 7, 1864, HL

Sigel continued to order the stores loaded for evacuation on railroad cars. At 9:00 a.m., a wagon train was filled with stores and ordered to Williamsport, Md. By 10:00 a.m., all rolling stock of the railroad was dispatched. As the wagon train moved up the road to Williamsport, it encountered trouble. McCausland captured a small guard at North Mountain Depot and continued to Hainesville where his brigade camped for the night, forcing the wagon train to turn back to Martinsburg. It would leave with the rest of the troops when Martinsburg was evacuated.[56]

By 11:00 a.m., Gilmor's cavalry was about two miles west of Martinsburg, destroying the railroad. At 11:30 a.m., it was reported that all remaining government stores, except for some forage, had been loaded and sent to Shepherdstown, W.Va. Anything that was not evacuated was ordered burned. All military personnel evacuated the town at roughly 12:00 noon on July 3; the sole exception was cavalry that followed at 1:00 p.m. Gilmor took possession of Martinsburg when the Union cavalrymen left.[57]

Sigel linked up with Mulligan's command at Kearneysville and together they marched to Shepherdstown. Sigel's force crossed the Potomac River at Boteler's Ford just south of Shepherdstown before midnight and took up a defensive position on the north side of the river bank to prevent the Confederates from following. In Petersburg, Grant continued to report that Early's corps was in front of him and the only possible threat to Sigel was Breckinridge and the remnants of the late Brigadier General William E. Jones' force. Union Assistant Secretary of War Charles Anderson Dana sent Stanton a message from Petersburg at 3:30 p.m. on July 3 that read:

> There is pretty good evidence that Early is now here, and all of Ewell's corps with him, but Breckinridge has not yet rejoined Lee's army. If he is moving down the Valley, as Sigel reports, it is possible that he may have with him 10,000 men of all sorts. Not more.[58]

While evacuating Martinsburg, Sigel contacted the Union Chief of Staff, Major General Henry Halleck, in Washington, for further instructions. Despite Hunter's failure to respond to any of Halleck's telegrams, Sigel was told to contact Hunter, advise him of the current situation and follow his orders. Halleck forwarded Sigel's message to

---

56 Hotchkiss, Diary, July 3, 1864, LOC; Meysenburg, Journal, July 3, 1864, DUL; *OR*, 37, s. 1, pt. 2, p. 16; Early, p. 384
57 Meysenburg, Journal, July 3, 1864, DUL; *OR*, 37, s. 1, pt. 2, p. 20; *OR*, 37, s. 1, pt. 1, p. 177-178
58 Meysenburg, Journal, July 3, 1864, DUL; *OR*, 37, s. 1, pt. 2, p. 15, 16, 20

Grant for his insight. Grant informed Halleck that if there was indeed a threat in Sigel's department, then Halleck could advise Sigel better than he could.[59]

The main body of Early's army moved at first light on July 3 and passed through Winchester on the Martinsburg Turnpike. About six miles north of Winchester, Ramseur's and Rodes' divisions turned off the turnpike and passed through Smithfield. Rodes bivouacked near the town and Ramseur bivouacked near Leetown. Early followed Ramseur and also camped near Leetown. Gordon's and Breckinridge's divisions continued down the turnpike toward Martinsburg. After the cavalry dispersed the remaining Union troops, Gordon entered Martinsburg late in the afternoon and bivouacked there with Gilmor's cavalry while Breckinridge stopped south of Bunker Hill, W.Va. Johnson's cavalry took part in a small skirmish near Shepherdstown in the evening before they fell back and camped between Leetown and Kearneysville. The army had covered a distance of about 25 miles.[60]

Harpers Ferry

At Harpers Ferry, Weber was desperately trying to ascertain the military situation. The last message he had received from Sigel was at 11:00 a.m. (July 3) when Martinsburg was being evacuated. All further attempts to contact him had failed. It was reported that a Confederate force of 10,000 to 20,000 men consisting of infantry, cavalry and artillery were moving toward the Potomac River and Williamsport. Weber prepared for an attack. Garrett kept the telegraph lines busy with requests for information about the military situation at Harpers Ferry. He wanted his railroad—especially the bridge—protected. Weber was directed to see Supervisor of Bridges F.W. Haskett, who instructed him how to disable the bridge with the least amount of damage. Weber was directed to destroy two spans of the trestle bridge on the West Virginia side of the Potomac River. Sigel finally sent a message about 10:00 p.m., roughly 10 hours after the evacuation of Martinsburg, informing Weber that the troops at Martinsburg and Leetown would cross the Potomac River during the evening, and move toward Harpers Ferry at 2:00 a.m., if possible.[61]

---

59 *OR*, 37, s. 1, pt. 2, p. 4, 15, 19

60 Hotchkiss, Diary, July 3, 1864, LOC; Early to Lee, July 7, 1864, HL; Bennette, Diary, July 3, 1864, UNC; Gilmor, p. 186; Beavans, Diary, July 3, 1864, UNC; Burrum, Diary, July 3, 1864, ETHS; McMurran, Diary, July 4, 1864, LOC; BG William Terry, Report, July 22, 1864, Chicago Historical Society (CHS); COL Thomas Toon, 20th NC, Diary, July 4, 1864, Thomas Toon Papers, North Carolina State Archives (NCSA)

61 *OR*, 37, s. 1, pt. 2, p. 20, 22, 32-33, 65

Rodes' and Ramseur's divisions moved at daylight on July 4 down the turnpike through Halltown and Charlestown, W.Va. Skirmishers from both divisions were deployed about 9:30 a.m. on the outskirts of Harpers Ferry and attacked the Union position at Bolivar Heights. After a brief engagement, the Union defenders fell back to the rifle pits on Camp Hill just above Harpers Ferry. Large quantities of stores were successfully evacuated across the Potomac River to Sandy Hook, Md., on 160 cars provided by the B&O Railroad. Weber was able to hold a portion of the town with infantry and cover their position from Maryland Heights with artillery. The engagement lasted throughout the day with no word from Sigel about his reinforcements. With only 400 troops and no reinforcements in sight, Weber withdrew his men from the town to Maryland Heights around 7:00 p.m. and destroyed two spans of the railroad trestle bridge on the Harpers Ferry side. The Confederates immediately took possession of the town, captured a number of commissary and quartermaster stores and proceeded to the banks of the Potomac River, but were unable to cross. Rodes' division moved along the turnpike with pickets advancing as far as the railroad bridge that crossed the Potomac River at Harpers Ferry. The division then followed the Winchester & Potomac (W&P) Railroad to the outskirts of town, where they bivouacked for the night. Ramseur's division moved along the B&O Railroad and bivouacked along the river.[62]

By 10:00 a.m. Sigel's command and wagon train were on the move through Pleasant Valley on the east side of Maryland Heights. At roughly 8:00 p.m. the lead elements of Sigel's force arrived at Maryland Heights while the wagon trains were forwarded to Frederick and on to Hanover, Pa. An hour later Union Colonel William Maulsby (13th Maryland Regiment) arrived with the rear guard. By 10:00 p.m. the infantry was positioned between Fort Duncan and Maryland Heights. Stahel's cavalry was kept in Pleasant Valley to protect the right flank. As the ranking officer, Sigel took command of the Heights.[63]

Breckinridge's division left around 3:00 a.m. on July 4 and passed through Bunker Hill, Darksville and Martinsburg. While in Martinsburg, both Gordon's and Breckinridge's divisions collected

---

62 *OR*, 37, s. 1, pt. 1, p. 185; Early to Lee, July 7, 1864, HL; Old, Diary, July 4, 1864, 1864, LOC; Hotchkiss, Diary, July 4, 1864, LOC; Whitaker, Diary, July 4, 1864, HL; Joseph C. Snider, 31st VA, Journal, July 4, 1864, Accession #29147, Miscellaneous Nr 341, LOV; *OR*, 37, s. 1, pt. 2, p. 17, 36, 65
63 *OR*, 37, s. 1, pt. 1, p. 177, 185-186; Meysenburg, Journal, July 4, 1864, DUL

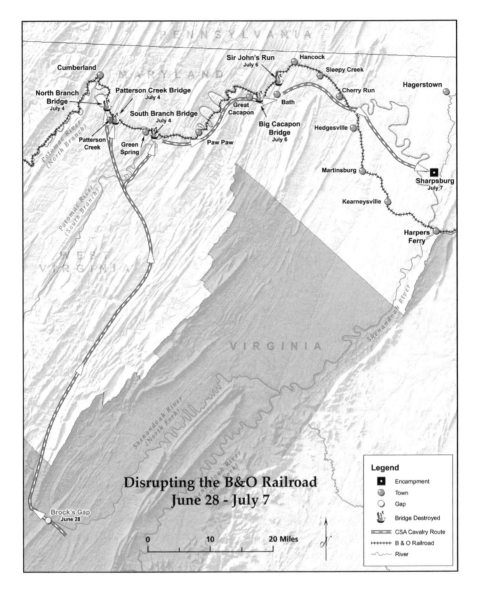

Disrupting the B&O Railroad
June 28 - July 7

Legend

■	Encampment
●	Town
○	Gap
🝙	Bridge Destroyed
====	CSA Cavalry Route
++++	B & O Railroad
～～	River

stores and secured shoes. Private Thomas E. Morrow, 8th Louisiana Infantry Regiment, wrote that:

> [T]he Yanks were in force there & expected to have a large 4th July dinner but they made no stand, run off & left a great quantity of commissary stores quarter masters goods & any amount of small arms. Our boy's got the 4th July Dinner. They had all kinds of fruits, preserves, sardines, oysters, wines & Liquors, & any amount of meats, our boy's enjoyed the delicacies as well as the substantials, it was a great treat.

About 3:00 p.m. both divisions left on the Shepherdstown Road. A brigade from Gordon's division was left to burn the railroad bridges at Martinsburg. After a few miles they turned toward Harpers Ferry and passed through Kearneysville and Halltown before they made their way to Duffield's Depot on the B&O Railroad. Here they tore up the railroad tracks before they camped. Gilmor's cavalry remained in Martinsburg until late in the day when they made their way to the Potomac River and crossed into Maryland.[64]

Disable the B&O Railroad

After being detached on June 28, Imboden's cavalry brigade (the 18th, 23rd Virginia Cavalry and 62nd Virginia Mounted Infantry) began to execute their orders while Harpers Ferry was attacked on July 4. Imboden had been tasked with destroying a number of bridges on the B&O Railroad between Martinsburg, W. Va., and Cumberland, Md., to delay any reinforcements coming East. The brigade was divided into detachments that attacked the South Branch, Patterson Creek and North Branch bridges. The detachment that attacked the North Branch Bridge was driven off without causing any damage. At Patterson Creek, another detachment was able to partially burn the bridge before being driven off. Imboden did the most damage at the South Branch Bridge. The attack began at about 6:00 a.m. and lasted for roughly five hours. The Confederates attacked the blockhouse and an ironclad railroad car with three pieces of artillery. The ironclad was abandoned when one end was knocked out with a "fire ball." This enabled the Confederates to destroy the blockhouse and set fire to the bridge, damaging the east span and about one-third mile of track. Several canal boats were burned, the railroad was torn up, and the horses and grain in the area were taken. Imboden's men were finally driven off when an engine with three ironclad cars arrived.[65]

Two days later on July 6, Imboden's brigade proceeded east and made another series of attacks on the railroad. They attacked Big Cacapon Bridge and Sir John's Run. The engine with three iron-

---

64 Gilmor, p. 187; Waldrop, Diary, July 4, 1864, UNC; Woolwine, Diary, July 4, 1864, VHS; 51st VA Record Book, July 4, 1864, VHS; COL Edmund N. Atkinson, Evan's Brigade, Report, July 22, 1864, James Eldridge Collection, HL; Early, p. 384; OR, 37, s. 1, pt. 2, p. 591; PVT Thomas E. Morrow, 8th LA, to His Father, August 2, 1864, Special Collection, Tulane University Library (TUL)

65 OR, 37, s. 1, pt. 2, p. 42-43, 49, 50-51; OR, 37, s. 1, pt. 1, p. 186-187; 38th Annual Report of the President and Directors to the Stockholders of the Baltimore and Ohio Railroad Co., For the Year Ending September 30, 1864 (Baltimore: J.B. Rose & Co.), p. 56

clad cars that had driven them from South Branch Bridge was on patrol between South Branch and Sir John's Run and drove the Confederates from both places, but not before they had set fire to the depot building and water station at Sir John's Run. On July 5, Imboden became sick with typhoid fever and relinquished command of the brigade to Colonel George Smith of the 62nd Virginia Cavalry Regiment. Smith took the brigade and linked up with Early on July 7 at Sharpsburg, Md. Overall, the operation accomplished

Brig. Gen. John D. Imboden

very little. The B&O Railroad repaired the Patterson Creek Bridge by July 7 and the South Branch Bridge was finished on the 8th.[66]

Confederate Colonel John Mosby and his cavalry assisted Early's movement by severing all communications by railroad and telegraph between Washington and Harpers Ferry at Point of Rocks, Md. On July 4, Mosby crossed the Potomac River at Mocks Ford under the protection of two pieces of artillery. During the crossing, Mosby's cavalry attacked and burned a canal boat that was returning to Washington from Harpers Ferry with men from the Treasury Department. Shortly thereafter, at about 1:00 p.m., a mail train returning to Baltimore, Md., from Harpers Ferry was alerted to the danger by smoke from the burning boat. When the engineer sighted Confederates, he stopped the train and reversed course. Mosby's men open fired on the train in an attempt to stop it, but failed. The Confederates pursued the train for some distance before breaking off the attack. Many of the passengers, fearing capture, jumped off the train to escape. The only casualty was the fireman, who was badly wounded. The train returned to Sandy Hook, Md., on the south side of Maryland Heights next to the Potomac River. Mosby then advanced on the

66 *OR*, 37, s. 1, pt. 1, p. 187; Early, p. 386; *38th Annual Report of the President and Directors to the Stockholders of the Baltimore and Ohio Railroad Co.*, p. 56-57

Union garrison stationed at Point of Rocks and drove them from the area without much of a struggle. After relieving stores of Union goods, Mosby burned the warehouse and the Union camp.[67]

Four freight trains containing mainly government supplies and a mail train were stranded at Sandy Hook with Mosby's force at Point of Rocks and Early's at Harpers Ferry. On July 5 at about 8:00 a.m., yard engine 31 conducted a reconnaissance mission to Point of Rocks and was fired on from the Virginia side of the Potomac River. The train quickly reversed direction, returned to Sandy Hook, and reported that the railroad had not been damaged yet. The railroad men decided to run the gauntlet of Mosby's force and continue on to safety. As the trains passed Point of Rocks, they came under fire, but all managed to pass through and arrive in Baltimore with virtually no damage.[68]

Stahel was ordered to Point of Rocks with his cavalry to engage Mosby's force, but upon arrival in the afternoon they found no sign of the Confederates. Mosby was camped on the Virginia side of the Potomac and withdrew from the area on the morning of July 6 to investigate reports of Union activity at Leesburg, Va.[69]

Reinforce Harpers Ferry

On July 3, Union Chief of Staff, Major General Henry Halleck, who was concerned about the safety of Harpers Ferry, sent reinforcements for Weber. Fifteen cars from the B&O Railroad were readied to take 470 artillery troops of the 170th Ohio National Guard at 3:00 a.m. on July 4 from Washington to Harpers Ferry. By 10:45 a.m., the 100 days-men still had not left. They were to be used as infantry and were waiting for rifles and ammunition from the arsenal. They finally left at noon without being issued any rifles or ammunition. The 170th Ohio made it as far as Monocacy Junction, where Union Brigadier General Erastus Tyler stopped the train and sent it east about 10 miles to Monrovia, Md. Tyler did not want to send the unarmed regiment forward without an escort, and held it there until one could be found. Later in the evening, the 170th Ohio was sent to the Baltimore Depot.[70]

Union Brigadier General Albion P. Howe, who was in Baltimore, was given command of the 170th Ohio, a battalion of dismounted cav-

---

67 *OR*, 37, s. 1, pt. 2, p. 37-38, 65; OR, 37, s. 1, pt. 1, p. 4; William E. Bain, ed. *The B&O in the Civil War* (Denver, CO.: Sage Books, 1966), p. 98-100, 102
68 *OR*, 37, s. 1, pt. 1, p. 4; *OR*, 37, s. 1, pt. 2, p. 63-64; Bain, p. 101-102
69 *OR*, 37, s. 1, pt. 1, p. 176; *OR*, 37, s. 1, pt. 2, p. 67-68
70 *OR*, 37, s. 1, pt. 2, p. 23, 33-34, 36, 37-38, 39, 55

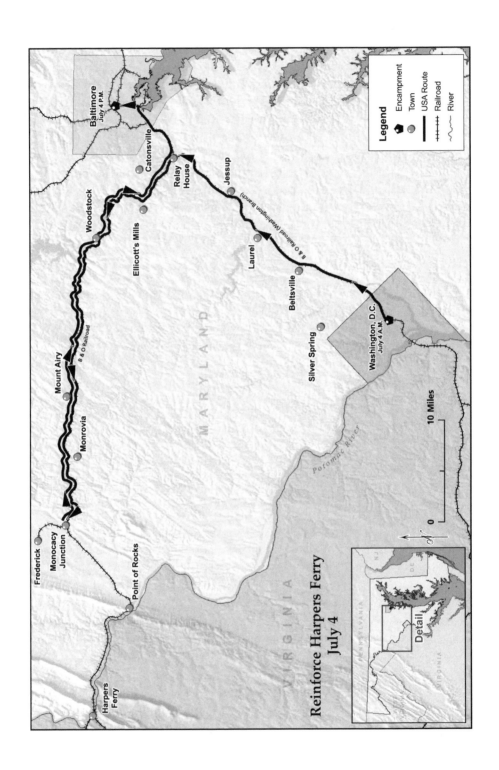

Reinforce Harpers Ferry
July 4

Legend

- Encampment
- Town
- — USA Route
- +++++ Railroad
- ∿ River

Baltimore
July 4 P.M.

Catonsville

Woodstock

Relay House

Jessup

Ellicott's Mills

Laurel

B & O Railroad (Washington Branch)

Beltsville

Mount Airy

Silver Spring

Monrovia

B & O Railroad

Washington, D.C.
July 4 A.M.

Frederick

Monocacy Junction

Point of Rocks

M A R Y L A N D

Potomac River

Harpers Ferry

V I R G I N I A

0   10 Miles

Detail

PENNSYLVANIA

NJ

DE

MD

VIRGINIA

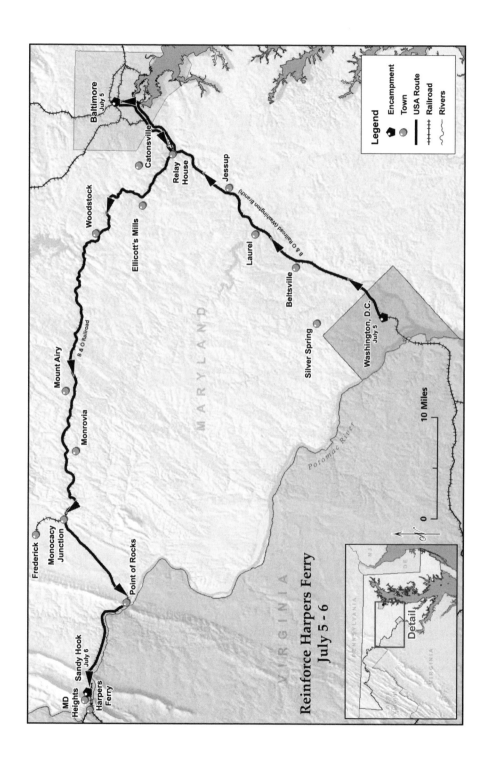

Reinforce Harpers Ferry
July 5 - 6

Legend
- Encampment
- Town
- USA Route
- Railroad
- Rivers

Baltimore
July 5

Catonsville

Relay House

Jessup

Woodstock

Ellicott's Mills

Laurel

B & O Railroad (Washington Branch)

Beltsville

Silver Spring

Washington, D.C.
July 5

MARYLAND

Mount Airy

B & O Railroad

Monrovia

Frederick

Monocacy Junction

Point of Rocks

Potomac River

Sandy Hook
July 6

MD Heights

Harpers Ferry

VIRGINIA

10 Miles

0

Detail

PENNSYLVANIA

VIRGINIA

39

Maj. Gen. Henry Halleck

alry (to be used as infantry) and a four-gun battery. He was given explicit orders to deliver these reinforcements by rail to Harpers Ferry and then return to Washington. On July 5, Howe linked up with the 170th Ohio that were now refitted as infantry, an artillery battery and about 1,800 dismounted cavalrymen in Baltimore. With a force of about 2,800 men, Howe arrived at Sandy Hook about 4:00 a.m. on July 6, and turned his command over to Sigel, who dispersed it to help defend different areas of the Heights. The artillery battery and 300 dismounted cavalrymen were kept at Sandy Hook, while the 170th Ohio and 1,500 dismounted cavalry pushed on to Maryland Heights, arriving about 1:00 p.m. After Howe turned the troops over, he returned to Washington, missing a message from Halleck that ordered him to remain at Maryland Heights and assist with the defense. On July 8 at about 1:00 p.m., Howe returned to Maryland Heights with orders to assume command of the force there—replacing Sigel, who was relieved of duty along with Major General Stahell—and report to Hunter.[71]

Hagerstown Ransom

On July 5, Brigadier General John McCausland left the Sharpsburg area with orders from Early to ransom Hagerstown, Md. As reports of Confederate activity filtered into Hagerstown on July 5, the 6th U.S. Cavalry posted pickets and advance scouts to watch the roads leading into town. Late in the afternoon, a small advance group of Confederate cavalrymen engaged the scouts and pickets under the command of Lieutenant H. McLean of the 6th Cavalry on the Sharpsburg Road and forced them back to

71 *OR*, 37, s. 1, pt. 2, p. 33-34, 59, 61, 62, 81, 98, 104; Meysenburg, Journal, July 4, 1864, DUL

Hagerstown. The Confederates pursued the Union cavalrymen into the town where they discovered a Union force of about 125 cavalrymen from various detachments. Their greater numbers allowed the Union cavalrymen to charge and drive off the Confederates for some distance. During the charge, Union Lieutenant Stanwood's force captured one Confederate lieutenant and two privates. Every effort was made to alert the civilians to the Confederate activity in the area, so they could hide their stock. All government animals, including 500 to 700 horses, were driven off to safety.[72]

LOC

Brig. Gen. John McCausland

The following day, McCausland led his brigade of about 1,200 cavalrymen and a battery of artillery toward Hagerstown and easily drove off the Union cavalrymen at about 1:00 p.m. As the Union cavalrymen retreated, they fought a rear guard action on their way to Muttontown, Md. They then rode on to Greencastle, Pa. where pickets were posted on the roads to await pursuing Confederates.[73]

McCausland presented Hagerstown's treasurer with a written demand for a ransom of $20,000 in greenbacks (rebel currency being refused) and additional supplies, including 1,500 suits, hats, shirts, pairs of socks, shoes or boots and 1,900 pairs of drawers. The town was given three hours to raise the money and four hours to provide the supplies. If the entire payment was not made by the deadline, the town would be burned.[74]

---

72 *OR*, 37, s. 1, pt. 1, p. 95-96, 337-338
73 *OR*, 37, s. 1, pt. 1, p. 338; "Rebel Operations in Hagerstown," *New York Times*, July 15, 1864
74 Richard R. Duncan, "Maryland's Reaction To Early's Raid In 1864: A Summer Of Bitterness," *Maryland Historical Magazine* (Fall 1969), p. 251; Daniel C. Toomey, *The Civil War In Maryland* (Baltimore, MD.: Toomey Press, 2004), p. 102; "Rebel Operations in Hagerstown," *New York Times*, July 15, 1864; "Tomorrow is 114th anniversary of Battle of Monocacy," *Frederick News Post*, July 8, 1978; Edward Delaplaine, "General Early's Levy on Frederick," *Monocacy: July 9, 1864 The Battle That Saved Washington Centennial July 9, 1964*, p. 44; *OR*, 37, s. 1, pt. 2, p. 116

Upon receiving the demand, the treasurer pleaded that the amount was exorbitant. McCausland ignored the pleas, and the treasurer was forced to comply. It was determined that the money would be levied from three banks. Before the banks agreed to pay the $20,000 ransom, a note was signed by city officials stating that the banks would be paid back in full. The Hagerstown Bank provided $10,000, and the First National Bank and Williamsport Branch Bank each contributed $5,000.[75]

With the money raised, the citizens only needed to provide the clothing. After four hours, they had failed to meet the demand, but were given a two-hour extension. Two hours later, they still had not collected enough clothing. McCausland was determined to burn the city; however, after pleas from citizens and a few of his soldiers, he was persuaded to take the money and the clothes that had been collected. The town was spared. Later it was discovered that McCausland had levied the wrong dollar amount. Early wanted $200,000 from Hagerstown, but the ransom note was missing a zero. Thus, the Confederates collected $20,000 and missed out on an additional $180,000.[76]

Shortly after McCausland left Hagerstown, Confederate Major Thomas Sturgis Davis, commander of the Maryland Battalion and not part of Early's invasion force, rode into town to set fire to stores of government hay and the Franklin Railroad Depot. Davis was acting on his own accord and ignored the fact that McCausland had already ransomed the town. To keep Davis from burning private warehouses, an agreement was reached: If all the government stores were burned and a $500 ransom was paid, he would leave. After the town was unable to raise the money, Davis settled for 10 pairs of boots.[77]

On July 7, McLean's cavalry force in Greencastle began patrolling toward Muttontown. They discovered the Confederates had left earlier in the morning, and so they rode toward Hagerstown, arriving there the evening of July 8. A small detachment was sent to reconnoiter the area, where they discovered and easily dispersed a few Confederates. The only major physical damage incurred by the town was the burning of the hay, some grain and the railroad depot. Several shops had also been plundered. After securing the town, pickets and patrols were sent out on the roads leading to town.[78]

75 Duncan, *Maryland Historical Magazine*, p. 251; Delaplaine, "General Early's Levy on Frederick," p. 44; "Tomorrow is 114th anniversary of Battle of Monocacy," *Frederick News Post*, July 8, 1978

76 Duncan, *Maryland Historical Magazine*, p. 251; Toomey, p. 102; "Tomorrow is 114th anniversary of Battle of Monocacy," *Frederick News Post*, July 8, 1978

77 Duncan, *Maryland Historical Magazine*, p. 252; Toomey, p. 103

78 *OR*, 37, s. 1, pt. 1, p. 338-339

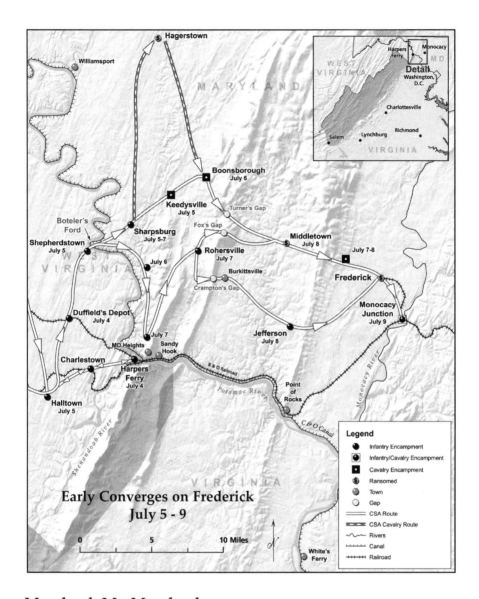

Early Converges on Frederick
July 5 - 9

Legend

●	Infantry Encampment
◉	Infantry/Cavalry Encampment
■	Cavalry Encampment
$	Ransomed
○	Town
○	Gap
═══	CSA Route
▭▭▭	CSA Cavalry Route
∿∿	Rivers
┼┼┼	Canal
✛✛✛	Railroad

Maryland, My Maryland

On the morning of July 5, Gordon's division left Duffield's Depot at roughly 8:00 a.m., followed by Breckinridge's division about two hours later. They moved down Shepherdstown Road to Boteler's Ford. Gordon crossed the Potomac River around 1:00 p.m. The water was about waist deep, which delayed the army's movement. Once across, Gordon took the road leading down the C&O Canal toward Maryland Heights and bivouacked near the iron works at Antietam Creek. Breckinridge's division crossed the river after Gordon and bivouacked at Sharpsburg. Johnson's cavalry brigade also crossed the river and made their way through Sharpsburg to Keedysville, Md., where they bivouacked about a half mile from the town, while Early's headquarters was at Shepherdstown.[79]

As Early's army entered Maryland, a General Order was issued outlawing all straggling, marauding and appropriation of property by unauthorized parties, and requiring its rigid enforcement by all commanding officers. Early demanded the strictest discipline of his soldiers. Any officer or enlisted man found guilty of committing depredations of any sort would be arrested and summarily punished.[80]

Ramseur's and Rodes' divisions remained in Harpers Ferry for the day, plundering the stores and exchanging shots with Union sharpshooters at Maryland Heights. Most of the fighting was confined exclusively to sharpshooters at long range. In the evening, both divisions withdrew, leaving Confederate Brigadier General William G. Lewis' brigade from Ramseur's division to demonstrate against the Union force on Maryland Heights. The two divisions made their way back to Halltown and bivouacked for the night.[81]

The next day (July 6), Ramseur's division left Halltown in the morning and marched toward Shepherdstown, where they crossed the Potomac River at Boteler's Ford. Now in Maryland, they passed through Sharpsburg and bivouacked on the east side of Antietam Creek. Rodes' division left late in the afternoon and also crossed at the ford, passed through Sharpsburg after dark and proceeded for another mile or two before bivouacking at Antietam Creek. Work parties were organized and sent out to destroy the aqueducts, locks and canal boats. Early also crossed the river with the artillery and wagon trains, and established his headquarters at Sharpsburg. Both Ransom's cavalry and Breckinridge's division remained in their camps throughout the day. At dusk, Breckinridge's division was ordered to the foot of Maryland Heights as the reserve for Gordon. The movement took all night, with the last regiments arriving early the next morning (July 7). Ransom also moved with the cavalry late in the day

79 Atkinson, Report, July 22, 1864, HL; Bennette, Diary, July 5, 1864, UNC; Terry, Report, July 22, 1864, CHS; Hotchkiss, Diary, July 5-6, 1864, LOC; Woolwine, Diary, July 5, 1864, VHS; Beverige, Diary, July 5, 1864, DUL; Frank Moore, ed. *The Rebellion Record: A Diary of American Events*, Vol. 10 (New York: D. Van Nostrand, 1869), p. 158

80 *OR*, 37, s. 1, pt. 2, p. 592

81 Beavans, Diary, July 5, 1864, UNC; Randolph, Diary, July 5, 1864, VHS; Hotchkiss, Diary, July 5, 1864, LOC; Old, Diary, July 5, 1864, LOC; *OR*, 37, s. 1, pt. 2, p. 65-66

down the road from Keedysville to Boonsboro, Md. and established a new camp.[82]

On July 6, Gordon's division led the army, with Brigadier General Clement Evans' brigade in front of the division. About 6:00 a.m., they marched down River Road toward Maryland Heights, where sharpshooters engaged Stahel's cavalry, which had been ordered to locate and confront the Confederates at Sharpsburg. Sharpshooters drove Stahel's men back to within two miles of the Heights, where a heavy line of Union skirmishers supported by a short line of battle and two pieces of artillery were located. Gordon deployed his division in a line of battle with Evans' brigade on the left flank, followed by Brigadier Generals Zebulon York's and William Terry's brigades. After the area was reconnoitered, it was discovered that the Union right could be flanked. About 2:00 p.m., Evans' brigade was sent by a difficult route to a point on the Boonsboro Road at the rear of the Union line. Once in position, Gordon posted a strong picket line on the Boonsboro Road to prevent any movement from that direction. The 26th and 60th Georgia Infantry Regiments were deployed as skirmishers at about 4:00 p.m., while the remainder of the brigade was held in support. The skirmish line successfully turned the Union right flank, and after a slight resistance, drove the defenders back near the fortifications on the Heights. The brigade moved forward to the skirmisher's position and established a new line of battle, with its left flank resting on the Heights.[83]

During the evening of July 6, a message was delivered by special courier from General Lee informing Early that an effort would be made on July 12 to release the Confederate prisoners at Point Lookout Prison and that he should assist. Early had received instructions on June 26 to release the prisoners, and the new message ordered him to unite his detachment with an unknown Confederate force to accomplish the same mission. Little more was known of the plan. Even Lee was not aware of all the details.[84]

On July 7, Johnson's cavalry was sent across South Mountain toward Frederick, Md., where they engaged the Union's 8th Illinois Cavalry Regiment, led by Lieutenant Colonel David Clendenin, east of

82 Randolph, Diary, July 6, 1864, VHS; Burrum, Diary, July 6, 1864, ETHS; Old, Diary, July 6, 1864, LOC; Hotchkiss, Diary, July 5-6, 1864, LOC; Beavans, Diary, July 6, 1864, UNC; Early, p. 385

83 Meysenburg, Journal, July 6, 1864, DUL; MG John Gordon, Report, June 28-July 9, 1864, J Ni 51, John Page Nicholson Collection, HL; OR, 37, s. 1, pt. 1, p. 177-178; Atkinson, Report, July 22, 1864, HL

84 Early to Lee, July 7, 1864, HL; Early, p. 385

Middletown, Md. Ramseur's division remained at Sharpsburg for the day, along with Early's headquarters. Rodes' division left camp about 5:00 a.m. and marched a few miles east to Rohersville, Md., blocking any possible Union retreat to the north from Maryland Heights. Gordon held a line west of Maryland Heights, blocking movement in that direction. Early hoped to force Sigel to retreat eastward and provide him with the opportunity to move directly along the river from Maryland Heights to Washington. Sigel, who felt it was "impossible, under the present circumstances, to make an aggressive movement from this point, having but two regiments that can be relied on," held his troops in position at the fortifications, which provided a formidable defensive position. Early decided to withdraw from the Heights and move the army through the gaps of South Mountain to Frederick and then to Washington. Early wrote:

> Maryland Heights are so thoroughly fortified and defended by so many and such heavy guns that I will not attempt to carry them though I am satisfied I could do so, but it would be with such loss as would cripple us to count for doing anything else.

Another possible maneuver would have been to move back across the Potomac and continue to Washington by way of Loudon County, Va. Early had already ruled out this route to Washington because there were no provisions in the area that could support the army.[85]

Lewis' brigade, which had been left at Harpers Ferry to demonstrate against Maryland Heights, was ordered to link back up with Ramseur. They left about 9:00 p.m. on July 7 for Shepherdstown, after burning the government stores that could not be carried off. The brigade marched through the night, crossed the Potomac River at Boteler's Ford, and made its way toward Sharpsburg. The next morning (July 8), at about 7:00 a.m., Harpers Ferry and Bolivar Heights were reoccupied by Union troops from Maryland Heights.[86]

Breckinridge's division (now commanded by Brigadier General John Echols, who had just reported for duty) and Gordon's division remained in their respective lines of battle on July 7. Several attacks on Gordon's left flank were easily repelled. Skirmishing and periodic artillery bombardment continued until dark, when orders were issued to prepare to withdraw. Before they left, the long-anticipated wagon

---

85 Early to Lee, July 7, 1864, HL; Early, p. 383-385; Hotchkiss, Diary, July 7, 1864, LOC; Randolph, Diary, July 7, 1864, VHS; Beavans, Diary, July 7, 1864, UNC; Jones, *Southern Historical Society Papers*, Vol. 1, p. 378; *OR*, 37, s. 1, pt. 2, p. 87

86 Old, Diary, July 7, 1864, LOC; Meysenburg, Journal, July 8, 1864, DUL; Beverige, Diary, July 7, 1864, DUL; *OR*, 37, s. 1, pt. 1, p. 185-186

train of shoes finally arrived from Staunton. After the shoes were distributed, Gordon's and Breckinridge's divisions took the Boonsboro Road at about 9:00 p.m. to Rohersville. They marched through the night and arrived at Rohersville around daylight, July 8.[87]

Once at Rohersville, Gordon's and Breckinridge's divisions rested for about two or three hours before they resumed their march. With Gordon's division in the lead, both divisions crossed South Mountain at Fox's Gap. Stahel's Union cavalry was ordered to Rohersville, and made a dash for the wagons before they crossed the gap, but Breckinridge's rear guard easily drove them off before they could reach them. The divisions continued to Middletown and bivouacked about one mile beyond the town at sunset. Rodes' division left the Rohersville area at daylight and crossed the mountain at Crampton's Gap, passed through Burkettsville, Md., and bivouacked near Jefferson, Md., on the army's right flank. From Sharpsburg, Ramseur's division started toward Middletown at about 3:00 a.m. with the wagon train. Lewis' brigade caught up with them on the Boonsboro Pike and provided the rear guard. It passed through Keedysville, Boonsboro, crossed South Mountain at Turner's Gap, and bivouacked near Middletown. At dark, the division moved a few miles closer to Frederick and established a new camp.[88]

Middletown Ransom

On July 7, Confederate Major Harry Gilmor, 2nd Maryland Cavalry Battalion, entered Middletown and demanded each family provide a loaf of bread and a piece of meat to the soldiers. The cavalrymen were provided with the food and they continued east toward Frederick. The following day, Major General Robert Ransom, with Johnson's brigade of cavalry, demanded that 8,000 rations be provided in two hours. The demand was met but depleted the town of most of its meat, sugar and coffee.[89]

The Confederates made a third demand on the citizens of Middletown later in the evening of July 8th. This time Burgess William J. Irving and another civilian visited Early, who demanded a $5,000

87 Atkinson, Report, July 22, 1864, HL; Terry, Report, July 22, 1864, CHS; Woolwine, Diary, July 7, 1864, VHS; McMurran, Diary, July 7, 1864, LOV; Early, p. 385

88 Hotchkiss, Diary, July 8, 1864, LOC; Old, Diary, July 8, 1864, LOC; Woolwine, Diary, July 8, 1864, VHS; Meysenburg, Journal, July 8, 1864, DUL; Terry, Report, July 22, 1864, CHS; Whitaker, Diary, July 8, 1864, HL; Snider, Journal, July 8, 1864, LOV; OR, 37, s. 1, pt. 1, p. 179; Early, Narrative of the War Between the States, p. 386

89 Duncan, Maryland Historical Magazine, p. 252; "Account of the Rebel Raid Through Middletown Valley," The Valley Register, July 22, 1864

ransom. Irving pleaded that the sum was too high for their small town to pay. Early slightly modified the ransom demand. He required payment of $1,500 by 7 a.m. on July 9 and the remaining $3,500 by 6 p.m.

The first part of the ransom was paid as the Confederate army began to move across the Catoctin Mountains into Frederick. Confederate Quartermaster Major J. R. Braithwaite issued a receipt for this part of the payment. Early left a brigade of infantry in Middletown to collect the second part of the ransom as his army moved east. As the deadline approached, Union cavalry activity in the brigade's rear caused them to leave Middletown and join the rest of the army. They left before the deadline and never collected the remaining $3,500.[90]

The Johnson's cavalry established camp between Middletown and Frederick on July 7, and skirmished with Clendenin's cavalry in the area on July 7 and 8. McCausland's brigade of cavalry arrived and was ordered to move to the right of the army during the afternoon of the 7th. The next day (July 8), he was ordered to cut the telegraph lines and railroad tracks connecting Maryland Heights with Washington and Baltimore. Then he was to cross the Monocacy River and, if possible, secure the bridge at Monocacy Junction.[91]

Early had every reason to be optimistic about taking Washington; after Salem, he had not encountered any major obstacles while moving down the Shenandoah Valley and crossing into Maryland. The army had been reorganized, traveled on average 20 miles a day, easily secured Martinsburg and Harpers Ferry, and captured large quantities of stores. It had crossed the Potomac River into Maryland, damaged the C&O Canal and B&O Railroad, and passed through the gaps of South Mountain to Middletown. Up to this point, there was no clear indication that Union forces were able to muster the manpower required to prevent or slow the Confederate march to Washington. Early's unobstructed movement, however, would soon change at the banks of the Monocacy River.

---

90 Duncan, *Maryland Historical Magazine*, p. 253; Delaplaine, "General Early's Levy on Frederick," Monocacy: July 9, 1864 The Battle That Saved Washington Centennial July 9, 1964, p. 45; "Tomorrow is 114th anniversary of Battle of Monocacy," *Frederick News Post*, July 8, 1978; "Account of the Rebel Raid Through Middletown Valley," *The Valley Register*, July 22, 1864
91 Early, p. 386

Chapter Three

SOUND THE ALARM

After forcing Union Major General David Hunter out of the Shenandoah Valley near Salem, Va., on June 19, 1864, the Confederates moved unopposed down the Valley toward Harpers Ferry. The Union was unaware of the event unfolding before them. On June 28, Captain John McEntee, Hunter's aid-de-camp, sent a message relaying the location of Early's army to Colonel George H. Sharpe, (Grant's intelligence chief), stating, "...they are probably at Richmond again by this." On the same day, Major General Franz Sigel sent a message to the Adjutant-General of the U.S. Army, saying, "I have no information as to any movements of the enemy in this Valley."[92]

The first indication of a problem was reported by B&O Railroad President John W. Garrett. Garrett, who was at the B&O headquarters at Camden Station in Baltimore,

LOC

**John W. Garrett
Pres., B&O Railroad**

Md., received telegrams from his agents on June 29 reporting that a Confederate force of 15,000 to 30,000 troops was moving down the Valley. He sent a message to Secretary of War Edwin M. Stanton that evening with this information. Part of the message read "I find from

---

[92] *U.S. War Department, The War of the Rebellion: A Compilation of the Official Records of the Union and Confederate Armies* (Washington, 1880-1901), 37, Series 1, pt. 1, p. 684, 686 (hereinafter cited as *OR* with references to volume, series, part and page)

various quarters statements of large forces in the Valley. Breckinridge and Ewell are reported moving up. I am satisfied the operations and designs of the enemy in the Valley demand the greatest vigilance and attention." No one realized that Early had replaced Ewell as II Corps commander in late May. The railroad was always a primary target of destruction; Garrett wanted it protected at all cost. On July 1, Lieutenant General Ulysses S. Grant, who was at City Point, Va., responded to these reports when he contacted Chief of Staff Major General Henry W. Halleck in Washington. The message said, "Ewell's corps has returned here, but I have no evidence of Breckinridge having returned." This misinformation continued to support the notion that there was no serious threat in the Valley.[93]

As the days passed, Garrett became more concerned about the protection of the railroad. By July 2, Sigel, who commanded Hunter's reserve division in the Martinsburg-Harpers Ferry area, reported that some of his cavalry was engaged at Winchester, Va. Refugees from the town stated that the Confederates were advancing in force. As a precaution, Sigel requested 150 railroad cars to evacuate the government stores in Martinsburg, W.Va. Early on July 3, Garrett learned that Union forces at Leetown, W.Va., had been attacked and that Sigel was in the process of abandoning Martinsburg. With this information, Garrett became convinced of the severity of the situation. Stanton received a message from Garrett at 9:15 a.m. on July 3 that stated, "I apprehend the information recently sent you of heavy forces in the Valley is about to prove correct." From this point, Garrett focused all his attention and resources to help the Union resist the Confederate invasion.[94]

After contacting Stanton, Garrett personally visited Major General Lew Wallace on July 3. Wallace was commander of the VIII Army Corps and Middle Department, headquartered in Baltimore. Garrett requested that Wallace send 1,000 troops to reinforce Harpers Ferry and protect the railroad, which was vital to the Union cause. Wallace refused to send troops on the grounds that he had only a limited number of men under his command. Sending 1,000 troops to another department would have meant relinquishing about a third of the available troops to protect his department; however, he at once sent a regiment of 100-days men to strengthen the line at Monocacy Junction, the western limit of the Middle Department. Garrett was thankful for the aid that Wallace promised. If Harpers Ferry could not be

93 *OR*, 37, s. 1, pt. 1, p. 694-695; OR, 37, s. 1, pt. 2, p. 3
94 *OR*, 37, s. 1, pt. 2, p. 16

reinforced, the next strategic point on the railroad was the iron bridge spanning the Monocacy River. Garrett ordered transportation to rapidly move the troops there. Two engines with 35 troop cars for 1,000 men were ready around 4:30 p.m. on July 3.[95]

Garrett and his Master of Transportation William Prescott Smith spent the remainder of the day telegraphing Harpers Ferry in an attempt to ascertain the military situation in that area. While relaying information to Halleck and Stanton in Washington, Garrett and Smith also tried to convince them to send additional reinforcements to Maryland Heights.[96]

LOC

Maj. Gen. Lew Wallace

Monocacy Junction

After meeting with Garrett on July 3, Wallace contacted Brigadier General Erastus Tyler, commander of the 1st Separate Brigade, VIII Army Corps. Tyler was directed to concentrate the 3rd Regiment Maryland Potomac Home Brigade (P.H.B.) at Monrovia, Md., six miles east of Monocacy Junction. If the junction was attacked, he was to reinforce that position with the regiment and any other available troops in the area; however, if the junction could not be held, he was not to risk the troops. Two companies were immediately ordered to Monocacy Junction to assist the force already stationed there with the construction of rifle pits. Upon completion of this task, two strong companies would remain to protect the area, while the remainder of the men would return to Monrovia. Tyler was also ordered to make arrangements to replace the 3rd P.H.B. with the 11th Maryland Regiment. Once they were replaced, the 3rd P.H.B. was to be held at the

95 *OR*, 37, s. 1, pt. 2, p. 17, 23; William E. Bain, ed. *The B&O in the Civil War* (Denver, CO.: Sage Books, 1966), p. 95

96 *OR*, 37, s. 1, pt. 2, p. 23

Relay House near Ellicott's Mills, Md. Tyler was further instructed not to send any troops beyond the Monocacy River without orders from Wallace or his headquarters.[97]

Wallace received word on July 4 that the Confederates were at Harpers Ferry. As reports of Confederate cavalry operating in the Middletown Valley filtered into his headquarters, he decided on July 5 to concentrate all available troops in his department at Monocacy Junction. That morning, Wallace left Baltimore for Monocacy Junction to personally take command of the force concentrating there. By July 7, Wallace's force consisted of the available soldiers, about 3,200

LOC

Brig. Gen. Erastus B. Tyler

men total, from the Middle Department, specifically 700 men from the 3rd P.H.B., about 887 from the 11th Maryland Infantry Regiment, 100 men of the 159th Ohio National Guard (mounted infantry), 660 men from seven companies of the 149th Ohio National Guard and three companies of the 144th Ohio National Guard, 200 men from the 1st P.H.B. and 162 men from Alexander's Baltimore Battery with six 3-inch guns. There were also 256 men from a detachment of mixed cavalry and 10 men from the 8th New York Heavy Artillery Regiment. All of the Ohio troops and the 11th Maryland were 100-days men.[98]

Monocacy Junction was an ideal location to establish a defense. The river covered the entire front and there were few fords, even when the river was low. The fords that existed were difficult for artillery and wagons to cross. The high ground was on the eastern side of the river, and the ground on the western side was nearly level, with a virtually unobstructed field of fire. There were also two blockhouses (fortified defensive buildings) positioned on the east and west banks near the railroad bridge.[99]

---

97 *OR*, 37, s. 1, pt. 2, p. 30-31, 54
98 *OR*, 37, s. 1, pt. 2, p. 72, 110; *OR*, 37, s. 1, pt. 1, p. 193-194, 214
99 *OR*, 37, s. 1, pt. 1, p. 193

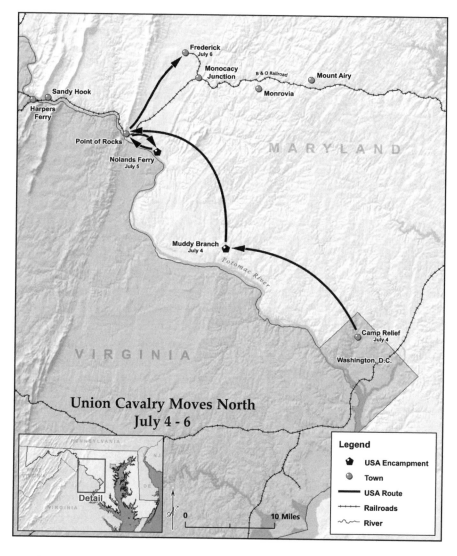

Union Cavalry Moves North
July 4 - 6

Legend
- 🏴 USA Encampment
- ⚪ Town
- ▬ USA Route
- �────── Railroads
- ∿∿∿ River

Confederate activity at Harpers Ferry prompted the authorities in Frederick, Md. to seek transportation to evacuate patients from the military hospital and the government stores. This was done as a precaution to prevent the men and supplies from falling into Confederate hands. General Hospital #1 had a capacity of 3,000 patients, and on July 3, authorities were trying to evacuate about 1,000 patients whose wounds or sickness were not considered life threatening. By the evening of July 8, all the sick and wounded soldiers who could be moved, as well as the stores, were evacuated.[100]

---

100 *OR*, 37, s. 1, pt. 2, p. 108-109, 138; *OR*, 51, s. 1, pt. 3, p. 1171; Bain, p. 91-93

Washington Investigates

On the evening of July 4, Halleck ordered five companies of the 8th Illinois Cavalry Regiment (Companies B, C, I, K and M), commanded by Lieutenant Colonel David R. Clendenin, to investigate the disruption of telegraph communications between Harpers Ferry and Washington in the vicinity of Point of Rocks. Halleck also wanted the 8th Illinois to escort Brigadier General Albion P. Howe's 2,800 reinforcements to Harpers Ferry. Howe was ordered to take reinforcements from Washington by railroad through Point of Rocks to Harpers Ferry. The 8th Illinois, consisting of 230 men, left Washington from Camp Relief at Meridian Hill on 7th Street about 7:00 p.m. They rode about 20 miles before camping near Muddy Branch at 1:00 the following morning. The ride was resumed about 6:00 a.m. and the cavalrymen reached Point of Rocks around 1:00 p.m. on July 5. There Clendenin bombarded Mosby's Confederate force, which was positioned across the Potomac River with two pieces of Union artillery. Over the next hour and a half, the two forces exchanged fire. Miss Ellen Fisher, who was standing in her doorway, was accidentally shot and killed by a Confederate round. The Confederates withdrew and proceeded south to Noland's Ferry, where they attempted to cross the river around 10:00 p.m. Clendenin's men followed and fought another light skirmish before Mosby's men withdrew.[101]

After spending the night at Noland's Ferry, the 8th Illinois returned to Point of Rocks on July 6. Companies C and K were sent to protect the railroad from Point of Rocks to Sandy Hook, and fought a small skirmish with a few Confederates. At 11:30 a.m., Clendenin received a telegram from Howe ordering him to report to Frederick and investigate a report of Confederates operating in the vicinity of Boonsboro, Md. Clendenin recalled his men and arrived in Frederick about 8:00 p.m. after covering a distance of about 16 miles. While in Frederick, Wallace ordered Clendenin to report in person at Monocacy Junction. Wallace had requested the use of Clendenin's cavalry from Halleck, and ordered Clendenin to take two artillery pieces from Alexander's Baltimore Battery, move across the Catoctin Mountains west toward Middletown, Md., reconnoiter the area, and report on Confederate activity.[102]

---

101 *OR*, 37, s. 1, pt. 1, p. 219; *OR*, 37, s. 1, pt. 2, p. 33-35, 43; George Hyland, Diary, July 4-5, 1864, 8th Illinois Cavalry File, Monocacy NB Archives (MNBA); Abner Hard, *History of the Eighth Cavalry Regiment Illinois Volunteers, During the Great Rebellion* (Aurora, IL: 1868), p. 295-296; Jeffrey D. Wert, *Mosby's Rangers* (New York: Simon & Schuster, 1990), p. 173
102 *OR*, 37, s. 1, pt. 1, p. 219; *OR*, 37, s. 1, pt. 2, p. 91; Hyland, Diary, July 6, 1864, MNBA; Hard, p. 295-296

Volunteers Needed

On July 4, a concerned Governor Andrew Curtin of Pennsylvania contacted Secretary of War Edwin Stanton about the reports of Confederate activity in the Harpers Ferry area. The governor wondered whether he should make a call for men to be mustered into service. On the morning of July 5, Stanton contacted the Governors of Pennsylvania and New York to request that 12,000 100-days men be raised from each state. This was done as a precaution to secure areas against Confederate detachments conducting raids into Maryland, and if required, to strengthen Grant's position at Petersburg, Va. Stanton assured the governors that he believed that Sigel would be able to hold the Confederate force in check at Maryland Heights with the reinforcements (inexperienced artillery-men used as infantry) that Howe was escorting from Washington. He also down-played the reports from Brigadier General Max Weber by stating:

LOC

Edwin M. Stanton
Secretary of War

> No reliable intelligence has yet been received indicating that the rebels operating on the Baltimore and Ohio Railroad are in any strong force. General Weber, from Harper's Ferry, gives much greater dimensions to the rebel force, but it is believed that his representations of numbers are much exaggerated.[103]

Grant's first indication that Early was not at Richmond, Va., came on July 4, when a deserter reported that Ewell's (Early's) corps and other forces operating in the Valley had entered Maryland. Grant advised Halleck to hold all forces assigned to reinforce the Army of the Potomac in Richmond. He made light of the report and said he

---

103 *OR*, 37, s. 1, pt. 2, p. 57, 70, 74, 78

had from similar authority information that Early was on the right of Lee's army. On July 5, Stanton informed Governors Andrew Curtin (Pennsylvania) and Horatio Seymour (New York) on behalf of President Abraham Lincoln that militia in as large numbers as possible should be organized for service in Washington. There they could meet any emergency that might arise in the vicinity. Both governors promised to answer the President's call for troops.[104]

A concerned Stanton telegraphed Hunter on July 5 and demanded that he report where and how his force was employed as well as take measures to deal with the threat that had developed in and around Harpers Ferry. Hunter had not provided his superiors with any information since June 29, but he immediately responded to Stanton. In the messages that followed, he informed Stanton and the Adjutant-General of the U.S. Army that his whole force was under orders to move to Parkersburg, W.Va., and from there they would promptly be sent to Martinsburg by railroad. Earlier in the day, 40 cars loaded with 1,300 infantry from Hunter had been sent to Cumberland to report to Brigadier General Benjamin Kelley. Hunter also added that if Sigel managed his force properly, he could drive the Confederates back.[105]

Misguided Notions

Though the military threat intensified at Harpers Ferry on July 5, Grant and Halleck still did not believe it was Early, despite a report from a Confederate deserter on the 4th. They were not overly concerned with the situation that had developed around Harpers Ferry, believing that Hunter would eliminate the threat. Hunter was in Parkersburg, W.Va., trying to move his army of about 18,000 men from Charleston, W.Va., to the Ohio River and up river to Parkersburg, where they would take the B&O Railroad to Martinsburg. Grant did tell Halleck that he was willing to send an army corps if the unknown Confederate force crossed into Maryland or Pennsylvania, and if Halleck felt that they were needed.

Halleck did not believe that Washington, Baltimore, Harpers Ferry, or Cumberland were in any serious danger. He was also certain Hunter could arrive in time to handle the situation. He did, however, request that a dismounted cavalry force be sent to Washington where it could be remounted and sent to Harpers Ferry. As a precaution, all available water transportation was sent to Fort Monroe, Va., on the James

---

104 *OR*, 37, s. 1, pt. 2, p. 33, 77, 91
105 *OR*, 37, s. 1, pt. 2, p. 59, 62, 63, 79

River. This would allow for the quick movement of the dismounted cavalry force and, if needed, the army corps that Grant promised.[106]

Additional reports came to Grant's attention on July 5 about the location of Early's army. Around 1:00 p.m., Major General George Meade sent a telegram to Grant concerning two Confederate deserters who reported that Early, Breckinridge and other forces were invading Maryland with the purpose of capturing Washington. Union Major General Benjamin Butler, at Bermuda Hundred, Va., telegraphed Grant at 2:55 p.m. with information gathered from deserters and prisoners. Butler told Grant he was inclined to believe that Early's corps, with Breckinridge, Imboden and Mosby, was currently making a raid near Harpers Ferry.[107]

With all this information in hand and additional reports from deserters, Grant determined at 11:30 p.m. on July 5, "there is no doubt that Ewell's Corps is away from here." He ordered Meade to send one good infantry division and all of the dismounted cavalry to Washington. Ships would be made ready to transport the soldiers between 11:30 p.m. and 2:00 p.m. the following day (July 6). Grant was now aware that Early's army was in Maryland, and he wanted it destroyed. Grant still did not grasp the severity of the situation, and only sent a single division without artillery, because he relied on information from Halleck that Hunter was swiftly moving his troops. Grant mistakenly believed that Hunter's army would intercept Early and defeat him, so he sent only one division to hold Harpers Ferry until Hunter's arrival.[108]

Grant Sends Reinforcements

At 11:30 p.m. on July 5, Grant ordered the 3rd Division, VI Corps to Locust Point, Md., located south of Baltimore. The division commander, Brigadier General James Ricketts, was ordered to report to Halleck by telegraph for further orders when he arrived. The division was sent without wagons, ambulances, artillery and ammunition (except for what they carried). It was assumed they would return to Virginia very soon; therefore, it was unnecessary to move the burdensome equipment back and forth.[109]

Ricketts received marching orders about 3:00 a.m. on July 6, and the division started the 12-mile march to City Point about 5:00 a.m.

---

106 *OR*, 37, s. 1, pt. 2, p. 58, 59
107 *OR*, 40, s. 1, pt. 3, p. 5, 18
108 *OR*, 37, s. 1, pt. 2, p. 60
109 *OR*, 37, s. 1, pt. 2, p. 74, 80; *OR*, 40, s. 1 pt. 3, p. 36

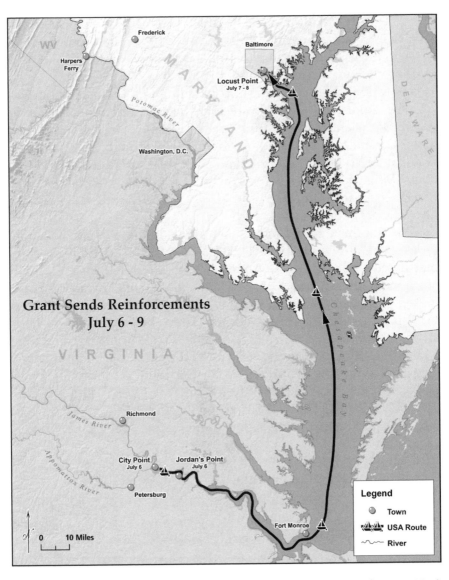

Grant Sends Reinforcements
July 6 - 9

Legend

● Town
▲▲▲ USA Route
∿ River

The march was very difficult. Private Abiel LaForge, 106th New York Infantry Regiment, described dust, "so thick that for 10 & 15 minutes at a time we could not see 20 feet from our selves, this added to the heat was dreadful." Private Josiah Hill, 110th Ohio Infantry Regiment, described the road as "the dustiest road I ever saw in my life." [110]

---

110 Abiel T. LaForge, Diary, July 6, 1864, 106th New York File, MNBA; Hill, Robin Gustin, ed. "A Civil War Diary kept by Josiah Lewis Hill from August 22, 1862 to July 1, 1865 and a History of the 110th Ohio Voluntary Infantry," (1986), 110th Ohio File, MNBA; Lewis Fuller, Diary, July 6, 1864, 106th New York File, MNBA

Ricketts' division of 12 regiments (roughly 4,400 men) arrived at City Point about noon, ate dinner and drew new clothing. The 1st Brigade immediately boarded transports, and as soon as additional transports became available, the 2nd Brigade followed. Ricketts and his staff embarked on one of the first transports, *Sylvan Shore*, along with the 14th New Jersey and 151st New York Infantry regiments. He left explicit orders to the commanding officers aboard each vessel that they were not to disembark until he arrived at Locust Point and gave the order. The last transports left City Point on the morning of July 7.[111]

Monocacy NB

Brig. Gen. James B. Ricketts

A few of the transports boarded by the division were the *Star, Daniel Webster, Thomas Powell, City Of Albany, Salvor, Louisa Moore, Leymour,* USS *Exchange* and USS *Columbia*. They steamed down the James River to Fort Monroe, located at the mouth of the river. Then they entered the Chesapeake Bay and continued north to Baltimore. The first transports to leave passed Fort Monroe about midnight on July 6. The voyage was relatively uneventful except for the loss of Private Joseph Warfield from Company I of the 110th Ohio Regiment, who fell overboard while sleeping. He had retired for the night by the gangway (where one enters and leaves the ship) and in the morning was missing. The transports traveled at varying rates of speed, causing them to spread out during the voyage and arrive at different times. The first vessel arrived at Locust Point about noon on July 7, anchored in the harbor and waited for Ricketts to arrive.[112]

---

111 *OR*, 37, s. 1, pt. 1, p. 195-196; *OR*, 40, s. 1, pt. 3, p. 44; Bain, p. 122-123; LT James Read, 10th VT, Diary, July 6, 1864, James B. Ricketts Collection, Manassas National Battlefield Park Archives (MNBPA); Daniel Long to His Wife, July 5, 1864, 151st New York File, MNBA; Newton Terrill, *Campaign of the Fourteenth Regiment New Jersey Volunteers* (New Brunswick: Daily Home News Press, 1884), p. 72

Garrett Takes Action

On July 7, Garrett made arrangements to have transportation waiting at Locust Point for the 3rd Division. He sent one of his best men to hasten the disembarking, loading and forwarding of the troops. Although the transports were hauled in and made ready for unloading, the officer in charge—Ricketts had not arrived—would not disobey his orders and unload the troops. Garrett sent a message to Stanton asking if his department could issue orders to countermand Ricketts and forward the troops to Monocacy Junction without delay.

Garrett's message also addressed the issue of Wallace's departmental lines. Garrett received a message from the railroad agent at Monocacy Junction who reported that Wallace and Tyler's actions were tentative west of the river due to departmental lines. Wallace's western limit of authority in the Middle Department ended at the Monocacy River. The agent probably sent the message when he overheard Wallace talking about operating outside his departmental lines. Halleck sent a telegram at 9:42 p.m. to the officer in charge at Baltimore that the troops from City Point should be sent upon arrival to the mouth of the Monocacy or Point of Rocks. Stanton resolved the issue of the departmental lines when he sent a telegram to Wallace at 10:00 p.m., telling him, "In the operations now in progress you will not restrict yourself to any departmental lines..."[113]

While Garrett was trying to rectify the situation at Monocacy Junction and Locust Point, a telegram informing Lieutenant Colonel Samuel Lawrence (Wallace's adjutant in Baltimore) that the forces at Monocacy were out of ammunition, and that more should be sent, came to Garrett's attention. Garrett contacted Lawrence immediately and offered a fast passenger train that would be ready in 20 minutes at Camden Station. Lawrence turned down Garrett's offer, saying that after an initial delay he had obtained some of the ammunition earlier and that the balance was on its way. In addition to the ammu-

---

112 *OR*, 37, s. 1, pt. 2, p. 100; *OR*, 37, s. 1, pt. 1, p. 208; *OR*, 40, s. 1, pt. 3, p. 31, 36; Read, Diary, July 6, 1864, MNBPA; Fuller, Diary, July 6, 1864, MNBA; SGT Francis Cordrey, Diary, July 6, 1864, 126th Ohio File, MNBA; George R. Prowell, *History of the Eighty-Seventh Regiment Pennsylvania Volunteers* (York, PA: Press of the York Daily, 1903), p. 175; Alfred S. Roe, *The Ninth New York Heavy Artillery* (Worcester, MA: 1899), p.120; COL John F. Staunton, 67th PA, to CPT A.J. Smith, 3rd Division AAG, August 8, 1864, COL Stanton Service Records, RG 94, NARA; "Army Correspondence," *Morgan County Herald*, Ohio, July 13, 1864; Daniel Long to His Wife, July 7, 1864, 151st New York File, MNBA; Thomas E. Pope, *The Weary Boys* (OH: The Kent State University Press, 2002), p. 69

113 *OR*, 37, s. 1, pt. 2, p. 100-101, 108, 111

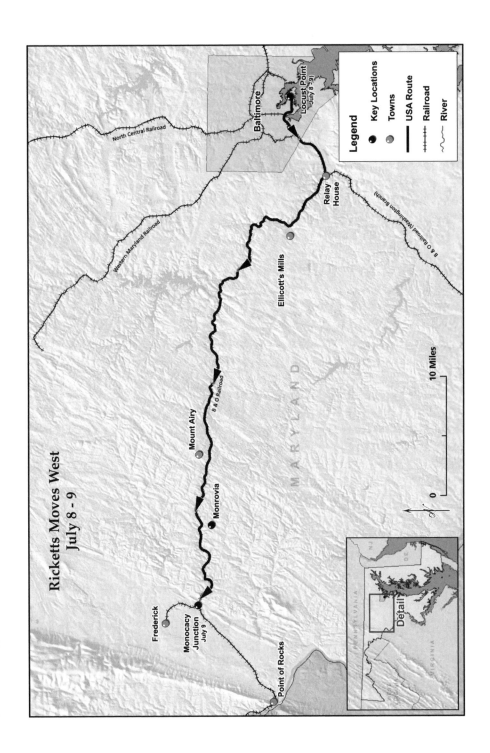

Ricketts Moves West
July 8 - 9

Legend
• Key Locations
● Towns
━ USA Route
┼┼┼ Railroad
〜 River

Baltimore

Locust Point
July 8 - 9

North Central Railroad

Relay House

B & O Railroad (Washington Branch)

Ellicott's Mills

Western Maryland Railroad

Mount Airy

B & O Railroad

Monrovia

MARYLAND

Frederick

Monocacy Junction
July 9

Point of Rocks

Detail

PENNSYLVANIA

N J

DE

VIRGINIA

N

0   10 Miles

nition train that Garrett offered, he ordered that an extra 120 telegraph repairers and roadmen remain on duty during the night between Monocacy Junction and Baltimore to ensure the safety of the
road, switches and telegraph lines. Garrett was utilizing all the tools
at his disposal to ensure the safety of the railroad.[114]

Race to Monocacy

Lawrence received Halleck's order around 10:00 p.m. on July 7,
directing the reinforcements to immediately take trains provided
by the B&O Railroad and report to the mouth of the Monocacy
River or Point of Rocks, with five days' rations. Colonel William
Truex, 1st Brigade commander, immediately complied with the new
orders. The 14th New Jersey, part of the 87th Pennsylvania and the
10th Vermont Infantry regiments, which had arrived on the first
transports, disembarked, loaded railroad cars and left Locust Point
at 12:50 a.m. on July 8. Truex was ordered to report to Wallace at
Monocacy Junction.[115]

Lawrence informed Ricketts, who arrived at Locust Point about
12:45 a.m. on July 8, of Halleck's order and that Truex had already left
for Monocacy Junction. Ricketts was also informed that he would
receive rations and ammunition when he arrived. The supplies would
be sent on a special train at 4:00 a.m. and on another train at 12:00
p.m. For unknown reasons, the trains did not leave Baltimore on the
8th. One train left on the morning of the 9th and arrived at Monocacy
Junction about 7:30 a.m. The remainder of the division left Locust
Point on railroad cars at 3:20 a.m., 7:45 a.m., 8:30 a.m., 9:40 a.m. and
4:00 p.m. on July 8.[116]

When Ricketts left Locust Point, he placed Colonel John Staunton,
commander of the 2nd Brigade, in charge. He was ordered to move the
rest of the division forward as rapidly as possible. By midnight of
July 8, three ships (*Louisa Moore*, *Leymour*, and *Exchange*) had failed to
dock at Locust Point. They contained the 67th Pennsylvania, 6th Maryland and part of the 122nd Ohio Infantry regiments (companies A, D,
G, H, most of F and all the officers from the regiment except one),
totaling about 1,050 soldiers. Staunton spent the night searching for
the missing regiments. Two ships (*Leymour* and *Exchange*) were found
anchored at Locust Point for the night and the third (*Louisa Moore*)

114 *OR*, 37, s. 1, pt. 2, p. 100-101, 112
115 *OR*, 37, s. 1, pt. 2, p. 110, 114, 115, 128-129; Read, Diary, July 8, 1864, MNBP;
    Terrill, p. 73
116 *OR*, 37, s. 1, pt. 2, p. 111, 113, 120-121, 127-128; Prowell, p. 180

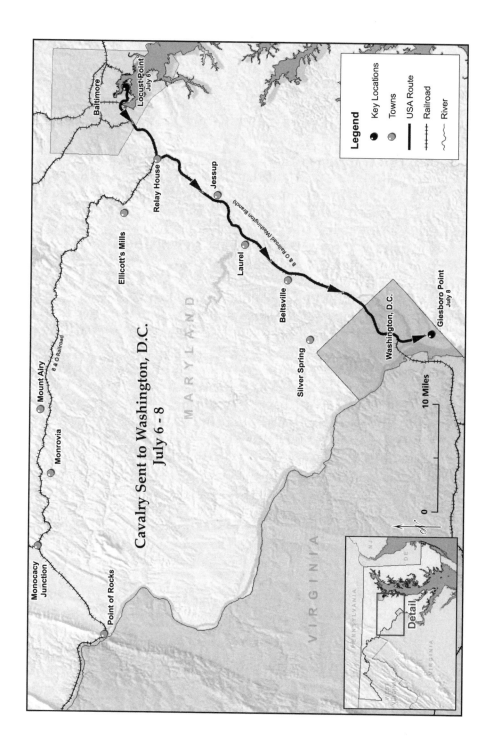

Cavalry Sent to Washington, D.C.
July 6 - 8

Legend
● Key Locations
◉ Towns
▬ USA Route
┼┼┼┼ Railroad
〜 River

Baltimore
Locust Point
July 6

Relay House
Jessup
Ellicott's Mills
Laurel
B & O Railroad (Washington Branch)
Beltsville
Silver Spring
Washington, D.C.
Giesboro Point
July 8

Mount Airy
B & O Railroad
Monrovia
Monocacy Junction
Point of Rocks

M A R Y L A N D

V I R G I N I A

10 Miles
0

Detail

PENNSYLVANIA
N.J.
DE.
VIRGINIA

63

had already disembarked its troops in the city. Once located, the troops were ordered to the trains that were waiting at Locust Point. The first train, with 23 cars, left at 6:45 a.m. on July 9, with Staunton and the balance of the men aboard. The second train, consisting of 13 cars, left at 7:30 a.m. loaded with stock, baggage and 100 men.[117]

The trains moved slowly, with the first train reaching Plane Number 4, 11 miles east of the junction, at about 11:00 a.m. on July 9. Both trains were delayed at Plane Number 4 for a few hours. The first delay was due to passing trains heading east on the tracks. Next, they were stopped by the superintendent of trains, who said his orders were that no trains moving west could pass. After that miscommunication was rectified, Staunton delayed the trains' progress once again when he issued rations to the troops. The movement was finally resumed around 4:00 p.m. The first train only proceeded a few miles from Monrovia when it was stopped again by soldiers who informed Staunton that the entire command was in retreat, having been defeated at Monocacy Junction. Staunton fell back to Monrovia, disembarked from the train and formed a line of battle on the edge of the town. During the movement to Baltimore, he received orders from Wallace to bring up the rear and collect stragglers.[118]

On August 23, 1864, a general court martial was convened. Staunton had three charges levied against him for his failure to appear with the remainder of the 3rd Division at the Battle of Monocacy on July 9. The first charge was disobedience of orders; the second charge, neglect of duty to the prejudice of good order and military discipline; and the third charge, misbehavior before the enemy. Staunton was found guilty on September 1 of the first two charges. He had failed to rapidly move the troops under his command, which resulted in their inability to reach the battle in time to render assistance. He was sentenced to be cashiered (discharged from the military) and forever disqualified from holding any office of honor, profit, or trust under the Government of the United States.[119]

Cavalry Reinforcements

Grant ordered Major General Philip Sheridan to send his dismounted cavalry of the Army of the Potomac north, because they could

---

117 COL John F. Staunton, 67th PA, Report, August 23, 1864, General Court Martial Proceedings, NARA; Staunton to Smith, August 8, 1864, NARA; Bain, p. 122-123; *OR*, 37, s. 1, pt. 1, p. 210

118 *OR*, 37, s. 1, pt. 2, p. 137, 138-139; Staunton, Report, August 23, 1864, NARA; Staunton to Smith, August 8, 1864, NARA

119 Staunton, Report, August 23, 1864, NARA

be equipped faster in Washington than at Petersburg. Once equipped, they could be placed into immediate service against Early's force. The cavalrymen were collected at Jordan's Point on July 6 for transport to Baltimore, and embarked after noon. The commanding officer, Major Myron Beaumont, 1st New Jersey Cavalry Regiment, was ordered to inform Halleck of his arrival at Locust Point.[120]

While the transports were on their way, Grant discovered that the dismounted cavalry was composed of detachments from all of the cavalry regiments. He had intended for organized regiments to be sent. In all, Sheridan had sent about 2,927 men; most of them had no weapons, and 2,496 were sick. Sheridan had not been told why the dismounted cavalry was being sent, and felt this was an excellent opportunity to have the ineffective men recuperate, be remounted and then be returned. Beaumont reported the arrival of his command at Locust Point, on July 8 at 9:00 a.m. At 10:40 a.m., Halleck ordered the dismounted cavalry to report to Major General Christopher Augur (commander of the XXII Corps and the Department of Washington) at the cavalry camp. Upon reporting in, he received new orders to report at Camp Stoneman on Giesboro Point in Washington. The cavalry boarded railroad cars in the evening and arrived at sunrise on the 9th.[121]

Doubts Rising

As the days passed, Halleck became increasingly concerned for the safety of the capital. Reports indicated that the Confederate force consisted of anywhere from 7,000 to more than 30,000 men. On July 6, Augur informed Halleck that "one regiment of heavy artillery should be returned to Washington, to be distributed among the 100-day's militia in the forts, as the latter are not sufficiently instructed in the use of heavy batteries." Halleck feared that rail damage caused by Imboden's Confederate cavalry brigade would slow Hunter's advance, but he remained confident that Hunter would intercept Early before he reached the defenses of Washington.[122]

By July 7, Halleck was fully aware of the situation that was escalating in Frederick. At 12:50 p.m., he received a telegram from Wallace informing him that Clendenin's cavalry was being driven back from Middletown to Frederick by a superior Confederate force with infan-

---

120 *OR*, 40, s. 1, pt. 3, p. 49-50
121 *OR*, 40, s. 1, pt. 3, p. 37, 50, 68, 92-93; *OR*, 37, s. 1, pt. 2, p. 111, 127, 129; "Dismounted Cavalry," *National Tribune*, August 9, 1900
122 *OR*, 40, s. 1, pt. 3, p. 32, 60; *OR*, 37, s. 1, pt. 2, p. 79

try, cavalry and artillery. Wallace also reported that he would hold the town until the Confederates had fully revealed their intentions. Later he reported that the Confederates had been pushed back after a four-hour battle that finally concluded as night fell.[123]

Wallace commanded the only army protecting Baltimore and Washington from the Confederates. He was facing a Confederate force of unknown strength, (possibly five times larger than his own army), and had just fought a four-hour battle with a force comprised mostly of 100-days men. Nevertheless, Halleck refused to recognize the severity of the situation and continued to believe that Hunter would arrive in time. At 9:40 p.m., Halleck ordered Wallace to use his men to gather all the horses fit for cavalry service that they could find in Maryland and the border counties of Pennsylvania. The horses were to be sent to the mouth of the Monocacy River for use by the dismounted cavalry force that was to arrive from Richmond. Halleck also ordered the 3rd Division, VI Corps beyond Wallace's position at Monocacy Junction to the mouth of the Monocacy River or Point of Rocks.[124]

As Garrett continued to send telegrams to Washington about Hunter's progress to Harpers Ferry, it was becoming increasingly apparent that Hunter would be unable to intercept Early. On the night of July 7, Garrett informed Secretary Stanton that only 3,000 troops had arrived at Parkersburg and been sent east on railroad cars. Garrett added, "The arrivals at Parkersburg are very slow; in consequence, it is stated, of the river being so low that the boats have great difficulty in getting up."

On July 8, Halleck sent a message to Grant at 2:30 p.m. to inform him that Hunter was moving too slow and the railroad was so damaged that Halleck did not believe Hunter would be able to provide much aid. In addition, the dismounted cavalry that arrived in Locust Point at 9:00 a.m. on July 8 had not yet arrived in Washington. To aid in the defense of the capital, Grant directed Halleck to order the 1st and 3rd battalions of the 9th New York Heavy Artillery Regiment, part of Ricketts' division, to Washington. Grant would also immediately send the 2nd Battalion, which had remained with his army. Halleck did not receive Grant's message until 7:40 a.m. on July 9; the 9th New York Heavies were at Monocacy Junction about to engage Early's force.

123 *OR*, 37, s. 1, pt. 2, p. 108-109, 110
124 *OR*, 37, s. 1, pt. 2, p. 108, 111
125 *OR*, 37, s. 1, pt. 2, p. 102, 119; Joseph Keifer, Official Report, November 1, 1864, Box OV1, Joseph Warren Keifer Collection, LOC

Halleck lacked artillery troops to operate the large guns in the defensive forts around Washington.[125]

A state of crisis erupted in Washington on the evening of July 8. At 8:00 p.m., Halleck received a telegram from Wallace regarding a strong column of Confederates that was moving down the Georgetown Pike to within six miles of Urbana, Wallace stated that he would position his force to cover Washington. Halleck also received a telegram at 9:40 p.m. from Major General Darius Couch (commander of Pennsylvania Department) that a deserter from McCausland's cavalry brigade reported the Confederates numbered about 30,000 troops with 125 pieces of artillery.[126]

Halleck relayed this information in a telegram to Hunter at 10:00 p.m., asking him to report the location and number of forces en route to Harpers Ferry. At 10:30 p.m., Howe, now in command at Harpers Ferry, reported that the main body of the Confederate force had crossed South Mountain into the Middletown Valley and numbered about 20,000. Halleck finally realized that Washington was in danger. When he had not received a reply from Hunter after 30 minutes, Halleck opted to report to Grant about the dangerous situation in Maryland. Hunter had often failed to respond to messages during the last few days, possibly because the telegraph lines had been disrupted by the Confederates. At 10:30 p.m., Halleck sent a telegram to Grant that read as follows:

> None of the cavalry sent up by you has arrived nor do we get anything from Hunter. ...If you propose to cut off this raid and not merely to secure our depots we must have more forces here. Indeed, if the enemy's strength is as great as represented, it is doubtful if the militia can hold all of the defenses. I do not think that we can expect much from Hunter. He is too far off and moves too slowly. I think, therefore, that very considerable re-enforcements should be sent directly to this place.[127]

At 11:00 p.m., Stanton asked Major General John Dix, military commander in New York, to report the status of the troops that had been raised under the President's call. Stanton informed Dix that Wallace had reported that an enemy force of 20,000 was about 30 miles from Washington. Dix replied on the afternoon of July 9 that 3,500 troops would immediately be sent to Washington. Hunter finally responded at 11:00 p.m. that his advance troops were expected to reach Hedgesville, W.Va., about 10 miles north of Martinsburg, sometime

---

126 *OR*, 37, s. 1, pt. 2, p. 127, 131
127 *OR*, 37, s. 1, pt. 2, p. 119-120, 124

during the evening. Hunter was moving too slowly, and it was now evident that he was not going to make it to Washington with sufficient forces to defend the capital. It was up to Wallace's small force and the speed of Grant in sending reinforcements.[128]

Battle of Frederick

Following orders from Wallace, the 8th Illinois Cavalry and a section (two guns) of Alexander's Battery left Frederick about 5:30 a.m. on July 7 to conduct a reconnaissance mission down the Hagerstown Pike to determine the strength and position of the Confederates. They encountered a Confederate detachment of about equal strength a few miles west of Frederick in the Middletown Valley and drove them back about a half mile before the Confederates rallied and held their position. Confederate Major Harry Gilmor observed this action and deployed his cavalry into the fields, waiting for Clendenin to attack. When no attack came, he advanced two squads from the 1st Maryland Cavalry Regiment (Confederate). The two guns with Clendenin began to shell the attacking Confederates, who were compelled to lie down, out of harms way. Clendenin established a skirmish line and charged, but found Gilmor's line reinforced and thus retreated to a defensive position. Gilmor counterattacked and drove Clendenin back to a pass in the Catoctin Mountains, where a strong defensive position was maintained with the aid of the artillery. The counterattack stalled and Gilmor's force was compelled to fall back.[129]

The remainder of Brigadier General Bradley Johnson's cavalry brigade and two artillery pieces moved down the pike to reinforce Gilmor and assist in disposing of Clendenin's force. They had just halted at the top of a little hill, in columns of four, when a shell fell into the second or third rank and exploded. Hospital Steward J. Kelley Bennette, 8th Virginia Cavalry Regiment, described the horrific effects of this destructive shot:

> One man (Moore) was struck by a large piece on the shoulder which passing out at his hip nearly severing his body in twain; thence thro' his saddle it finished its mission by killing his horse. Another large fragment struck Mitchell Co. (B) on the left side, producing a wound into which it was easy to pass the hand, divided the spleen, lacerated the left lobe of the liver & passed out at the right hypochondrium carrying with it a large portion of the intestines & a piece of the right

---

128 OR, 37, s. 1, pt. 2, p. 119-120, 123, 133, 154-155
129 OR, 37, s. 1, pt. 1, p. 194, 219, 223; OR, 37, s. 1, pt. 2, p. 108; OR, 51, s. 1, pt. 1, p. 1172-1173

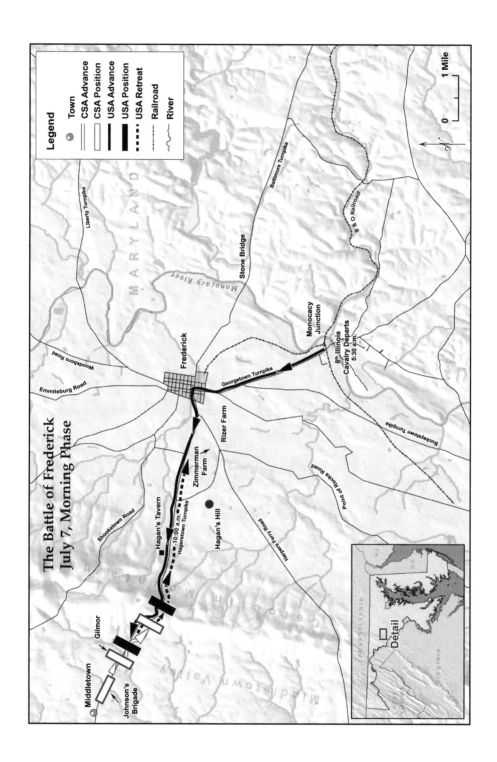

The Battle of Frederick
July 7, Morning Phase

Legend

- Town
- CSA Advance
- CSA Position
- USA Advance
- USA Position
- USA Retreat
- Railroad
- River

MARYLAND

Liberty Turnpike

Woodsboro Road

Emmitsburg Road

Frederick

Monocacy River

Stone Bridge

Baltimore Turnpike

B & O Railroad

Monocacy Junction

8th Illinois Cavalry Departs 5:30 a.m.

Georgetown Turnpike

Rizer Farm

Buckeystown Turnpike

Point of Rocks Road

Shookstown Road

Hagan's Tavern

10:00 a.m.

Hagerstown Turnpike

Zimmerman Farm

Hagan's Hill

Harper Ferry Road

Middletown

Gilmor

Johnson's Brigade

Middletown Valley

Detail

PENNSYLVANIA

N J

DE

VIRGINIA

0   1 Mile

lobe of the liver. Yet strange to say with this frightful wound he lived over three hours perfectly rational all the time. Another piece struck Sgt. Wright (B) on base of the nose producing an ugly tho' not a dangerous wound. Another of Co. (B) (Fitzgerald) was paralyzed by the concussion but will be able for duty tomorrow. Another piece struck a member of Maj. Gilmor's Batt under the chin severing both sides of the jaw-bone & dividing the inferior maxillary & sublingual arteries & inflicting what may yet prove a mortal wound. Another small fragment struck Stockton Co. (I) over the epigastrium penetrating the stomach & inflicting a mortal wound. ...Another piece struck Wilson Co. (D) on the head fracturing his skull & scattering his brains on all near him & yet he lived tho' insensible several hours. The same shell killed and wounded several horses. ...Since the beginning of the war I have seen death in many of its horrid forms but never have I seen so frightful a wound as that of Mitchell & Moore.

After approximately five hours of fighting, the dismounted Confederates advanced a strong skirmish line toward the center of Clendenin's line of battle on the mountain, while additional forces moved on his flanks. Clendenin observed the movement on his flanks and, lacking sufficient numbers to hold his position, gradually fell back toward Frederick. Most of the Confederates were hampered by the rough terrain, and some delay took place in regrouping and giving pursuit.[130]

About 10:00 a.m., Clendenin sent a message to Wallace stating he was currently engaged with 1,000 Confederates and gradually falling back to Frederick. Wallace decided that Frederick could be defended without jeopardizing the security of the railroad bridge, and at 11:00 a.m., ordered an additional artillery piece with ammunition along with the 3rd P.H.B. and the 159th Ohio Mounted Infantry Regiment (about 96 men, commanded by Captain Edward H. Lieb, 5th U.S. Cavalry) to the west side of Frederick. Clendenin was pursued by a few Confederates who were easily dispersed when an artillery piece was deployed on the road and fired on the head of the pursuing column. By 12:30 p.m., the additional artillery piece arrived, followed by Colonel Charles Gilpin and the 3rd P.H.B., which had taken a train from Monocacy Junction into town.[131]

Just before the engagement at 3:40 p.m., Wallace received word from Garrett that the veteran reinforcements had arrived at Locust

---

130 J. Kelly Bennette, 8th VA Cavalry, Diary, July 7, 1864, Collection 886, UNC; Harry Gilmor, *Four Years In The Saddle*, (NY: Harpers, 1866) p. 188-189; *OR*, LI, s. 1, pt. 1, p. 1172-1173; *OR*, 37, s. 1, pt. 1, p. 219

131 *OR*, 37, s. 1, pt. 1, p. 194, 219-221, 221, 223; Gilmor, p. 188-189

Point and would immediately be sent to Monocacy Junction. Garrett also stressed the importance of the railroad bridge for forwarding reinforcements to Harpers Ferry. Wallace replied at 4:55 p.m., "I will hold the bridge at all hazards. Send on the troops as rapidly as possible."[132]

About three miles west of Frederick, the Confederates formed a line of battle on the Hagerstown Pike. The 8th and 36th Virginia Cavalry regiments were positioned to the right of a macadamized road, while the remainder of the regiments formed on the road. The Confederates covered the ground between the Hagerstown Pike and Harpers Ferry Road. Their artillery was positioned southwest of Frederick on Hagan's Hill near a barn. As senior officer, Gilpin assumed command of the Union force and established a skirmish line across the Hagerstown Pike. The 3rd P.H.B. was positioned on a hill about half a mile west of town, and the three pieces of artillery were placed at various points in Zimmerman's field. The 159th Ohio was ordered to support the artillery, while the 8th Illinois Cavalry was sent to the left of the line.[133]

The skirmish started about 4:00 p.m. as an artillery duel began with both sides firing intervals until dark. One piece under the command of Lieutenant Parkins was handled with such expertise that he was able to damage one of the Confederate artillery. At roughly 5:00 p.m., the 8th Illinois Cavalry dismounted for the engagement. At the same time, Gilpin requested ammunition for the cavalry regiment, which had nearly exhausted its supply from skirmishing nearly all day. As the engagement was on the outskirts of the town, many citizens ventured close to the action to catch a glimpse of the battle in progress.[134]

The Confederates pressed the Union left flank and succeeded in taking Rizer's Barn, but were forced to relinquish control. The engagement seemed to yield no results until about four hours after it started (8:00 p.m.), when Gilpin lead a charge into the Confederate lines, causing them to fall back. With the onset of night, and believing the Union force had been reinforced or would be during the night, the Confederates withdrew to Catoctin Mountain. Here they en-

---

132 *OR*, 37, s. 1, pt. 2, p.100

133 *OR*, 37, s. 1, pt. 1, p. 194, 219-220, 221, 223; *OR*, 51, s. 1, pt. 1, p. 1171, 1172; Bennette, Diary, July 7, 1864, UNC; "The Fight at Frederick on the 7th," *New York Times*, July 10, 1864; William R. Quynn, ed. *The Diary of Jacob Engelbrecht* (Frederick, MD: The Historical Society of Frederick County, 1976), p. 997

134 *OR*, 37, s. 1, pt. 1, p. 194; Bennette, Diary, July 7, 1864, UNC; "The Fight at Frederick on the 7th," *New York Times*, July 10, 1864; Quynn, p. 997

camped near Johnson's headquarters at John Hagan's Tavern and prepared a defense, as the Confederate infantry had not yet arrived. Gilpin was ordered to hold his ground and make no movement to pursue the Confederates. The Union soldiers wounded in the engagement were evacuated on railroad cars and taken to the hospital in Annapolis, Md. Wallace was very proud of the events that had unfolded and sent a message to Lawrence that read, "Think I have had the best little battle of the war."[135]

At 12:00 a.m. on July 8, the 159th Ohio was ordered to return to the junction to protect the Georgetown Pike Bridge that spanned the gap over the railroad. At the same time, Wallace was concerned that the Confederates would return in force that morning, and so he ordered Tyler to reinforce the troops at Frederick. The 149th Ohio National Guard (Companies B, C, D, E, G, I and K) and the 144th Ohio National Guard (Companies B, I and G) moved at daylight with a combined strength of about 660 men. They marched to the west side of Frederick, took possession of the deserted Confederate lines and posted skirmishers. About 9:00 a.m., the three remaining artillery pieces in Alexander's Battery arrived in Frederick and resupplied the three artillery pieces that had engaged the Confederates the previous day. Some artillerymen ventured out toward Middletown to observe the battlefield. Private Frederick Wild, of Alexander's Battery wrote,

> We saw long trenches where the dead had been hastily buried; A curious sight was that of a dead horse that had been shot through the abdomen by one of our shells, the rotary motion of the shot, had caught in the entrails of the horse, dragged them through the wound, and stretched them out some twenty feet on the ground.

The regiments remained in a line of battle on July 8 and did not engage the Confederates.[136]

A portion of the 8th Illinois Cavalry was sent forward on the morning of July 8 to reconnoiter the roads west of Frederick and conduct delaying actions against the Confederates. One company patrolled Harpers Ferry Road, while Companies B and C skirmished on the Hagerstown Pike throughout the day. Company M skirmished with the Confederates on the Shookstown Road. The 159th Ohio Mounted

---

135 *OR*, 37, s. 1, pt. 1, p. 223; *OR*, 37, s. 1, pt. 2, p. 108, 110; Gilmor, p. 188-189; Bain, p. 114-115; Bennette, Diary, July 7, 1864, UNC; "The Fight at Frederick on the 7th," *New York Times*, July 10, 1864; Quynn, p. 997

136 *OR*, 37, s. 1, pt. 1, p. 194, 214, 216, 220-221, 223; *OR*, 51, s. 1, pt. 1, p. 1171; Frederick W. Wild, *Memoirs and History of Capt. F.W. Alexander's Baltimore Battery of Light Artillery* (Loch Raven, MD: The Maryland School for Boys, 1912), p. 120

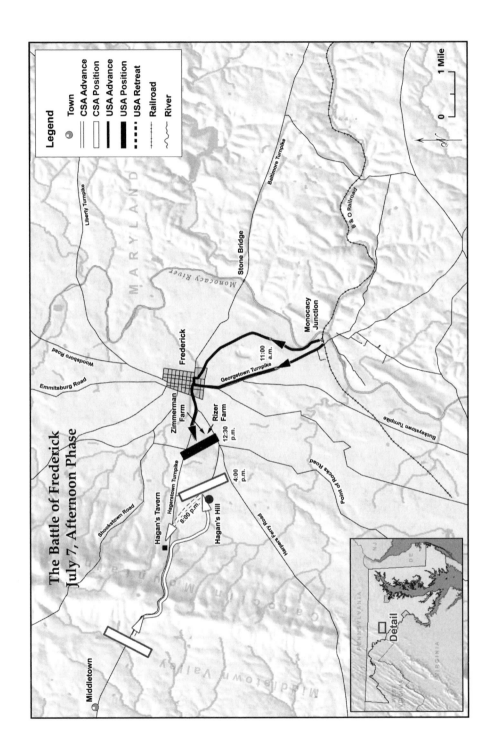

The Battle of Frederick
July 7, Afternoon Phase

Legend
- Town
- CSA Advance
- CSA Position
- USA Advance
- USA Position
- USA Retreat
- Railroad
- River

0   1 Mile

MARYLAND

Liberty Turnpike

Woodsboro Road

Emmitsburg Road

Frederick

Baltimore Turnpike

Stone Bridge

Monocacy River

Monocacy Junction

B & O Railroad

Georgetown Turnpike

11:00 a.m.

Zimmerman Farm

Rizer Farm
12:30 p.m.

Buckeystown Turnpike

Point of Rocks Road

Shookstown Road

Hagerstown Turnpike

Hagan's Tavern

Hagan's Hill
4:00 p.m.

8:00 p.m.

Harpers Ferry Road

Middletown

Middletown Valley

Catoctin Mountain

PENNSYLVANIA

VIRGINIA

Detail

Infantry—now joined by 256 men from various cavalry regiments commanded by Major Charles A. Wells, the 1st New York Veteran Cavalry Regiment and the Loudon Rangers—were ordered to support and watch the flanks of the 8th Illinois Cavalry. The companies were engaged for most of the day and warded off several charges. Eventually, the Confederates were driven back into the mountains.[137]

Prepare for Battle

When the first regiments of the 3rd Division, VI Corps arrived at Monocacy Junction on the morning of July 8, they expected to draw five days' rations and proceed to the mouth of the Monocacy River or Point of Rocks as ordered; however, Wallace had decided against sending the veterans away from Monocacy Junction. They would serve no purpose if sent forward. Wallace knew his inexperienced and outnumbered force had little hope of successfully defending the routes to Washington and Baltimore, and his men had already fought Confederates west of Frederick. With the aide of a division of veterans, he could possibly delay the Confederate advance and provide the time needed for reinforcements to reach Washington.

At daybreak on July 8, the first trains arrived at Monocacy Junction with the 14th New Jersey and part of the 10th Vermont and 87th Pennsylvania regiments. The first two ammunition trains also arrived in the morning. Wallace informed Colonel William W. Henry (commander of the 10th Vermont Regiment) that the Confederates were located on the west side of Frederick with artillery, infantry and cavalry, and that the previous day his army had successfully fought a battle against the lead elements of Early's army. The 14th New Jersey was sent to march around in a circuit (circle) to make it appear as if more troops were at the junction. Later in the afternoon, they formed a line of battle. The 10th Vermont was also ordered to march around Frederick and form a line of battle north of the Hagerstown Pike. The 87th Pennsylvania was ordered to the west side of town, and formed a line of battle on the Hagerstown Pike. Wallace had instructed the regiments to march through the town in an effort to deceive the Confederates as to their true strength.[138]

---

137 *OR*, 37, s. 1, pt. 1, p. 220; Hard, History of the Eighth Cavalry Regiment Illinois Volunteers, p. 297

138 *OR*, 37, s. 1, pt. 1, p. 194; Terrill, p. 73; Bain, p. 115; Read, Diary, July 8, 1864, MNBPA; Prowell, p. 175-176; Roe, p. 122, 124; Lemuel A. Abbott, *Personal Recollections and Civil War Diary 1864* (Burlington, VT: Free Press, 1908), p. 94; Will Clark, Letter, July 11, 1864, 14th New Jersey File, MNBA

After sending the veterans to Frederick, Wallace conducted a reconnaissance around the town. Lieutenant Colonel L. Catlin and the 11th Maryland Regiment remained at the junction to secure the area and stop other trains caring the veteran troops of the 3rd Division. Once in Frederick, Wallace sent a message to Catlin ordering him to forward the 11th Maryland by train into Frederick from the junction. From there they would march through the city to the western edge of town. He also wanted the next troop train that arrived to continue into Frederick. From there the reinforcements would also march through the town to the western side. With an adequate force present in Frederick, Wallace ordered Catlin to hold all troops arriving at Monocacy Junction until the Confederate threat had been resolved. As the remaining trains arrived from Locust Point, the regiments disembarked and established camps near the junction.[139]

About 4:00 p.m. on July 8, Colonel Allison L. Brown, commander of the 149th Ohio National Guard, was ordered to withdraw from Frederick with his seven companies. The regiment was directed to move east on the Baltimore Pike to guard the Stone Bridge that crossed the Monocacy River. After reaching the bridge, one company was posted at Hughes Ford about one mile north of the bridge to prevent the regiment from being flanked on its right.[140]

About 6:00 p.m., Catlin informed Wallace that three Confederate deserters had told him a Confederate force was moving toward Urbana by way of Buckeystown Pike, which would place them behind Wallace's defensive position on the Georgetown Pike. Tyler immediately ordered the 159th Ohio, which had been relieved by a regiment of the 3rd Division, to reconnoiter Buckeystown Pike and determine the validity of the report. Wallace had also learned that Early and Breckinridge were moving on Frederick with 30,000 men. With the reported threat to his rear and 30,000 men reportedly at his front, Wallace decided to withdraw to Monocacy Junction, a far better defensive position. At 8:00 p.m., he telegraphed Halleck that Breckinridge was moving on the Georgetown Pike, which was not yet the case, and added that he would position his force to cover the road. The 159th Ohio reconnoitered for about five miles before being recalled, and returned about midnight.[141]

139 OR, 51, s. 1, pt. 1, p. 1174; OR, 37, s. 1, pt. 2, p. 195; LaForge, Diary, July 8, 1864, MNBA
140 OR, 37, s. 1, pt. 1, p. 214, 216-217
141 OR, 51, s. 1, pt. 1, p. 1174; OR, 37, s. 1, pt. 1, p. 195, 221-223; OR, 37, s. 1, pt. 2, p. 127

About 10:00 p.m., the troops in Frederick were ordered to with-draw to Monocacy Junction by way of the Baltimore Pike, which would take them east. Wallace wanted to give the Confederates the impression that the army was heading to Baltimore and leaving the road to Washington clear. As the army withdrew from Frederick, Clendenin had his cavalry regiment (8th Illinois), along with the mounted men of the 159th Ohio, cover the rear of the column. They left Frederick between 1:00 and 2:00 a.m. on July 9, and arrested two citizens for attempting to signal the Confederates of the movement. Once across the Stone Bridge, the army turned to the right and followed the river south to the junction.[142]

The march from the Stone Bridge to Monocacy Junction was difficult and marred by a number of delays. The artillery wagons had an especially hard time with the movement. One delay occurred when a sapling caught one of the wagon wheels, making it impossible for the wheel to move forward or back. The tree was cut down and the movement continued. In darkness and unfamiliar territory, the soldiers made a wrong turn, making it necessary to unlimber all of the artillery, turn them around by hand, hook up the horses and return to the proper road. The final mishap occurred when one of the caissons rolled down a ravine. It was righted and pulled back onto the road, ready to resume the march. The last train of 3rd Division veterans who would fight at Monocacy arrived about 2:00 a.m. on the morning of July 9. A few hours later, at about sunrise, the rear guard of the column from Frederick reached the junction.[143]

Ricketts arrived at Monocacy Junction late on July 8 and met with Wallace. He knew nothing of Early's presence in the area and was informed of the use of his division during the day at Frederick and the vicinity. Lacking orders to remain at Monocacy Junction, Ricketts questioned Wallace as to his intentions. Wallace told Ricketts that he had three objectives. First, he had to determine whether Early's goal was Baltimore or Washington. Second, he needed to determine how many men Early had. Reports ranged anywhere from 15,000 to 30,000 men. Third, if Early's objective was Washington, Wallace would have to delay him for 20 to 30 hours, allowing time for reinforcements to reach the capital. Recognizing that he had been sent to Maryland to

142 *OR*, 37, s. 1, pt. 2, p. 138; *OR*, 37, s. 1, pt. 1, p. 220, 221; Fuller, Diary, July 8, 1864, MNBA; Hard, p. 298; Abbott, p. 98

143 Wild, p. 121-122; *OR*, 37, s. 1, pt. 1, p. 220; "Army Correspondence," *Morgan County Herald*, Ohio, July 13, 1864; Read, Diary, July 8, 1864, MNBPA

help confront the Confederate threat, and that it would have been unwise to continue toward Harpers Ferry, which the Confederates had already passed, Ricketts placed his division under Wallace's command and accepted his orders. Ironically, Halleck amended Ricketts' orders at 11:40 p.m., and ordered him to report to Wallace. If the Confederates were indeed moving on Urbana, Ricketts was to assist Wallace with delaying the Confederate advance.[144]

By the morning of July 9, Wallace was confident that he could mount a delaying action. Although outnumbered, he held an excellent defensive position and had been reinforced by a veteran division. His small force was the last obstacle between Early and the defenses of Washington. Halleck realized Hunter would be too late to render any assistance; in order to protect the capital from the Confederate army; he was forced to request additional reinforcements from Grant in Petersburg. The success of Early's operation depended on how fast he could dispose of Wallace's force and move on the capital. Washington's fate would be determined at the Battle of Monocacy.

---

144 MG Lew Wallace to Senator Frye, April 13, 1896, Lew Wallace Collection, Indiana Historical Society (HIS); *OR*, 37, s. 1, pt. 2, p. 128

CHAPTER FOUR

THE BATTLE:
MONOCACY JUNCTION

Confederate Lieutenant General Jubal Early's army broke camp near Middletown, Md., at sunrise on July 9 and resumed its march along the Middletown Pike toward Frederick. Confederate Assistant Surgeon J. Kelley Bennette, 8th Virginia Cavalry Regiment, described the movement, "The veteran infantry are pouring down the mountain in a continuous stream and take the road direct to the city."

Major General Stephen D. Ramseur's infantry division led the way and entered the town from the west at 6:00 a.m. Brigadier General Robert Lilley's brigade, consisting of the 13th, 31st, 49th, 52nd and 58th Virginia regiments, spearheaded the march. They moved east, beyond the town, on the Baltimore Pike, while the remaining two brigades (commanded by Brigadier Generals Robert D. Johnston and William G. Lewis) turned to the right and proceeded down the Georgetown Pike. After emerging from the town, Lilly deployed skirmishers and engaged the Union skirmishers near the Stone Bridge, which carried the Baltimore Pike across the Monocacy River. The wagon train, which extended in length, more than nine miles, began to move through Frederick about 8:00 a.m. and for roughly four or five hours, 400 to 500 wagons passed. Once through the town, all of the wagons waited in a large field (probably the fairgrounds) on the east side of town.[145]

Johnston's brigade (5th, 12th, 20th and 23rd North Carolina regiments) led Ramseur's division down the Georgetown Pike, followed by Lewis'

---

145 U.S. War Department, *The War of the Rebellion: A Compilation of the Official Records of the Union and Confederate Armies* (Washington, 1880-1901), Vol. 37, Series 1, Part 1, p. 217 (hereinafter cited as *OR* with references to volume, series, part and page); J. Kelly Bennette, 8th VA Cavalry, Diary, July 9, 1864, Collection 886, University of North Carolina (UNC); CPT William Old, Early's Adjutant, Diary, July 9, 1864, Manuscript Division, Library of Congress (LOC); William R. Quynn, ed. *The Diary of Jacob Engelbrecht* (Frederick, MD: The Historical Society of Frederick County, 1976), p. 997; Robert U. Johnson and Clarence C. Buel, eds. *Battles and Leaders of The Civil War,* Vol. IV (New York: The Century Co., 1887-1888), p. 499

brigade (6th, 21st, 54th and 57th North Carolina regiments). Johnston deployed skirmishers, hoping to secure the wooden covered bridge where the pike crossed the Monocacy River at Monocacy Junction. Securing the bridge would allow the army to easily and quickly cross the river and continue down the pike toward Washington.[146]

LOC

Maj. Gen. Stephen D. Ramseur

The Junction Defense

The Union defense on the Frederick side of the Monocacy River at the junction consisted of 200 men from Companies C and K of the 1st Maryland P.H.B. and 75 men from the 10th Vermont Regiment. The detachment had been posted since about 7:00 a.m., with the 1st Maryland P.H.B. positioned along the railroad and in the blockhouse located near the covered bridge. There was a second blockhouse located across of the river near the railroad bridge. The men from the 10th Vermont were held in reserve, and there were no pickets out in front of the defensive line. Roughly 3,000 veterans of the 3rd Division, VI Corps were deployed in two lines of battle across the river behind the detachment at the junction. The Union officer in charge of this detachment was Lieutenant Colonel Charles G. Chandler of the 10th Vermont, but he was unaccounted for and command fell to Captain Charles J. Brown of the 1st Maryland P.H.B.[147]

Frederick Ransom

When Early entered Frederick that morning, he went to the home of Dr. Richard Hammond on the northwest corner of Market and Second streets and wrote a ransom demand at approximately 8 a.m. The

146 Johnson and Buel, Vol. IV, p. 499

147 Edwin M. Haynes, *A History of the Tenth Regiment Vermont Volunteers* (Lewiston, ME: The Tenth Vermont Regimental Association, 1870), p. 191-192; *OR*, 37, s. 1, pt. 1, p. 215-216; Lemuel A. Abbott, *Personnel Recollections and Civil War Diary 1864* (Burlington, VT: Free Press, 1908), p. 98-99, 104-105

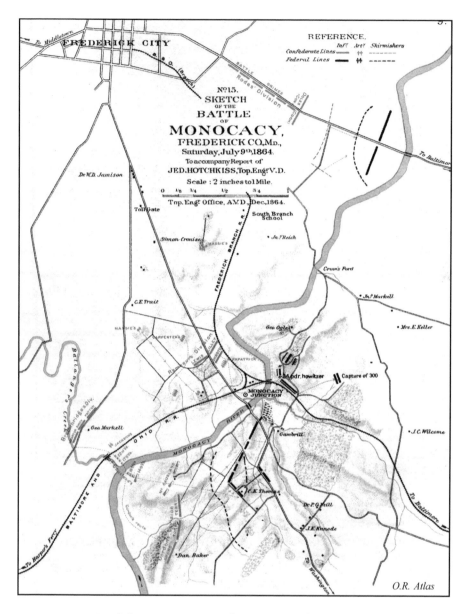

ransom required the town to pay $200,000 or face burning. The note was delivered to Mayor William G. Cole. A separate demand was also issued by the Chief of Commissary Major Wells J. Hawks for 500 barrels of flour, 6,000 pounds of sugar, 3,000 pounds each of coffee and salt, and 20,000 pounds of bacon.

Cole contacted four leading citizens—Judge Richard H. Marshall, former Associate Judge of the Circuit Court; Lawrence J. Brengle, a former delegate who served in the Maryland General Assembly; R. H. Macgill;

and Joseph Baugher—to ask their advice. Believing the sum was too high, especially for a town of 8,000 inhabitants, the citizens decided to send a petition requesting sympathy and fairness. A section of the petition read, "The assessment made in other places in Maryland is relatively much less than that imposed upon our City…" It appears that news of the Hagerstown and Middletown ransoms had reached the citizens of Frederick. They did not know that Early had also intended Hagerstown to pay $200,000 and the request was denied.[148]

The Board of Aldermen and the Board of Common Council were called together to decide how the ransom would be raised. The group concluded that the money would be borrowed from five of the town banks. The banks were assured that they would be reimbursed at the earliest possible moment. The Farmers and Mechanics Bank provided $28,000; the Frederick County Bank, $33,000, the Central Bank, $44,000; the Frederick Town Savings Institution, $64,000; and the Franklin Savings Bank, $31,000.[149]

The payment was delayed until late in the afternoon in the hope that Union Major General Lew Wallace's force, located a few miles south on the Georgetown Pike, would drive the Confederates out of the city before the ransom was paid. About 4:00 p.m. news reached the city that the Confederates were gaining the upper hand and would soon defeat Wallace. The $200,000 was placed in baskets and transported in a wagon provided by the Confederates. The Quartermaster, Major J. R. Braithwaite, filled out a receipt for the town that ensured all property in the city, including that of the Federal governments, would be spared.[150]

Frequent attempts for reimbursement had been made by members of Congress from the Sixth District of Maryland; all claims were denied by the Federal government. The municipal government solely

---

148 Daniel C. Toomey, *The Civil War In Maryland* (Baltimore, MD: Toomey Press, 2004), p. 106; Glenn Worthington, *Fighting For Time* (Shippensburg, PA: White Mane, 1985), p. 104; Edward Delaplaine, "General Early's Levy on Frederick," *Monocacy: July 9, 1864 The Battle That Saved Washington Centennial July 9, 1964*, p. 49, 51-52; "Tomorrow is the 114th anniversary of Battle of Monocacy," *Frederick News Post*, July 8, 1978; "Ransom documents on display," *Frederick News Post*, June 23, 1989; Thomas John Chew Williams and Folger McKinsey, *History of Frederick County Maryland*, Vol. 1 (Baltimore, MD: Regional, 1967; reprinted Genealogical, 2003), p. 386; B. Franklin Cooling, *Monocacy: The Battle That Saved Washington* (Shippensburg, PA: White Mane Publishing, 2000), p. 97
149 Worthington, p. 105; "Ransom of Frederick," *Frederick News Post*, June 23, 1989; Delaplaine, p. 53; Cooling, p. 98
150 Delaplaine, p. 54; "Tomorrow is the 114th anniversary of Battle of Monocacy," *Frederick News Post*, July 8, 1978; Williams and McKinsey, Vol. 1, p. 386; Cooling, p. 98

reimbursed the banks for the full $200,000 plus interest. Half of the total principal debt was repaid by 1868 with the issuing of bonds, and a slight reduction of city taxes that lasted through 1896 also reduced some of the debt. The City of Frederick made the final repayment installment to the banks on September 29, 1951, more than 87 years after the ransom was paid. The exact interest has never been determined, but it is estimated between $200,000 and $600,000. Middletown's claim for reimbursement by the Federal government was also denied.[151]

The Battle Begins

At 7:00 a.m., Dr. Barr, Surgeon-in-Chief of the 3rd Division, VI Corps; Surgeon Joseph Rutherford; Captain Henry Kingsley; and Chaplain Edwin Haynes of the 10th Vermont were on their way to Frederick for breakfast. The four men had paid for lodging and breakfast at a hotel in Frederick the day before and were unable to spend the night because Wallace had ordered the town evacuated on the evening of July 8. The soldiers instead spent the night at the junction with the army. The next morning, as they rode toward town, they saw a squad of cavalrymen in blue uniforms in the distance. In fact, they were Confederates who opened fire when they noticed the four Union soldiers advancing toward them. The hungry men were compelled to abandon the breakfast they had paid for and hastily return to the Union line. Upon their arrival at the junction, they reported their encounter with the Confederate cavalrymen. A squad of 8th Illinois cavalrymen was sent to investigate. They exchanged a few shots with the Confederate cavalrymen about a mile from the junction before they were outnumbered and forced to fall back. The squad crossed the river and linked up with the rest of their regiment on the Thomas Farm.[152]

At roughly 8:30 a.m., Confederate skirmishers advanced down the Georgetown Pike toward the junction. As the Confederates advanced, Captain Brown, the Union officer commanding the small force at the junction, refused to order his men to engage them. He could see the men were in blue uniforms and misidentified them as reinforcements, despite repeated warnings from First Lieutenant George E. Davis of

---

151 "Ransom documents on display," *Frederick News Post*, June 23, 1989; Delaplaine, p. 54; Cooling, p. 213; *OR*, 37, s. 1, pt. 1, p. 337

152 Haynes, p. 191; *OR*, 37, s. 1, pt. 1, p. 220; George G. Benedict, *Vermont in the Civil War: A History Of The Part Taken By The Vermont Soldiers And Sailors In The War For The Union 1861-5*, Vol. 2 (Burlington, VT: The Free Press Association, 1888), p. 309

the 10th Vermont. When the Confederates opened fire and killed one soldier and wounded several others; Brown was surprised by the turn of events and urged Davis to take command of the detachment. [153]

Davis quickly strengthened the line with his Vermonters and sent pickets up and down the river. The defense extended from the railroad bridge, along the railroad tracks, to the viaduct bridge where the Georgetown Pike crossed the railroad. There, it turned sharply left toward the river and continued toward the covered bridge. The blockhouse and the railroad cut provided excellent protection for the defenders. Earlier in the day, Wallace had ordered Davis, "to hold the two bridges across the river at all hazard, and to prevent the enemy from crossing."[154]

At 9:00 a.m., the commander of the 9th New York Heavy Artillery, Colonel William Seward, Jr., son of Secretary of State William Seward, was ordered to send two companies across the river to reinforce the junction. Though the 9th New York Heavies had originally been trained to operate the big guns in the defense of Washington, Grant needed infantry, and so they were converted. Lieutenant Chauncy Fish was sent with Company B to guard the covered bridge and the left flank of Davis' line. Captain Anson Wood was ordered to take Company M and seven men from Company E, a total of 100 men, for picket duty. Wood crossed the bridge with his men and advanced up the Georgetown Pike toward Frederick. They almost immediately came under fire from Confederate skirmishers on the Best Farm. A short time later, they discovered that a skirmish line had been established to the left of the pike by a few men that were commanded by an unidentified captain. Wood quickly reinforced the line, and within a few minutes, and without warning, the captain and his men fell back to the defenses at the junction.[155]

Captain Parker, commander of the 106th New York Regiment's Company F, later crossed the river and took position to the left of Wood. Parker was ordered to establish a picket line with two companies consisting of about 150 men. The pickets were posted about three fourths of a mile in front of the junction facing north. Although rein-

153 Haynes, p. 192, 197; "A Day's Skirmish," *National Tribune*, March 18, 1897; Abbott, p. 104-105; Benedict, p. 309-310; Joseph B. Mitchell, *Badge of Gallantry: Letters from Civil War Medal of Honor Winners* (New York: Macmillan, 1968), p. 37-38

154 Haynes, p. 197, 198

155 Alfred S. Roe, *The Ninth New York Heavy Artillery* (Worcester, MA: 1899), p.128-131; Frederick W. Wild, *Memoirs and History of Capt. F. W. Alexander's Baltimore Battery of Light Artillery* (Loch Raven, MD: Press of the Maryland School for Boys, 1912), p. 124

forced, the Union pickets were forced to withdrawal when the Ramseur's line of battle advanced in force. They fell back to the railroad and protected the left flank of the line established by Davis.[156]

Artillery Engaged

As the Confederates continued to pour down the Georgetown Pike, several artillery batteries were brought forward around 9:00 a.m. One section (two guns) of Massie's Battery (Nelson's Battalion) was positioned about one mile northwest of the junction on the Best Farm. The other section was located on the extreme left of Ramseur's division, about one mile from Crum's Ford, and was not engaged. The first shots impacted around Gambrill Mill on the east side of the river, mortally wounding two soldiers of the 151st New York Regiment and wounding several soldiers of the 87th Pennsylvania Regiment. As the battle continued, Kirkpatrick's Battery (Nelson's Battalion) took up a position on the northeast side of the Georgetown Pike, with the junction to their immediate front. Carpenter's Battery (Braxton's Battalion) was positioned on the northwest side of the Georgetown Pike. Both batteries were on the Best Farm. The Confederates thus positioned a total of 12 guns in the fields north of the junction.[157]

Union artillery consisted of Alexander's Baltimore Battery with three 3-inch rifles on the east side of the river and left of the Georgetown Pike on the Thomas Farm. They protected the Union left flank at the junction. A 24-pounder howitzer was located on the east side of the river on a knoll near the train tracks and blockhouse. The howitzer, which replaced a smaller 12-pounder on May 21, was manned by roughly 10 men from the 8th New York Heavy Artillery. They had been detached from their regiment to train the soldiers at the junction on how to fire the weapon. Alexander's remaining three 3-inch rifles were located farther east of the blockhouse at various vantage points. Together with the gun at the blockhouse, they covered the approaches to the two bridges.

As the action at the junction escalated, the artillery aided in checking the attack, and after roughly an hour (9:30 a.m.), the Confederates eased the pressure at the junction. Ramseur's men had reconnoitered

---

156 Abiel T. LaForge, Diary, July 9 & 10, 1864, 106th New York File, Monocacy National Battlefield Archives (MNBA); Roe, p.130; Haynes, p. 197; "From the 106th," *The Daily Journal*, Ogdensburgh, New York, July 19, 1864

157 Haynes, p. 197; George B. Davis, Leslie J. Perry and Joseph W. Kirkley, *The Official Military Atlas of the Civil War* (New York: Gramercy Books, 1983), plate LXXXIII, map 9; David G. Martin, *The Fluvanna Artillery* (Lynchburg, VA: H.E. Howard, Inc., 1992), p. 105-106

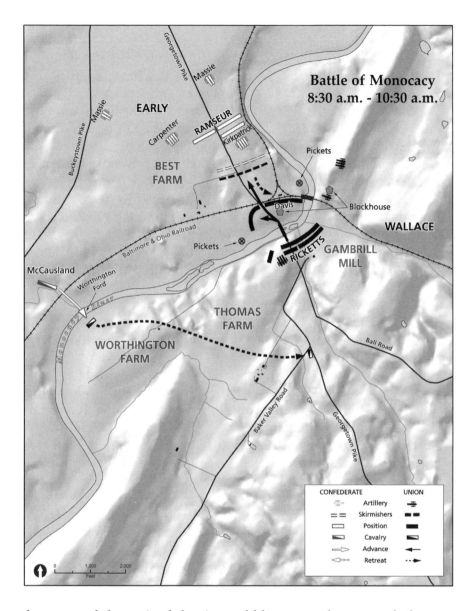

Battle of Monocacy
8:30 a.m. - 10:30 a.m.

EARLY

Massie

Georgetown Pike

Buckeystown Pike

Massie

Carpenter

RAMSEUR

Kirkpatrick

Pickets

BEST FARM

Davis

Blockhouse

WALLACE

Baltimore & Ohio Railroad

Pickets

RICKETTS

GAMBRILL MILL

McCausland

Worthington Ford

Monocacy River

THOMAS FARM

Ball Road

WORTHINGTON FARM

Baker Valley Road

Georgetown Pike

CONFEDERATE		UNION
	Artillery	
= =	Skirmishers	
	Position	
	Cavalry	
	Advance	
	Retreat	

0   1,000   2,000
Feet

the area and determined that it would be too costly to assault the covered bridge. The risk of losing a large number of men and supplies required to assault the defenses of Washington was too great, and a different means of crossing the river would be found, though Ramseur would continue to pressure the Union force at the junction.[158]

---

158 *OR*, 37, s. 1, pt. 1, p. 196, 224; Wilbur R. Dunn, *Full Measure of Devotion: The Eighth New York Volunteer Heavy Artillery,* PART II (Kearney, NE: Morris Publishing, 1997), p. 380, 390

The Second Attack

The Confederates mounted a second attack at the junction at roughly 11:00 a.m. The 23rd North Carolina Regiment, commanded by Colonel Charles Blackwell, attempted to attack the right flank of the Union line near the railroad bridge and capture the blockhouse by moving along the west bank of the river. This route was hidden from view by foliage, but well-positioned Union pickets detected the movement and informed Davis of the advancing troops. Davis recalled the pickets and fortified his flank where they were "perfectly protected." As the 23rd North Carolina attempted to storm the railroad bridge, they came under a "racking fire from the heavy battery on the other side of the river." Davis' men fired along the entire length of the advancing soldiers, forcing the Carolinians to fall back and abandon the attack. As the danger subsided, Davis redeployed the pickets. During this attack, Lilly's brigade was relieved by Rodes' division at the Stone Bridge on the Baltimore Pike. They moved through Frederick and south on the Georgetown Pike, where they linked back up with their division. Ramseur now had his three brigades, more than 2,000-men strong.[159]

During the 11:00 a.m. attack, Confederate sharpshooters also pressured Davis' left flank. They had taken up positions in a barn on the Best Farm and in trees and grain fields that effectively concealed them and provided commanding views of the Union troops. Private Daniel B. Freeman of the 10th Vermont Regiment, who was posted near a rail fence at the Pike Bridge, wrote that, "...every time I raised my head above a certain rail a bullet would hit the rail, embankment of dirt, or go whistling past." The sharpshooters were able to pin down and inflict a number of Union casualties. Private George Douse of the 10th Vermont Regiment was with Freeman and was shot in the face. Douse was taken to a field hospital and it was later discovered that the bullet had passed through his check and lodged in his back teeth.[160]

Eventually, Union artillerymen noticed the small puffs of smoke from the sharpshooter's rifles coming from the Best's barn and directed a number of shots at it. Private Frederick Wild of Alexander's Baltimore Battery described what happened:

---

159 Haynes, p. 198-199; "A Day's Skirmish," *National Tribune*, March 18, 1897; H.C. Wall, 23rd NC, p. 31-32, C.S.A. Archives, Army Units, Duke University Library (DUL); Old, Diary, July 9, 1864, LOC

160 "A Day's Skirmish," *National Tribune*, March 18, 1897; Wild, p. 124-125; Hal Douse, January 9, 2007, Email to Brett Spaulding, 10th Vermont File, Douse Folder, MNBA

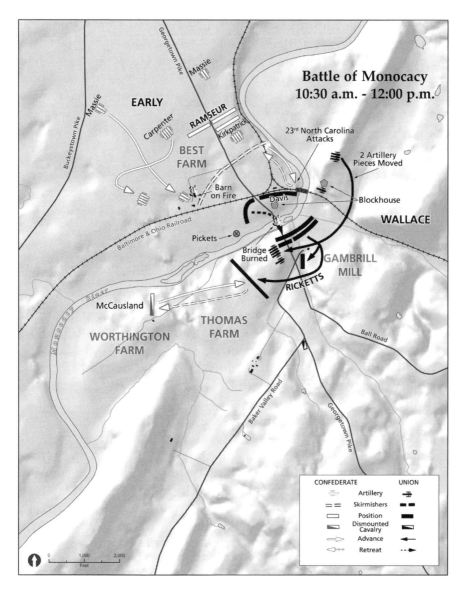

Battle of Monocacy
10:30 a.m. - 12:00 p.m.

EARLY

Massie

Massie

Carpenter

RAMSEUR

Kirkpatrick

23rd North Carolina
Attacks

2 Artillery
Pieces Moved

BEST
FARM

Barn
on Fire

Davis

Blockhouse

WALLACE

Baltimore & Ohio Railroad

Pickets

Bridge
Burned

GAMBRILL
MILL

RICKETTS

McCausland

THOMAS
FARM

Ball Road

WORTHINGTON
FARM

Baker Valley Road

Georgetown Pike

CONFEDERATE   UNION

Artillery

Skirmishers

Position

Dismounted
Cavalry

Advance

Retreat

0   1,000   2,000
Feet

... that barn was filled with sharpshooters so we directed our attention to them, the second shot burst inside the barn, and so did the third, and the fourth; the barn was soon on fire, and we had the satisfaction of seeing some of them being carried away on a litter, and put in an ambulance.[161]

Sometime during this attack, the 24-pounder howitzer, commanded by Captain William H. Wiegel of Brigadier General Erastus

---

161 Wild, p. 125

Tyler's staff, was improperly loaded, which jammed it. A soldier inadvertently dropped a shell down the tube before the powder was inserted. A number of attempts were made to clear the weapon, but they failed. The soldiers did not have the immediate means to dislodge the shell, and so the howitzer was out of action for the remainder of the battle.[162]

Burn the Bridge

The Confederate cavalry had found a ford across the Monocacy and attacked Ricketts' men across the river. With his force fully engaged, Wallace feared Ramseur would mount a frontal attack on the junction, and sometime between 11:00 a.m. and 2:00 p.m., ordered Seward to burn the wooden covered bridge. Seward forwarded the order to Lieutenant Fish, who was detached at the junction, and Privates Alven Sova and Samuel Mack, along with Sergeant Albert Smith, were ordered to burn the bridge. They gathered sheaves of wheat from a nearby field, placed them under the southeast corner of the bridge's roof and ignited the fuel. The soldiers executed the order to the letter, and the bridge was soon engulfed by flames. As the bridge burned, the 9th New York Heavy Artillery troops guarding it withdrew across the river, leaving the detachment's left flank unprotected.[163]

Wallace's aide, Major James R. Ross, attempted to recall Davis' detachment just before the bridge was ignited, but they were too far off and engaged with the Confederates. If they had been recalled, the Confederates would have pursued them and possibly captured the bridge before it could be burned. Thus, the detachment was stranded at the junction with the railroad bridge as their only means of retreat. Also during this attack, the 106th New York Regiment and 9th New York Heavy Artillery soldiers under the command of Wood and Parker fell back. As the covered bridge burned, they retreated across a ford located near the bridge. Davis continued to skirmish with Ramseur's troops and eventually saw the bridge burning. He continued to protect the junction and waited for further orders, which did not come.[164]

162 Dunn, p. 389; *OR*, 37, s. 1, pt. 1, p. 215; Lew Wallace, *Lew Wallace An Autobiography*, Vol. II (New York: Harpers & Brothers', 1906), p. 758, 776-777
163 Roe, p. 128; Wallace, p. 777-778; Mitchell, p. 38; Haynes, p. 199
164 Haynes, p. 199; Cooling, p.120; Wallace, p. 777-778; Roe, p. 131; LaForge, Diary, July 10, 1864, MNBA

When Confederate Brigadier General John McCausland's cavalry brigade, which had crossed the river at a ford, began an assault toward the covered bridge from the Worthington Farm, Wallace ordered Brigadier General James Ricketts, commander of the 3rd Division, VI Corps, to eliminate the threat. Ricketts shifted the 1st Brigade from its position on the east side of the river facing the junction to the Thomas Farm, and easily checked McCausland.[165]

Reposition the Artillery

Two of the three artillery pieces of Alexander's Baltimore Battery, located to the right of the blockhouse on the eastern side of the river, were ordered to redeploy to the Thomas Farm sometime around 12:00 p.m. when more Confederate guns and infantry appeared on the left. They linked up with the three 3-inch rifles already there. Once in position, they assisted the infantry with defending both the Thomas and Best Farms.[166]

Around 1:00 p.m., the Confederate guns on the Best Farm moved forward. The section of Massie's Battery moved about three-fourths of a mile to the southeast. This placed them closer to the train tracks and the Best House. Carpenter's Battery also moved closer to the railroad tracks, but farther west of the Best House. Kirkpatrick's Battery was moved to the west side of the Georgetown Pike and set up on a hill in the field. About 2:00 p.m., McLaughlin and Lowry's batteries were ordered by Breckinridge to cross the Worthington Ford behind Major General John Gordon's division. The ford crossing was more difficult than suspected, and it was felt that it would be more prudent to rush Lowry's Battery into action than take the time to cross the river behind McLaughlin's Battery. McLaughlin's Battery was positioned around the Worthington House, while Lowry's Battery was positioned on the Best Farm near the viaduct bridge. From this position, Lowry's Battery provided enfilading fire to the right and rear of the 110th Ohio Regiment, which was across the river on the Thomas Farm.[167]

---

165 Haynes, p. 198; Wallace, p. 766

166 *OR*, 37, s. 1, pt. 1, p. 196, 224; Wallace, p. 781

167 Davis, Perry and Kirkley, *Atlas*, plate LXXXIII, map 9; LTC J. Floyd King to MAJ J. Stoddard Johnston, July 22, 1864, Box 34, James Eldridge Collection, Huntington Library, San Marino, CA (HL); Martin, p. 106; William H. Runge, ed. *Four Years in The Confederate Artillery: The Diary of Henry Robinson Berkeley* (Chapel Hill: University of North Carolina Press, 1961), p. 86; Wallace, p. 782

The Final Attack

The third and final attack at the junction began around 3:30 p.m. and coincided with the third attack on the Thomas Farm, led by Confederate Major General John Gordon. This attack by Ramseur's troops was larger than the first two and lasted for nearly an hour. The hole created when the men of the 9th New York Heavy Artillery and 106th New York Regiment pulled out remained unfilled because of Davis' limited number of men. Corporal John G. Wright of the 10th Vermont's Company E was sent to relieve a scout in the cornfield to the west of the blockhouse, and report on Confederate activity. Once in position, Wright stood up to assess the situation and was immediately shot in the head and killed.[168]

As the attack continued, the 1st Maryland P.H.B. was ordered by Tyler to retreat across the river. Brown retreated across the railroad bridge and occupied the rifle pits on the east side of the river. As the last of Brown's men left the blockhouse, they torched it to prevent it from falling into Confederate hands. All remaining rations were also ordered burned for the same reason. Tyler then ordered the men of the 1st Maryland P.H.B. north to the Stone Bridge, where the Baltimore Pike crossed the river, to assist the regiments engaged there.[169]

Ramseur's men managed to coordinate a successful assault when the 20th North Carolina Regiment, which had been held in reserve until around 4:00 p.m., was ordered to attack the junction along with the 12th and 23rd North Carolina regiments. While the regiments pressured the Union defense in the railroad cut, one company from the 23rd North Carolina passed under the viaduct bridge and opened fire on the Union left flank. Davis could see the 3rd Division headquarters flag across the river retreating as the last Union defenders on his left flank were forced from the railroad. Knowing that his only means of retreat would soon be cut off and he would be overrun, Davis ordered what was left of his Vermonters to retreat over the railroad bridge. Freeman wrote the following about one of his comrades during the retreat, "As I neared the depot and looked back along the railroad I saw one of my comrades under the pike bridge fighting a dozen Johnies charging down the railroad toward him. He was riddled with lead."[170]

---

168 Haynes, p. 199; Daniel B. Freeman, 10th VT, to Secretary of War, October 2, 1897, NARA
169 Haynes, p. 199; OR, 37, s. 1, pt. 1, p. 215; Wallace, p. 788, 808
170 Haynes, p. 199; H.C. Wall, 23rd NC, p. 31-32, DUL; COL Thomas Toon, 20th NC, to CPT Halsey, August 1, 1864, Thomas Toon Papers, North Carolina State Archives (NCSA); OR, 37, s. 1, pt. 1, p. 215; Wallace, p. 793; "A Day's Skirmish," National Tribune, March 18, 1897

About 4:30 p.m., Davis and his Vermonters retreated across the railroad tracks under fire from the pursuing Confederates. During this retreat across the bridge, 40 feet above the water, there were several casualties from falls off the bridge into the river. Davis wrote that he was, "… pursued so close by the enemy that five of my own Company were seized forcibly by the enemy grabbing the coat collar, so close to me that if one more man had been taken, it would have been me."[171]

Monocacy NB

Lt. George E. Davis

The Confederates closely pressed what remained of Davis' force, and as he reached the eastern bank of the river, the lead elements of the 20th North Carolina began to cross the bridge. As Davis reached the opposite bank and passed the rifle pits, he noticed that Brown and his Marylanders had already withdrew from that position, too. Confederate Colonel Thomas Toon of the 20th North Carolina wrote:

> I cross my regt over the R.R. under a concentrated fire from the bridge with the loss of three men wounded- and charged the Enemy from their works- some of my men charged across the river but the water being too deep to ford I took the flag and lead the Regt across the R.R. Bridge in pursuit of the routed enemy.[172]

Davis led his men to the Baltimore Pike and then to Monrovia, Md., where they connected with the remainder of the division. The Confederates pursued them for about two miles before returning to the junction, where they camped until the next morning. By the end of the day, Davis detachment had lost roughly one-third of its number in wounded, killed and captured. Most of the regiments in Ramseur's division were held in reserve and not engaged during the battle. This resulted in the division taking only about 50 casualties.[173]

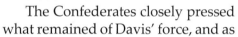

171 Haynes, p. 199; Benedict, p. 315; Abbott, p. 104; Wallace, p. 794; George E. Davis, 10th VT, Pension Record, NARA
172 Haynes, p. 199; Toon to Halsey, August 1, 1864, NCSA
173 Haynes, p. 199

CHAPTER FIVE

THE BATTLE:
McCAUSLAND ATTACKS

At roughly 8:00 a.m. on July 9, 1864, Confederate Major General Stephen Dodson Ramseur's division advanced down the Georgetown Pike toward Monocacy Junction. As the Confederates moved down the pike, the Union force, under Major General Lew Wallace, formed battle lines on the east side of the river. The covered bridge that carried the pike across the river and the railroad junction were located to the Union front. The 2nd Brigade of the 3rd Division, VI Corps moved to the high ground on the pike, with the 110th Ohio Infantry Regiment on the left of the first line of battle, and the 126th and 122nd Ohio Infantry regiments to their right. A little more than five companies (B, C, E, I, K and a few men from F) of the 122nd Ohio were present. The remainder of the 122nd Ohio, the 6th Maryland and the 67th Pennsylvania Infantry regiments were expected to arrive in the afternoon by train. They failed to arrive and did not take part in the battle. The 1st and 3rd Battalions of the 9th New York Heavy Artillery Regiment, which at this point in the war were used as infantry, formed a second line to the rear of the 110th, with the 138th Pennsylvania Infantry Regiment to their right. The 1st Brigade (14th New Jersey, 106th New York, 151st New York, 87th Pennsylvania and 10th Vermont Infantry regiments) had just drawn rations from a supply train and were waiting for further orders in the field near Gambrill Mill. A detachment of 10th Vermont soldiers were at the junction to assist with its defense.[174]

---

174 U.S. War Department, *The War of the Rebellion: A Compilation of the Official Records of the Union and Confederate Armies* (Washington, 1880-1901), Vol. 37, Series 1, Part 1, p. 207-208, 210-211 (hereinafter cited as *OR* with references to volume, series, part, page); Daniel Long to His Wife, July 9, 1864, 151st New York File, Monocacy National Battlefield Archives (MNBA); George R. Prowell, *History of the Eighty-Seventh Regiment Pennsylvania Volunteers* (York, PA: Press of the York Daily, 1903), p. 180; Osceola Lewis, *History of the One hundred and Thirty-Eighth Regiment, Pennsylvania Volunteer Infantry* (Norristown, PA: Iredell & Jenkins, 1866), p. 115; Robert U. Johnson and Clarence C. Buel, eds. *Battles and Leaders of The Civil War,* Vol. IV (NY: The Century Co., 1887-1888), p. 499

Early in the morning, Companies B and I of the 8th Illinois Cavalry Regiment, commanded by Lieutenant Colonel David Clendenin, rode toward Frederick, Md. to ascertain the location of Early's Confederates. Early's advance elements were encountered, and soon after the first shots were fired, they found themselves outnumbered and so recrossed the Monocacy River. The five companies (B, C, I, K and M) were sent to guard the fords and destroy two bridges south of the junction. Company B, commanded by Lieutenant George W. Corbit, was sent to the Worthington Ford about one and a half miles downriver from the covered bridge. Company C, commanded by Lieutenant John Sergeant, was sent downriver to burn a bridge and guard some additional fords. A short time later, Companies I, K and M, commanded by Major John M. Waite, were sent farther down river to burn another bridge and support Company C.[175]

The Battle Begins

Light skirmishing took place at the junction until Confederate artillery was engaged about 9:00 a.m. The first shot fell in the field between Bush Creek and Gambrill Mill, mortally wounding two soldiers of the 151st New York Regiment. Several more shells landed in the area; one exploded near the Gambrill House, wounded three soldiers of the 87th Pennsylvania Regiment. When the artillery barrage started, the train that had brought rations moved down the track toward Baltimore. The 151st New York Regiment was ordered to support three guns of Alexander's Baltimore Battery that was located on a hill overlooking the river to the left of the Georgetown Pike on the Thomas Farm. The regiment was positioned to the left of the artillery. Private Philip Cooke, Company F, 151st New York, described the position, "The east bank there was considerable higher than the west bank and we had a good view of the surrounding country." The 2nd Brigade remained to the right of the artillery, while the balance of the 1st Brigade was positioned to the right of the 2nd Brigade and extended to the railroad. The 10th Vermont Regiment was held in reserve near the mill.[176]

175 Abner Hard, *History of the Eighth Cavalry Regiment Illinois Volunteers, During the Great Rebellion* (Aurora, IL: 1868), p. 298-299; Edwin M. Haynes, *A History of the Tenth Regiment Vermont Volunteers* (Lewiston, ME: The Tenth Vermont Regimental Association, 1870), p. 191

176 *OR*, 37, s. 1, pt. 1, p. 205; Prowell, p. 180-181; Helena A. Howell, comp. *Chronicles of the One hundred fifty-first Regiment New York State Volunteer Infantry 1862-1865* (Albion, NY: A.M. Eddy, 911), p. 86-87; Frederick W. Wild, *Memoirs and History of Capt. F. W. Alexander's Baltimore Battery of Light Artillery* (Loch Raven, MD: Press of the Maryland School for Boys, 1912), p. 123

Ramseur concluded that a frontal assault aimed at capturing the covered bridge would be too costly in terms of casualties, given the excellent Union position. He engaged a small number of men to maintain the pressure at the junction, and waited for another division to sweep the Union defenders from the eastern side of the river. Meanwhile, Confederate Brigadier General John McCausland's cavalry brigade, consisting of the 14th, 16th, 17th and 22nd Virginia Cavalry regiments, moved north along Buckeystown Pike and searched for a suitable place to cross the Monocacy River. McCausland had been ordered by Early on July 7 to cut the telegraph lines and railroad tracks between Maryland Heights and the cities of Washington and Baltimore. The brigade spent July 8 carrying out the orders and camped at Jefferson, Md., for two nights. At dawn on July 9, the brigade moved from the southwest along Buckeystown Pike toward the junction with plans to carry out the second part of Early's orders. Early wanted McCausland to cross the river and secure the covered bridge on the Georgetown Pike.[177]

Ford the Monocacy

At roughly 10:30 a.m., lead elements of McCausland's brigade found the Worthington Ford, located near the mouth of Ballenger Creek. They met stiff resistance from the 8th Illinois Cavalry Regiment's Company B. The Confederates were able to push through the defenders when the entire brigade came forward and overwhelmed the Union company. Corbit withdrew his outnumbered men in the direction of the Thomas House and established a new position on the south side of Baker Valley Road, where they covered the left flank of the Union line.[178]

From the heights near the blockhouse and railroad bridge, Wallace could hear the engagement at the ford. When the firing ceased, he speculated that the Confederates had gained control of the ford and were crossing the river. A short time later, he could see the Confederates forming a line of battle near the Worthington House. Wallace ordered Brigadier General James Ricketts, commander of the 3rd Division, to meet the threat. Ricketts ordered the 106th New York, 14th

---

177 Jubal Early, *Narrative of the War Between the States* (Wilmington, NC: Broadfoot, 1989), p. 386; Alexander St. Clair, 16th VA Cavalry, to S.C. Graham, October 5, 1916, Tazewell County, Historical Society Newsletter 1989, Virginia Historical Society (VHS); Johnson and Buel, Vol. IV, p. 499

178 Hard, p. 299; *OR*, 37, s. 1, pt. 1, p. 220; Lew Wallace, *Lew Wallace An Autobiography*, Vol. II (NY: Harpers & Brothers', 1906), p. 763

New Jersey and 87th Pennsylvania regiments of the 1st Brigade on the double quick to the left to establish a battle line on the Thomas Farm facing west, in the direction of the Worthington Farm. The three regiments connected with the left of the 151st New York and extended from the river a little west of the covered bridge and south toward the Georgetown Pike. The new position subjected the right flank of this line to a severe enfilade from the Confederate artillery batteries located across the river on the Best Farm. After forming the line, some relief was found from the Confederate artillery when the line advanced a short distance and extended in the direction of the Thomas House and Baker Valley Road. Ricketts reported that he had moved four regiments and recommended that "all the artillery should be moved to the left of the road at present, as it seems there should be no further necessity for it on the right."[179]

The First Attack

As the 1st Brigade shifted around 11:00 a.m., Colonel Matthew R. McClennan, the temporary 2nd Brigade commander, ordered Lieutenant Charles J. Gibson, acting commander of the 122nd Ohio Regiment, to provide 50 men for another line on the Thomas Farm. Gibson sent Company C and part of Company B. Companies A, D, F and I of the 138th Pennsylvania were also detailed to the new line by McClennan. These companies were positioned at the intersection of the Georgetown Pike and Baker Valley Road.[180]

The 1st Brigade's battle line was established behind a fence that ran southwest from the left flank of the 2nd Brigade to the north side of the Thomas House. On the east side of the fence was a wheat field, and on the west side of the fence was a cornfield to the north that had grown to about waist high and a grain field to the south. The soldiers lay behind the fence in the wheat field with the corn and grain fields to their front, which concealed their position from the Confederate advance. Extending from the right (near the river) to the left was the 151st New York, 106th New York, 14th New Jersey and 87th Pennsylvania regiments. The extreme left of the line extended toward the house, with the 106th New York Regiment positioned across the wheat field from where the Georgetown Pike turns at an angle.[181]

179 *OR*, 37, s. 1, pt. 1, p. 196, 205; *OR*, 51, s. 1, pt. 1, p. 1175-1176; Wallace, Vol. II, p. 764-765; Haynes, p. 192-193; LT James Read, 10th VT, Diary, July 9, 1864, James B. Ricketts Collection, Manassas National Battlefield Park Archives (MNBPA); Haynes, p. 193

180 *OR*, 37, s. 1, pt. 1, p. 211; Lewis, p. 115; Read, Diary, July 9, 1864, MNBPA

The Confederate cavalrymen rode to the Worthington House and were ordered to dismount. Corporal Alexander St. Clair of the 16th Virginia Cavalry Regiment's Company I explained what happened:

> As a rule, when the cavalry dismount to fight, every fourth man is detailed to take charge of the horses, to hold or move them as the exigencies of the battle may require. On this occasion when we reached the "brick house" every man was ordered to dismount, tie his horse to the fence or turn him loose. No one could be spared to hold the horses. We fully realized that this meant serious work, as this command had never before been given us.[182]

Hoping to attack the Union left flank, the brigade immediately formed a line of battle near the Worthington House. It was believed that the troops at the bridge were poorly trained and inexperienced 100-days men that would easily be defeated. The officers remained on horseback and the brigade advanced in two lines through a cornfield located in front of the Worthington House. The farm fields were bisected by a number of fences that separated the fields, one of which McCausland's dismounted cavalry brigade was forced to climb over. After clearing the fence, the brigade halted to regain the proper alignment of their battle lines and then continued the advance. Wallace observed the movement and described the scene that unfolded before him:[183]

> Then at a signal, the array having attained its proper front, it started forward slowly at first; suddenly, after a passage of a space arms were shifted and, taking to the double quick, the men raised their battle cry, which, sounding across the field and intervening distance, rose to me on the heights, sharper, shriller, and more like the composite yelping of wolves than I had ever heard it. And when to these were presently super added a tempestuous tossing of guidons, waving of banners, and furious trampling of the young corn that flew before them like splashed billows the demonstration was more than exciting-it was really fearful. A brave spectacle it was indeed.[184]

When McCausland's brigade approached to within 125 yards of the skirmish line, Ricketts, who was the only Union soldier on horse-

181 Wallace, Vol. II, p. 767; "Monocacy, Terrible Experience of a 14th N.J. Boy in that Battle," *National Tribune*, April 15, 1886; Alfred S. Roe, *The Ninth New York Heavy Artillery* (Worcester, MA: 1899), p.128; "Monocacy, and the Gallant Stand of the 106th New York Against Early," *National Tribune*, January 24, 1884
182 St. Clair to S.C. Graham, October 5, 1916, VHS
183 Wallace, Vol. II, p. 768; Lemuel Abbott, *Personnel Recollections and Civil War Diary 1864* (Burlington, VT: Free Press, 1908), p. 100
184 Wallace, Vol. II, p. 767-768

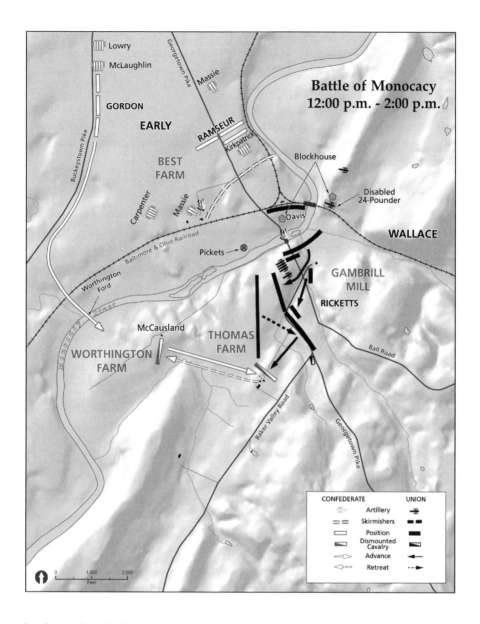

Battle of Monocacy
12:00 p.m. - 2:00 p.m.

Lowry
McLaughlin
GORDON
EARLY
Massie
RAMSEUR
Kirkpatrick
BEST
FARM
Carpenter
Massie
Georgetown Pike
Buckeystown Pike
Baltimore & Ohio Railroad
Blockhouse
Disabled
24-Pounder
Davis
Pickets
WALLACE
GAMBRILL
MILL
RICKETTS
Worthington
Ford
McCausland
THOMAS
FARM
WORTHINGTON
FARM
Ball Road
Baker Valley Road
Georgetown Pike

CONFEDERATE		UNION
	Artillery	
==	Skirmishers	
	Position	
	Dismounted Cavalry	
	Advance	
	Retreat	

0   1,000   2,000
Feet

back, ordered the entire line to rise and fire. The veteran soldiers
rested their weapons on the fence rails and unleashed a volley of lead
that ripped through the Confederates, causing a significant number
of casualties. The entire Confederate line disappeared from view, leaving only a few riderless horses and mounted officers visible. Those
not wounded quickly lay down to escape the attack and attempted to
return fire, while the wounded crawled roughly 400 yards back toward the Worthington Farm to safety. The order to fire at will was

given, and after a few minutes, the Union line swooped down upon the cavalrymen. The rout was complete and McCausland's brigade was driven back under heavy fire and closely pursued by Union skirmishers. John Worthington watched the attack from a second-story window of his home and later stated that he, "could not understand why the confederates went forward as if on parade." From his vantage point, he could see the Union line waiting to spring their trap upon the unsuspecting cavalrymen.[185]

Ricketts' ambush was performed perfectly, and his men celebrated their success with a cheer that could be heard by Wallace on the Heights. With the loss of a number of officers and the ease with which the Union forces warded off their attack, it was a long time before McCausland was able to reorganize his brigade and try again. Lieutenant Peter Robertson of the 106th New York Regiment's Company C reported that his regiment "captured one Lieutenant Colonel, one captain, two lieutenants, and twenty privates." After regrouping, Ricketts had the skirmishers establish a new line "running parallel with the pike and some distance to the west of it." Here they waited for the Confederates next attack.[186]

Sometime between the first attack (11:00 a.m.) and 2:00 p.m., the wooden bridge over the Monocacy River was burned to prevent the Confederates from crossing in Ricketts' rear and cutting off his primary route of retreat. Most of the soldiers who had been sent across the river earlier in the day were recalled to rejoin their regiments. Ricketts could now focus on the new threat coming from the direction of the Worthington Farm. Ironically, the burning of the bridge inadvertently cut off the primary route of retreat for about 300 men remaining at the junction.[187]

Union Cavalry Recalled

After McCausland's failed attack, Clendenin sent a message that recalled Waite and Companies M and K back to the Georgetown Pike. Upon their return, they assisted Corbit with protecting the left flank

---

185 Wallace, Vol. II, p. 769-670; "Army Correspondence," *Morgan County Herald*, OH, July 13, 1864; St. Clair to Graham, October 5, 1916, VHS; Glenn Worthington, *Fighting For Time* (Shippensburg, PA: White Mane, 1985), p. 120

186 Haynes, p. 193; Wallace, Vol. II, p. 770; "Monocacy, and the Gallant Stand of the 106th New York Against Early," *National Tribune*, January 24, 1884; George B. Davis, Leslie J. Perry and Joseph W. Kirkley, *The Official Military Atlas of the Civil War* (NY: Gramercy Books, 1983), plate LXXXIII, map 9

187 Roe, p. 128; Wallace, Vol. II, p. 777-778

of the line and patrolling the surrounding roads for Confederate activity. Company I, which had initially been sent with Waite, was ordered to assist Company C with the burning of the bridges farther down the river. Then both companies were to return. After carrying out their orders, however, they were cut off and unable to reconnect with the rest of the regiment. The companies, commanded by Captain Albert Wells, fell back by way of Sugar Loaf Mountain, rode to Barnesville, Md., and then traveled cross country with the intention of moving north on the Georgetown Pike to link up with their regiment. This route also was blocked by Confederates, and on July 10, Wells and his men fell in with a Union cavalry force from Washington that was patrolling the road.[188]

When McCausland crossed the ford, he solved Early's problem of finding an alternate river crossing. Early immediately had his second in command, Major General John Breckinridge, order one of his division commanders to move to the ford and cross the river. Major General John Gordon was ordered to move his division from Frederick down Buckeystown Pike to the Worthington Ford.[189]

Militarily, the situation could not have been better for Wallace and his force. They were still holding the junction and stone bridge (located about three miles north of the junction on the Baltimore Pike) and had easily repelled an attack on the Thomas Farm. Most importantly, they had delayed the Confederate army for roughly six hours. There were some serious problems for Wallace. The biggest was the loss of the 24-pounder howitzer that covered the approach to the junction, which had been improperly loaded and was disabled for the remainder of the battle. There was also no means of communicating with Washington or other towns as the civilian telegraph operator had left the area when the battle intensified. Likewise, the train that Wallace had intended to use for evacuating the wounded had left. Finally, the 67th Pennsylvania, 6th Maryland and the rest of the 122nd Ohio regiments—a total of about 1,100 men—still had not arrived. Without a telegraph operator, Wallace, who was expecting further attacks, was unable to find out when and if the reinforcements would arrive.[190]

---

188 *OR*, 37, s. 1, pt. 1, p. 220, 248; Hard, p. 299
189 Early, p. 387
190 *OR*, 37, s. 1, pt. 1, p. 196; William E. Bain, ed. *The B&O in the Civil War* (Denver, CO: Sage Books, 1966), p. 122-123; Wallace, Vol. II, p.774, 775, 778-779, 783, 802

McCausland Attacks Again

After the first disastrous attack on the Thomas Farm, McCausland's brigade was forced to fall back to the Worthington Farm. McCausland now knew that he was not in a fight with poorly led and trained 100 days-men, but battle-hardened veterans. The troops were quickly reorganized to defend against a Union counterattack. In spite of this, Ricketts elected not to follow up the attack, but to remain on the defensive, so McCausland chose to launch a second attack. This time, instead of blindly leading his brigade across the fields into the Union force, he took the time to reconnoiter the area.

McCausland and his staff surveyed the Union position as sporadic skirmishing continued. Wallace mentioned in his memoirs that after the first attack, he noticed mounted men leisurely riding along a cornfield, stopping to survey Ricketts' positions on the Thomas Farm. After gathering precise information about the whereabouts of the Union force McCausland devised a new plan of attack.[191]

About 2:00 p.m., McCausland advanced his dismounted brigade in a southeast direction toward the Thomas Farm house. Formed in two lines of battle, the dismounted brigade passed south of the Worthington Farm house at a double time. Undaunted by the failure of their first attack, the Confederate cavalrymen shouted their menacing battle cry as they moved over the fields separating the two farms.

Corporal Roderick Clark, 14th New Jersey Regiment, described the scene, "It was certainly a grand sight as they advanced, in good order, with their numerous battle-flags waving in the breeze." Lieutenant Lemuel Abbott, 10th Vermont Regiment, wrote that, "I for one looked on the scene with mingled feelings of bitterness, dread and awe, for they were so far away there was nothing else to do." Ricketts' line opened fire on the left of McCausland's brigade, but once the Confederates had closed to within a few hundred yards, the order was given to fall back.[192]

The two lines of cavalrymen were far beyond the extreme left of Ricketts' battle line, leaving him in the precarious position of having his left flank turned. This would have threatened the rest of the division. To counteract this movement, the 87th Pennsylva-

---

191 Wallace, Vol. II, p. 775-776; Abbott, p. 100

192 Abbott, p. 100-102; "Monocacy, Terrible Experience of a 14th N.J. Boy in that Battle," *National Tribune*, April 15, 1886; Davis, Perry and Kirkley, *Atlas*, plate LXXXIII, map 9; "Army Correspondence," *Morgan County Herald*, OH , July 13, 1864

nia, 14th New Jersey, 106th New York and 151st New York regiments that formed the line from left to right were ordered to fall back to the Georgetown Pike. The battle line was not able to shift, however, as the Confederates were moving too fast and would have been on top of them before they were able to move far enough to the left. McCausland's brigade took control of the Thomas House and surrounding outbuildings.[193]

When the regiments fell back to the Georgetown Pike, McClennan's 2nd Brigade, which was positioned on the pike in two lines of battle facing north along the Monocacy River, was ordered to shift to their left. This shift placed every regiment, except for the reserve, on a single line of battle facing west, from the river toward Baker Valley Road. The shift positioned the 110th Ohio Regiment on the extreme right, with a portion of the 9th New York Heavy Artillery to their left followed by the 138th Pennsylvania Regiment. The 126th and 122nd Ohio regiments were ordered to extend the line to the left of the 106th New York Regiment.[194]

Counterattack

When McCausland's brigade took the house, Wallace noticed that their right flank faltered. He sent his aide, Major James R. Ross, to find Ricketts and suggest that he charge the Confederate position. While en route, Ross encountered Colonel William Truex's aide, Captain William H. Lanius, who took the suggestion in the form of an order; instead of delivering the message, he rode up in full view of the Confederate sharpshooters in the Thomas House and ordered the 87th Pennsylvania and 14th New Jersey regiments on the left of the line to charge the Confederate positions in and around the house. After driving the Confederates off, Ricketts' men were to establish a new position with their right flank resting at the house.[195]

The two regiments dashed forward around 3:00 p.m., while the 106th and 151st New York regiments provided cover fire. Major Peter Vredenburgh, 14th New Jersey Regiment, described the attack, "Our men at Thomas' gate then charged up his yard & across his fields right up to his house & fought the rebels around the corner behind the trees and everywhere else. Till they retired behind the barn..."

---

193 *OR*, 37, s. 1, pt. 1, p. 205; "Monocacy, Terrible Experience of a 14th N.J. Boy in that Battle," *National Tribune*, April 15, 1886; "Monocacy, and the Gallant Stand of the 106th New York Against Early," *National Tribune*, January 24, 1884
194 *OR*, 37, s. 1, pt. 1, p. 208, 209, 210-211
195 Wallace, Vol. II, p. 779-780; Prowell, p. 182

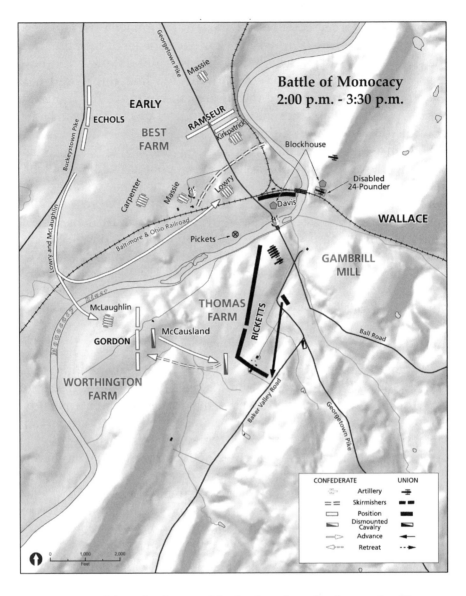

Battle of Monocacy
2:00 p.m. - 3:30 p.m.

EARLY

ECHOLS

BEST
FARM

RAMSEUR

Georgetown Pike

Massie

Kirkpatrick

Blockhouse

Disabled
24-Pounder

Carpenter

Massie

Lowry

Davis

WALLACE

Baltimore & Ohio Railroad

Pickets

GAMBRILL
MILL

Buckeystown Pike

Lowry and McLaughlin

McLaughlin

THOMAS
FARM

RICKETTS

GORDON

McCausland

Ball Road

WORTHINGTON
FARM

Baker Valley Road

Georgetown Pike

CONFEDERATE   UNION

Artillery
Skirmishers
Position
Dismounted
Cavalry
Advance
Retreat

0   1,000   2,000
Feet

Upon reaching the house, Vredenburgh, who knew the Thomas family, searched for them and "found them in the cellar frightened to death." He had become very good friends with the family in 1862 when the 14th New Jersey Regiment was tasked with guarding the junction for nine months. After checking on the family, Vredenburgh went through the house to lock drawers and some doors and brought down a basket of silver that they had packed up and left upstairs. He also brought down water and a wounded Confederate soldier for the family to tend.[196]

In the attack, the two regiments turned McCausland's right flank, forcing the Confederate brigade to relinquish control of the house and surrounding structures, and set them in retreat toward the Worthington Farm. With the house area secured, the order was given for the rest of the division, which was now on the line, to move forward and drive any remaining Confederates back. The division advanced about a fourth of a mile and established a new battle line. Two artillery pieces were also detached from the hill near the blockhouse and sent to the Thomas Farm where three artillery pieces were already located. Once in position, they joined the artillery barrage in progress.[197]

As the line moved forward and established its new position, the right flank was exposed to an intense artillery fire from across the river, with shells coming from their front, rear and right. Wallace wrote, "The shells seemed to be in flight from every direction." The extreme right was forced to fall back and seek some protection in an old road cut. The battle line was now established, with the right flank anchored on the Monocacy River just south of the covered bridge. The battle line extended obliquely from the river toward the Thomas House and outbuildings, where it formed an obtuse angle and extended to Baker Valley Road.[198]

Once the regiments were in position, the 10th Vermont Regiment, which was held in reserve at the turn in the Georgetown Pike, was ordered to the extreme left flank of the battle line. This placed every man that Ricketts had on the line with orders to hold at all cost. The 1st Brigade solely bore the brunt of each of McCausland's attacks and had taken a number of casualties during the engagements. Truex, 1st Brigade commander, reported to Ricketts that he could not hold his side of the line without additional men, and requested 300 troops. Ricketts detached the requested number of men from the 2nd Brigade and sent them to the left to reinforce Truex.[199]

Unconcerned about being forced to fall back to the Worthington Farm, McCausland quickly reformed the two battle lines and ad-

196 MAJ Peter Vredenburgh, 14th NJ, to His Mother, July 12, 1864, Collection 1, Folder 3, Peter Vredenburgh Papers, Monmouth County Historical Association Library & Archives, Freehold, NJ (MCHALA); OR, 37, s. 1, pt. 1, p. 224; Read, Journal, July 9, 1864, MNBPA

197 Wallace, Vol. II, p. 781; OR, 37, s. 1, pt. 1, p. 224; "Army Correspondence," Morgan County Herald, OH, July 13, 1864

198 OR, 37, s. 1, pt. 1, p. 208, 209, 210-211; Wallace, Vol. II, p. 777, 780; Ervin Dunbar to George Douse, August 24, 1913, 10th Vermont File, MNBA

199 Haynes, p. 193; OR, 37, s. 1, pt. 1, p. 205-206

vanced. Meanwhile, Ricketts' brigade held its fire until the Confederate cavalrymen were roughly 100 yards out. Then the order passed along the line and volley after volley was poured into McCausland's men, causing the ranks to break and fall back once again. When the men reached the Worthington Farm, they were again reformed, only this time with more difficulty. Once the line was established, they advanced over the same ground, and Ricketts' brigade delayed firing until the enemy had reached the same spot, then they opened fire again. The second attack was more fierce and protracted, but like the first, it pushed back the Confederates, who sustained heavy losses.[200]

Captain Adam E. King, Assistant Adjutant General to Ricketts, who was on horseback, led the 10th Vermont Regiment on the final counterattack and drove the last of McCausland's cavalrymen from the field. Exposing himself to great danger while encouraging his men forward, King was shot twice, once through the arm and again in his side, the second a serious but not mortal wound. When King was wounded, the Vermonters returned to the line and waited for further orders. Lieutenant Enoch Cowart, 14th New Jersey Regiment, later noted that during these attacks:

> Some 6 mounted officers of theirs dashed forward to rally their men and were all shot down. Our standard bearer [Sergeant William B. Cottrell] dashed forward in front of our Regmt and waved it in the faces of the rebs, but the brave little fellow was shot dead; another of our men caught it up and went forward, but soon shared the same fate.

The engagement ended around 3:30 p.m., at which time Truex requested additional men to reinforce his position. Unable to pull additional troops from the 2nd Brigade, Ricketts denied the request. McCausland had made his last attack now that infantry under the command of Major General John B. Gordon had crossed the river.[201]

Wallace wrote that during this second series of attacks, the two sides were engaged for roughly 40 minutes, which seems a little short for this type of battle. Regardless, Ricketts was compelled to shift his entire division to the left, and he eventually forced McCausland's brigade to retire once again. Wallace was elated about delaying the Con-

---

200 Prowell, p. 183; Read, Journal, July 9, 1864, MNBPA
201 LT James M. Read to His Father, July 19, 1864, 10th Vermont File, MNBA; Enoch Cowart to Mary Ann Dackus, August 10, 1864, Box 1, Folder 1, Cowart Family Papers, MCHALA; *OR*, 37, s. 1, pt. 1, p. 205

federates a while longer; he calculated that the attack had delayed them for a total of eight hours. He also held hope that the missing regiments from Ricketts' division would arrive at any moment to reinforce the battle line on the Thomas Farm. As the minutes passed, however, his expectations that they would arrive in time diminished. The situation would soon change for Wallace, now that Gordon was poised for attack.[202]

202 Wallace, Vol. II, p. 781, 789

CHAPTER SIX

THE BATTLE: GORDON'S ATTACK

As the Battle of Monocacy raged on, Major General John Gordon's division of roughly 3,500 troops received orders at about 2:00 p.m. to march down Buckeystown Pike and cross the Monocacy River. The division had been in a line of battle, about one mile south of Frederick, since around 8:00 a.m. Brigadier General Clement Evans' brigade (13th, 26th, 31st, 38th, 60th and 61st Georgia Infantry regiments and the 12th Georgia Infantry Battalion) led the division down the pike followed by the brigades of Brigadier Generals Zebulon York (1st, 2nd, 5th, 6th, 7th, 8th, 9th, 10th, 14th and 15th Louisiana Infantry regiments) and William Terry (2nd, 4th, 5th, 10th, 21st, 23rd, 25th, 27th, 33rd, 37th, 42nd, 44th, 48th and 50th Virginia Infantry regiments). Due to huge losses in the Overland Campaign that spring, York and Terry's brigades were forced to consolidate multiple regiments to become combat effective. McLaughlin's and Lowry's artillery batteries, consisting of four guns each, were attached to the division and brought up the rear of the line.[203]

After a few miles, the division turned off the pike, crossed the B&O Railroad tracks and began to traverse the Monocacy River at Worthington Ford. Brigadier General John McCausland's cavalry brigade had located this crossing earlier in the day and driven off a squad of Union cavalry guarding it. The ford was extremely rocky and slowed the movement of both the infantry and artillery. As McLaughlin's Battery crossed behind the infantry, it was determined that it would be more prudent to have Lowry's Battery rushed into action on the Best Farm, rather than take the time to cross the ford. Lowry's Battery was positioned near the viaduct bridge where the Georgetown Pike crossed the railroad. Here it provided enfilading

---

203 BG Zebulon York, Report, July 22, 1864, Ni 51, John Page Nicholson Collection, Huntington Library, San Marino, CA (HL); BG William Terry, Report, July 22, 1864, Chicago Historical Society (CHS); Robert U. Johnson and Clarence C. Buel, eds. *Battles and Leaders of The Civil War,* Vol. IV (NY: The Century Co., 1887-1888), p. 499

National Archives

Maj. Gen. John B. Gordon

fire on the right and rear of the 110th Ohio Infantry Regiment on the Thomas Farm.[204]

At the Worthington Farm, Gordon ordered the division to file to the left and face in an easterly direction toward the Union lines. This placed Evans on the extreme right, York in the middle and Terry on the left. The left of the line was about a fourth of a mile from the river. While the division crossed the river and reformed on the other side, Gordon reconnoitered the Thomas Farm. He could see the fields were separated by fences and the wheat fields had been cut and were littered with a number of wheat shocks. The Union defense was well posted behind one of the fences and around the farm buildings. There was also a skirmish line in front of the battle line and what appeared to be a second battle line in support of the first. The farthest line was actually the reserve (the 10th Vermont Infantry Regiment), which had just been ordered to the left flank of the Union battle line. Gordon decided to attack en echelon by brigades from the right. Evans' brigade would hit the Union left flank, followed by York's attack in the center and Terry's on the Union right flank. As soon as McLaughlin's Battery crossed the ford, it would be positioned at several vantage points around the Worthington House and directed to fire at the Thomas House and surrounding area. The attack took place under the supervision of Major General John Breckinridge.[205]

---

204 Lew Wallace, *Lew Wallace An Autobiography*, Vol. II (NY: Harpers, 1906), p. 784; LTC Floyd King to MAJ J. Stoddard Johnson, July 27, 1864, Thomas Butler King Papers, Southern Historical Society Collection, University of North Carolina (UNC)

205 U.S. War Department, *The War of the Rebellion: A Compilation of the Official Records of the Union and Confederate Armies* (Washington, 1880-1901), 37, Series 1, pt. 1, p. 350-352 (hereinafter cited as *OR* with references to volume, series, part and page); Terry, Report, July 22, 1864, CHS; Wallace, Vol. II, p. 791

The Union Defense

The Union defense on the Thomas Farm was commanded by Brigadier General James Ricketts of the 3rd Division, VI Corps with roughly 3,300 troops positioned in a line of battle west of the Georgetown Pike. By 3:00 p.m., every regiment in the division was on line and prepared for the next Confederate attack. The right flank was anchored on the Monocacy River just south of the covered bridge, which had been ordered burned by Major General Lew Wallace earlier in the day. The defense extended obliquely from the river toward the Thomas House and outbuildings, where it formed an obtuse angle and extended to Baker Valley Road where the left flank rested. The 1st Brigade (10th Vermont, 87th Pennsylvania, 14th New Jersey, 106th New York and 151st New York Infantry regiments), commanded by Colonel William Truex, was on the left of the battle line, and the 2nd Brigade (138th Pennsylvania, 122nd and 126th Ohio, 9th New York Heavy Artillery and 110th Ohio Infantry regiments), commanded by Colonel Matthew McClennan, was on the right. Posted in front of this line were skirmishers. Five artillery pieces from Alexander's Baltimore Battery were positioned on a hill west of the Georgetown Pike near the covered bridge.[206]

Evans' Georgians

As Gordon's division organized for attack, McCausland's cavalry brigade, which had been engaged since about 2:00 p.m., began to fall back from the Thomas Farm house. Two attacks had failed to dislodge Ricketts' defenders. The dismounted cavalrymen made their way to the Worthington Farm, which had served as a staging area for both attacks, and was now being used by Gordon in the same fashion. As the cavalrymen fell back, Private Nathaniel Harris, 16th Virginia Cavalry Regiment, overheard Evans inspiring his men by telling them, "Come on, Georgians, follow me-we will show these cavalrymen how to fight. These are only 100-days men and they can't stand up against our troops," an indication that Gordon's men did not know they faced veterans.[207]

---

206 Johnson and Buel, Vol. IV, p. 499; Edwin M. Haynes, *A History of the Tenth Regiment Vermont Volunteers* (Lewiston, ME: The Tenth Vermont Regimental Association, 1870), p. 193; Ervin Dunbar to George Douse, August 24, 1913, 10th Vermont File, Monocacy National Battlefield Archives (MNBA); David G. Martin, ed. *The Monocacy Regiment: A Commemorative History of the Fourteenth New Jersey Infantry in the Civil War 1862-1865* (Highstown, NJ: Lonstreet House, 1987), p. 181

207 Nathaniel E. Harris, *Autobiography: The Story of an Old Man's Life, with Reminiscences of Seventy-five Years* (Macon, GA: J.W. Burke, 1925), p. 90

LOC

Brig. Gen. Clement Evans

At roughly 3:30 p.m., the command to advance was given. Evans and his officers, who were on horseback, led the brigade over Brook's Hill south of the Worthington House. Two battle lines advanced over the steep slope and used the dense woodland that covered a portion of the hill to obscure their movement. The division skirmishers, commanded by Captain Benjamin F. Keller of Evans' brigade, were in advance of the brigade. Evans instructed his regiments to advance quietly until they emerged from the woods at the crest of the hill, and when the Union line came into view, to attack with a yell. Meanwhile, Ricketts' division was given orders to hold their positions at all hazards. Truex again requested additional troops to reinforce the left of the battle line. This time, unlike the first, no troops were sent. All available troops had already been sent from the right side of the battle line.[208]

The Georgians emerged from the wood line about 700 yards in front of the left flank of the Union defense and moved down Brooks Hill, where they were fired upon by the five artillery pieces from Alexander's Baltimore Battery. After a few minutes, the artillery had nearly exhausted the last of their ammunition, and Ricketts ordered them to limber up and withdraw toward the Baltimore Pike. When the Confederates reached a fence and began to climb over, the Union skirmishers answered their yells with a volley, followed by the command to fire at will.[209]

208 MG John B. Gordon, Report of Operations, June 28-July 9, 1864, Ni51, John Page Nicholson Collection, HL; *OR*, 37, s. 1, pt. 1, p. 205-206; I.G. Bradwell, "In The Battle Of Monocacy, MD," *Confederate Veteran*, Vol. XXXVI, February 1928, p. 56; I.G. Bradwell, "The Battle Of Monocacy, MD," *Confederate Veteran*, Vol. XXXVII, October 1929, p. 382-383; *OR*, 37, s. 1, pt. 1, p. 205-206

209 *OR*, 37, s. 1, pt. 1, p. 223-224, 350-352; I.G. Bradwell, *Confederate Veteran,* Vol. XXVIII, May 1920, p. 177; Wallace, Vol. II, p. 791-792; Helena A. Howell, comp. *Chronicles of the One hundred fifty-first Regiment New York State Volunteer Infantry 1862-1865* (Albion, NY: A.M. Eddy, 911), p. 87

While under fire, a few of Evans' men tore down a section of fence to allow the mounted officers to pass. Sometime within these first few minutes, Evans, who was riding along the lines urging the brigade forward, was shot from his horse while in front of the 31st Georgia Infantry Regiment, his old command. He was hit twice: the first through his left arm; the second, more serious wound, was in his left side. Two soldiers, alerted to what had happened, placed Evans on a litter and carried him across the river, where a field hospital had been established. That evening, the surgeon operated on Evans, who refused any anesthesia. He had heard the horror stories of captivity, and due to the severity of his wound, feared he would be left behind and captured if sedated. While probing the wound for the bullet, the surgeon discovered that it had hit some straight pins in Evans' side pocket, and the impact scattered the broken pieces in the wound. The bullet was removed, but since the surgeon operated in haste, he sewed the wound shut without removing the broken pins. The next morning, Evans procured an ambulance and remained with the army until it crossed back into Virginia.[210]

In addition to Evans, a number of regimental commanders were wounded or killed. Both Colonel John Lamar and Lieutenant Colonel David Van Valkenburg, 61st Georgia Infantry Regiment, were killed. The initial shock of losing Evans and other ranking officers caused a brief delay until Colonel Edmund Atkinson, commander of the 26th Georgia Infantry Regiment, took command of the brigade.[211]

As his brigade was under fire, Atkinson found it necessary to change its direction. He ordered the brigade to make a left-wheel movement (where the left side of the line pivots and the right side swings around), which threatened the Union left flank. As the Confederates moved forward, the Union skirmishers fell back to the battle line that was positioned behind a fence, in a sunken road, west of the Thomas House. As the Georgians advanced through a wheat field and maneuvered around the wheat shocks, they inadvertently caused the alignment of the battle lines to fall into disarray. Once through the field and over a second fence, Atkinson ordered the brigade to halt and reestablish the battle lines. Then he gave the order to charge.[212]

---

210 John B. Gordon, *Reminiscences Of The Civil War* (NY: Scribner's, 1903), p. 311; Robert Stephens, *Intrepid Warrior Clement Anselm Evans Confederate General from Georgia: Life, Letters, and Diaries of the War Years* (Dayton, OH: Morningside, 1992), p. 425-427

211 *OR*, 37, s. 1, pt. 1, p. 351

212 Bradwell, *Confederate Veteran*, Vol. XXVIII, May 1920, p. 177; Gordon, Report, HL; COL Edmund N. Atkinson, Evan's Brigade, Report, July 22, 1864, Box 2, James Eldridge Collection, HL; Gordon, p. 312

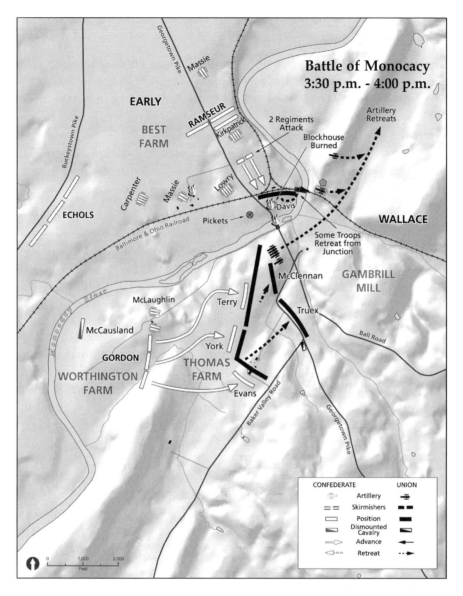

Battle of Monocacy
3:30 p.m. - 4:00 p.m.

EARLY

Massie

Georgetown Pike

RAMSEUR

Kirkpatrick

BEST FARM

2 Regiments Attack

Artillery Retreats

Blockhouse Burned

Carpenter

Massie Jr

Lowry

Davis

ECHOLS

Baltimore & Ohio Railroad

Pickets

WALLACE

Some Troops Retreat from Junction

McClennan

GAMBRILL MILL

McLaughlin

Terry

Truex

Ball Road

McCausland

York

GORDON

THOMAS FARM

WORTHINGTON FARM

Evans

Baker Valley Road

Georgetown Pike

CONFEDERATE		UNION
	Artillery	
== ==	Skirmishers	■■ ■■
▭	Position	■
	Dismounted Cavalry	
⇨	Advance	◀
⟨⇤	Retreat	◀- -

0   1,000   2,000
Feet

The Georgians rushed forward, determined to dislodge and rout the Union defenders. Truex ordered his men to hold their fire until the Confederates were approximately 125 yards out. Colonel William Henry, commander of the 10th Vermont Infantry Regiment, ordered his men to, "Wait, boys, don't fire until you see the C.S.A. on their waist belts and then give it to 'em." When the Georgians were within range, the order to fire was given and the soldiers of the 1st Brigade transformed into a line of smoke and fire as shot after shot was sent into the Confederate ranks, resulting in many casualties.

111

Major Peter Vredenburgh, 14th New Jersey Infantry Regiment, described the attack:

> It was really magnificent to see how heroically they charged. I never saw such a bold movement before. They evidently thought we were recruits and walked right up to us in this open field without shrinking dodging or running as soldiers usually do in the open on a charge.

The attack was thwarted, and it was evident to Atkinson that the Georgians could not dislodge Truex's men without reinforcements.[213]

York's Louisianans

Atkinson's Georgians were in a desperate situation and ready to fall back when York's Louisiana Tigers appeared on their left flank. The Louisianans engaged the soldiers of the 106th and 151st New York Infantry regiments and methodically pushed back the right of Truex's brigade from the sunken road. His left flank maintained its position, which was well protected in and around the Thomas House and grove. But, McLaughlin's Battery started to bombard the house and surrounding area with such great effect that the Georgians' attack was reenergized. Seven shells struck the house, one of which crashed through the dining room wall. The entire attack had lasted for about 30 minutes. Finally, Truex's brigade was driven back toward the Georgetown Pike, while McClennan's brigade, on Truex's right, maintained its position behind the crest of a hill.[214]

After dislodging Truex, a brief halt was ordered at the sunken road, which the Union line had just occupied. During the halt, Truex hastily established a second battle line in the open fields between the Georgetown Pike and the Thomas House. The two Confederate brigades of Georgians and Louisianans charged, again. This time the combined strength of the two brigades easily forced Truex back to the

---

213 Martin, p. 181; "Monocacy, and the Gallant Stand of the 106th New York Against Early," *National Tribune*, January 24, 1884; Haynes, p. 194; G. W. Nichols, *A Soldier's Story of his Regiment (61st Georgia) and incidentally of the Lawton-Gordon-Evans brigade* (Jessup, GA: 1898), p. 171; MAJ Peter Vredenburgh to His Mother, July 12, 1864, Collection 1, Peter Vredenburgh Papers, Folder 3, Monmouth County Historical Association Library & Archives, Freehold, NJ (MCHALA)

214 Bradwell, "Early's March To Washington In 1864," *Confederate Veteran,* Vol. XXVIII, May 1920, p. 177; Martin, p. 181; *OR*, 37, s. 1, pt. 1, p. 350-352; Mary A. Giunta, ed. *A Civil War Soldier of Christ and Country: The Selected Correspondence of John Rodgers Meigs 1859-1864* (Urbana and Chicago: University of Illinois Press, 2006), p. 234

Brig. Gen. Zebulon York

pike, where a third battle line was established along the cuts of the road. The sunken pike provided Truex's men with good natural breastworks. Private George Nichols of the 61st Georgia Infantry Regiment wrote, "We could not see a yankee on our part of the line during the whole advance. All that we could shoot at was the smoke of their guns, they were so well posted."

Private Isaac G. Bradwell, 31st Georgia Infantry Regiment, wrote that "the enemy was well protected and presented nothing to shoot at except their heads." The Confederate line had taken position in a "dry ditch" directly in front of the Union defensive position. From this point, the Confederate line was reformed and attacked on two separate occasions. Each time it was forced back. As the afternoon progressed, the two Confederate brigades could not break the line, and York's brigade received severe flanking fire on the left from McClennan's brigade.[215]

Terry's Virginians

Gordon, who was directing the attack, noticed the stalemate that had developed along the Georgetown Pike, and ordered Terry to break it by attacking the Union right flank. Terry's Virginians moved across the Thomas fields to the left of York's brigade. They had gone only a few feet through a corn field when a line of Union soldiers lying behind a post-and-rail fence came into view, about 125 yards to their front. They were from McClennan's brigade, which had not been heavily engaged to this point, but were feeling the effects of the artil-

215 Gordon, p. 312; *OR*, 37, s. 1, pt. 1, p. 351; Nichols, p. 171; Bradwell, "In The Battle Of Monocacy, MD," *Confederate Veteran*, Vol. XXXVI, February 1928, p. 57; "Monocacy, and the Gallant Stand of the 106th New York Against Early," *National Tribune*, January 24, 1884; BG Zebulon York, Report, July 22, 1864, Ni 51, John Page Nicholson Collection, HL; "The Battle of Monocacy: Holding at Bay Early and His Raiders," *National Tribune*, October 27, 1898

lery bombardment from the Best Farm located across the Monocacy River. Both sides opened fire, and after a few minutes, the 9th New York Heavy Artillery and 110th Ohio Infantry regiments located on the extreme right flank were ordered to fall back. While falling back, the regiments also shifted to the left to escape the artillery bombardment, thus leaving a gap of about 100 yards or more between the river and the battle line. The regiments established a new position in an old roadbed that had banks about two-feet high and provided them with a little protection.[216]

In an effort to reestablish their old line, the regiments were ordered to counterattack. The soldiers dashed forward, determined to reoccupy their former position. But the Confederate artillery and small-arms fire proved to be too much and McClennan's men were forced back to the old roadbed. The left of the line by the Thomas House was still locked in a heated fire fight, with neither side willing to yield. Henry described this:

> Their sharpshooters were firing on us quite lively from the second story windows. Sergeant Pike was one of our best sharpshooters, and was having all the fun he wanted firing at those rebs in the window, while I was watching them with my glass and giving him points. Soon I saw a head and gun coming in sight around one of the window casings, and directed Pike where to look, and almost at the same instant both fired, I felt a bullet go under my chin, and the reb pitched out of the window. The brave Color Sergeant, Billy [William] Mahoney, was watching us, and in a moment he caught me by the coat-tail and pulled me to the ground…and a moment after the brave Sergeant Pike dropped upon us, shot dead.[217]

Gordon recognized the strong defensive position that Ricketts' division commanded and sent two staff officers in succession to report to Breckinridge at the Worthington Farm. Per Gordon's instructions, they requested a brigade of reinforcements to be used in a flank attack. After sending the officers, Gordon soon determined that the reinforcements could not be deployed quickly enough, and instead ordered Terry to make another attack on the extreme right flank of the Union line. Terry split his brigade and ordered Colonel John Funk to take the five consolidated regiments of the Stonewall Brigade to

---

216 *OR*, 37, s. 1, pt. 1, p. 351; James A. Hutcheson, "Saved The Day At Monocacy," *Confederate Veteran*, Vol. XXIII, February 1915, p. 77; Terry, Report, July 22, 1864, CHS; Wallace, Vol. II, p. 793; Martin, p. 184; Alfred S. Roe, *The Ninth New York Heavy Artillery* (Worcester, MA, 1899), p.132; Howell, p. 87
217 Haynes, p. 203; *OR*, 37, s. 1, pt. 1, p. 351; Terry, Report, , July 22, 1864, CHS

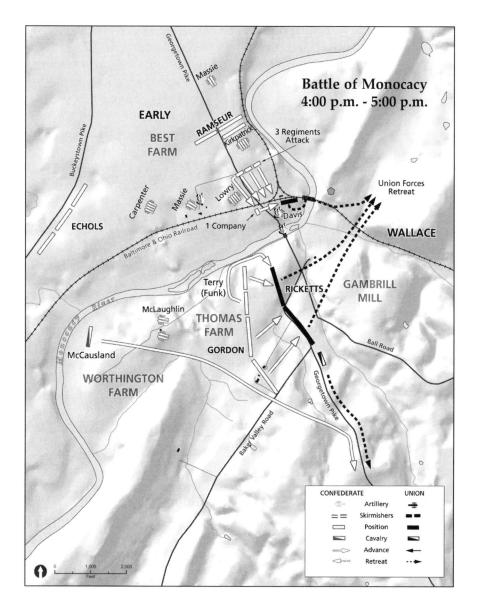

Battle of Monocacy
4:00 p.m. - 5:00 p.m.

EARLY

BEST
FARM

RAMSEUR

Massie

Kirkpatrick

3 Regiments
Attack

Union Forces
Retreat

ECHOLS

Carpenter

Massie

Lowry

Davis

1 Company

Baltimore & Ohio Railroad

WALLACE

Terry
(Funk)

RICKETTS

GAMBRILL
MILL

McLaughlin

THOMAS
FARM

McCausland

GORDON

Ball Road

Monocacy River

WORTHINGTON
FARM

Baker Valley Road

Georgetown Pike

CONFEDERATE		UNION
	Artillery	
==	Skirmishers	▬ ▬
▭	Position	▬
	Cavalry	
	Advance	◄—
	Retreat	- -►

0   1,000   2,000
Feet

his left and swing around behind the remainder of the brigade. Funk then led the regiments toward the river and moved along the river bank. When they reached a position below the Union right, they moved up a hill where they could enfilade the Union line.[218]

As the battle wore on, Ricketts' division became desperate for ammunition. Chaplain Edwin Haynes of the 10th Vermont Regiment

---

218 *OR*, 37, s. 1, pt. 1, p. 351-352; Haynes, p. 195; Terry, Report, July 22, 1864, CHS

stated that, "many had fired their last cartridge and were borrowing of their dead and wounded comrades." About 4:20 p.m., Major General Lew Wallace recognized that the battle was lost and ordered Ricketts to fall back toward the Baltimore Pike. Funk had exploited the gap on the Union right flank and caused the defense in that area to crumble as it was pushed toward Gambrill Mill. By 5:00 p.m., Ricketts' entire division was retreating and closely pursued by Gordon's division.[219]

Brig. Gen. William Terry

With Confederates hot on their trail, confusion spread and prevented any chance of an orderly withdrawal. It took about 15 to 20 minutes from the time Terry's brigade pushed McClennan's brigade from the fence to the retreat of the entire Union line along the Georgetown Pike. The Confederates pursued Ricketts' men for about two miles before returning to the battlefield and camping for the night. The attack by Gordon's division lasted for about an hour and a half.[220]

Throughout the day, there was a lack of communication among the Confederate soldiers. At first they were unaware that most of the Union troops they engaged were not 100-days men, but battle-hardened veterans. Nichols noted this when he wrote, "It was said that it was raw troops that we were fighting, but I never saw old soldiers shoot better." Early also wanted to keep his army intact as much as possible to continue the march toward the prime target: Washington. As a result, only a small fraction of Early's army was engaged, and the battle lasted the entire day. This would greatly benefit the Union in the days to come. Nevertheless, with the Battle of Monocacy, the Confederacy had obtained its first undisputed success on Union soil, and the road to Washington now lay open.[221]

219 Haynes, p. 194, 195; Wallace, Vol. II, p. 796; Roe, p.132

220 Hutcheson, "Saved The Day At Monocacy," *Confederate Veteran*, Vol. 23, February 1915, p. 77; Roe, p.132

221 Nichols, p. 171; "The Battle of Monocacy," *The Charleston Mercury*, Charleston, South Carolina, August 11, 1864

CHAPTER SEVEN

THE BATTLE:
THE STONE BRIDGE

As the Confederates advanced toward Frederick, Md., on the morning of July 9, Major General Lew Wallace established a defense along the eastern bank of the Monocacy River that covered the routes to Washington and Baltimore. The veterans of the 3rd Division, VI Corps were positioned on either side of the Georgetown Pike, and the soldiers of the Middle Department were periodically positioned at strategic points along the bluffs that lined the east side of the river from the B&O Railroad north to the Stone Bridge that carried the Baltimore Pike across the Monocacy River.

The 3rd Maryland P.B.H., commanded by Colonel Charles Gilpin, had Companies A, B, C, D, E and K positioned at various points between the B&O Railroad and the Stone Bridge. Companies H and I were mounted and used as scouts—Company I at Monocacy Junction and Company H at Monrovia, six miles east along the railroad. Companies F and G were stationed at the blockhouse on the east side of the Monocacy River near the junction. Captain Robert Bamford and Companies B, G and H of the 1st Maryland P.H.B., under Gilpin's command, were at Crum's Ford, about a mile north of the railroad bridge.[222]

The 11th Maryland Infantry Regiment, a new 100-days unit commanded by Colonel William T. Landstreet, was marched down the Georgetown Pike toward Frederick and the picket line. After a quick conference with the officer in charge of the pickets, the 11th Maryland was marched back toward the junction, over the railroad bridge, and up the road the regiment had used when they fell back from Frederick the night before.

---

222 U.S. War Department, *The War of the Rebellion: A Compilation of the Official Records of the Union and Confederate Armies* (Washington, 1880-1901), Vol. 37, Series 1, Part 1, p. 214, 215 (hereinafter cited as *OR* with references to volume, series, part and page); Frank Moore, ed. *The Rebellion Record: A Diary of American Events,* Vol. 11 (NY: D. Van Nostrand, 1869), p. 624-627; Lew Wallace, *Lew Wallace An Autobiography,* Vol. II (NY: Harpers & Brothers', 1906), p. 775

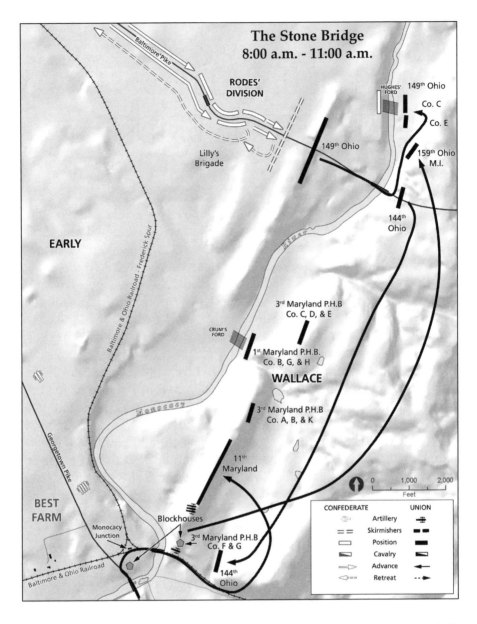

The Stone Bridge
8:00 a.m. - 11:00 a.m.

RODES' DIVISION

HUGHES' FORD

149th Ohio
Co. C
Co. E

149th Ohio

Lilly's Brigade

159th Ohio M.I.

144th Ohio

EARLY

3rd Maryland P.H.B Co. C, D, & E

CRUM'S FORD

1st Maryland P.H.B. Co. B, G, & H

WALLACE

3rd Maryland P.H.B Co. A, B, & K

11th Maryland

BEST FARM

Monocacy Junction

Blockhouses

3rd Maryland P.H.B Co. F & G

144th Ohio

CONFEDERATE		UNION
	Artillery	
	Skirmishers	
	Position	
	Cavalry	
	Advance	
	Retreat	

0   1,000   2,000
Feet

They traveled about a mile and a half, and Companies A and G took up a position in what appeared to be an old mill race. The position provided excellent protection, with natural breastworks about five feet high and a number of large trees. The remainder of the regiment extended south toward the B&O Railroad, with the left flank supporting Alexander's Baltimore Battery just behind the brow of a hill. Along this line the regiment was held in reserve. To prevent information about Wallace's numbers and deployment from reaching the Confederates, civilians were not permitted to enter the lines unless they were providing information on Confederate movements. Likewise, they were not permitted to leave unless they had a pass from headquarters.[223]

The Union Defense

Colonel Allison L. Brown, commander of the 149th Ohio National Guard, was ordered to guard the Stone Bridge the afternoon of July 8. The two regiments in his command, the 144th and 149th Ohio National Guard, arrived at sundown and went into camp. The 149th Ohio's Company C was sent to Hughes Ford, about one mile north of the bridge, to protect the right flank. Shortly after arriving at the bridge, the 144th Ohio, which consisted of companies B, G and I, was ordered to Monocacy Junction. At daylight on July 9, the 149th Ohio established a skirmish line on the crest of a ridge on the west side of the Monocacy River and prepared to receive the Confederate's advance on the Baltimore Pike.[224]

Captain Edward H. Lieb, 5th U.S. Cavalry Regiment, was detailed to command the 159th Ohio National Guard, a mounted infantry unit. Lieb reported at Monocacy Junction on the morning of July 9 after assisting the 8th Illinois Cavalry Regiment with the rear guard during the withdrawal from Frederick. He was ordered to hold Hughes Ford and assist Brown with the defense of the Stone Bridge. About 10:00 a.m., Confederate cavalry, probably the 8th Virginia Cavalry Regiment from Brigadier General Bradley Johnson's brigade, attempted to cross the Monocacy River at Hughes Ford and engaged the 149th Ohio's Company C, commanded by Captain Charles W. McGinnis. To reinforce McGinnis, Brown sent Company E, of the 149th Ohio, commanded by Captain Thomas B. Jenkins. Lieb arrived with his mounted men during the engagement and assisted McGinnis and Jenkins in successfully repelling the attack. The Confederates did not attempt to cross Hughes Ford again, and left only a light skirmish line there. After positioning the 159th Ohio at the ford, Lieb set out for the Stone Bridge to assist Brown.[225]

---

223 William H. James, "Blue and Gray: A Baltimore Volunteer of 1864," *Maryland Historical Magazine*, Vol. XXXVI, March 1941, p. 25-26, 28-29; *OR*, 51, s. 1, pt. 2, p. 1176
224 *OR*, 37, s. 1, pt. 1, p. 216
225 *OR*, 37, s. 1, pt. 1, p. 217, 221-222

Rodes' Division

Confederate Major General Robert Rodes' division was comprised of four brigades commanded by Brigadier Generals Bryan Grimes (32nd, 43rd, 45th and 53rd North Carolina Infantry regiments and 2nd North Carolina Infantry Battalion), Phillip Cook (4th, 12th, 21st and 44th Georgia Infantry regiments), William Cox (1st, 2nd, 3rd, 4th, 14th and 30th North Carolina Infantry regiments) and Colonel Charles Forsyth (3rd, 5th, 6th, 12th and 61st Alabama Infantry regiments). Forsyth commanded Brigadier General Cullen Battle's division while he was on leave recuperating from a wound received at the Battle of Spotsylvania, May 11-12.

Meade Album

Maj. Gen. Robert Rodes

The division camped on the right flank of Early's army near Jefferson, Md., and started for Frederick soon after sunrise on July 9, entering the town from the southwest at about 11:00 a.m. Rodes was ordered to move down the Baltimore Pike and relieve Lilley's brigade (Ramseur's division), which was engaged with Brown's skirmishers. Lilley returned to the Georgetown Pike, where Ramseur's division was attempting to dislodge the Union defenders at Monocacy Junction. Initially, Lilley's skirmishers were replaced with the Rodes' sharpshooters who engaged Brown's Ohioans while the remainder of the division was held in reserve. Rodes' objective was to make a feint at the Stone Bridge and draw as many troops away from Monocacy Junction as possible.[226]

---

226 Jubal Early, *Narrative of the War Between the States* (Wilmington, NC: Broadfoot, 1989), p. 387; R.A. Brock, ed. *Southern Historical Society Papers,* Vol. XXII (Richmond, VA: The Society, 1894), p. 378; SGM John G. Young, 4th NC, Diary, Collection #1076, NC State Archives (NCSA); Brandon Beck, *Third Alabama!: The Civil War Memoir of Brigadier General Cullen Andrews Battle* (Tuscaloosa, AL: The Univ. of Alabama Press, 2000), p. 114; Cullen Battle to John Campbell, July 14, 1864, RG 109, Register of Confederate Records, Telegrams Received by the Confederate Secretary of War, NARA, Washington D.C.; Robert U. Johnson and Clarence C. Buel, eds. *Battles and Leaders of The Civil War,* Vol. IV (NY: The Century Co., 1887-1888), p. 499

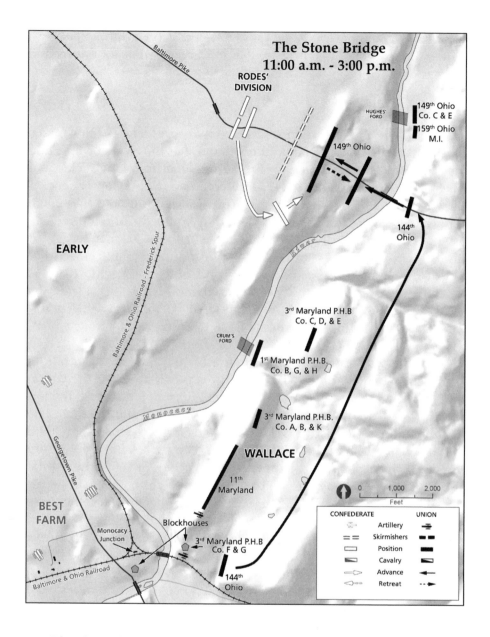

The Stone Bridge
11:00 a.m. - 3:00 p.m.

The sharpshooters occupied a strong position about 500 yards west of the Union line atop a parallel ridge with a valley between them. Some of them had taken a position in the log house of Mr. Simpson's near the Baltimore Pike. The structure provided excellent protection, and with the chinking between the logs removed, the sharpshooters were able to pick away at the Union skirmish line. Lieutenant Edward Goldsborough, a former officer discharged due to illness, volunteered his service and was made a temporary aide-de-camp to General Tyler during the crisis, wrote: "So accurate was their fire that it was dangerous for our men to even show their heads above the hilltop."[227]

Take the Bridge

About 11:30 a.m., Brown discovered that an effort was being made, in force, to turn the left flank of his defense at the Stone Bridge, and he requested reinforcements. Brigadier General Erastus Tyler sent the three companies of the 144th Ohio, commanded by Major Ebenezer Rozell, from Monocacy Junction. Brown decided to hold these men in reserve at the Stone Bridge where they could easily reinforce any point of the line. Brown had a total force of about 760 men located at the bridge and Hughes Ford. He sent five mounted infantrymen from the 159th Ohio to observe and report on Confederate activity on his left. These men were quickly discovered and had to retreat from the area when they were fired on. They delayed reporting their withdrawal for some time, leaving the flank exposed, with no one watching the Confederates.[228]

The Confederates took advantage of this lack of observation, and using the terrain to mask their movement, attacked the Union left flank. They were able to force the Union defenders on the left portion of the line back to within 100 yards of the bridge. The Confederates occupied this part of the deserted line and wreaked havoc on the remainder of the Union force by a raking fire down the line. To reestablish the defensive position, Brown ordered the 149th Ohio's Company B to fix bayonets and charge. The counterattack failed and Company B fell back. Brown then ordered the three companies of the 144th Ohio to charge. Assisted by Lieb, who had just arrived from Hughes Ford, the second attack successfully drove the Confederates back and restored the line. Brown reported that, "During this charge my loss was quite severe, owing to the fact that the enemy was posted behind the fence, while my men were compelled to charge across an open field, up the hill in fair view, and within short range of his guns."[229]

---

227 Edward Goldsborough, *The Battle of Monocacy* (Frederick, MD: Historical Society 1898), p. preface, 18

228 *OR*, 37, s. 1, pt. 1, p. 217; William A. Butler Letter, Company G 144th Ohio Volunteer Infantry, August 5, 1864, Civil War Newspapers: Wyandot County Correspondents, Center for Archival Collections, Bowling Green State University (BGSU)

229 *OR*, 37, s. 1, pt. 1, p. 217, 222

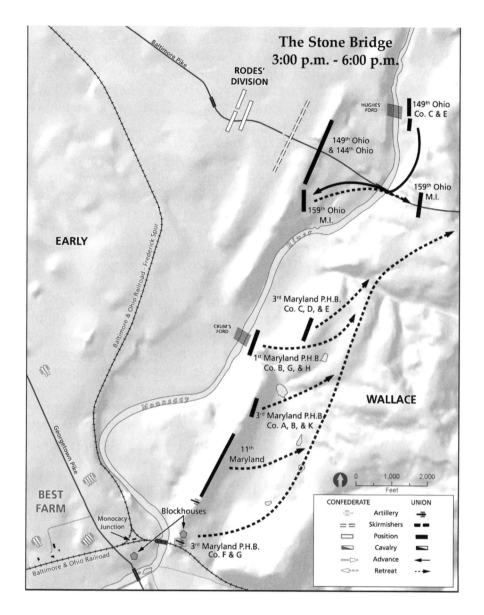

The Stone Bridge
3:00 p.m. - 6:00 p.m.

RODES'
DIVISION

HUGHES'
FORD

149th Ohio
Co. C & E

149th Ohio
& 144th Ohio

159th Ohio
M.I.

159th Ohio
M.I.

EARLY

3rd Maryland P.H.B.
Co. C, D, & E

CRUM'S
FORD

1st Maryland P.H.B.
Co. B, G, & H

WALLACE

3rd Maryland P.H.B.
Co. A, B, & K

11th
Maryland

BEST
FARM

Monocacy
Junction

Blockhouses

3rd Maryland P.H.B.
Co. F & G

Baltimore & Ohio Railroad

0   1,000   2,000
Feet

CONFEDERATE		UNION	
	Artillery		
	Skirmishers		
	Position		
	Cavalry		
	Advance		
	Retreat		

Cover the Retreat

Brown extended the line and moved the entire command forward, minus the two companies of the 149th Ohio at Hughes Ford. The 159th Ohio had been ordered back from Hughes Ford and positioned on the extreme left of the line. Lieb said, "The position was a very good one. The enemy tried hard to take it, but at every point [was] driven back." At 4:00 p.m., Wallace ordered Brigadier General James Ricketts to withdraw his division on the Thomas Farm to Baltimore Pike. By this time, Tyler had already begun to march his reserve regiments, (the 11th Maryland and 3rd Maryland P.H.B.), to the Stone Bridge. When Tyler received a message from Wallace, he ordered Companies C and K of the 1st Maryland P.H.B., which had been engaged in the defense of Monocacy Junction on the west side of the river, to disengage, cross the river and reinforce the regiments at the Stone Bridge.

These two companies did not make it to the Stone Bridge, but instead retreated with Ricketts' division from the Thomas Farm. Tyler rode ahead of the reserves and took overall command of Brown's force, while Brown remained in command at the bridge. Sometime between 4:00 and 5:00 p.m., as the head of Ricketts' division reached the Baltimore Pike, Brown was ordered by Wallace to hold the bridge "to the last extremity." Wallace reported that, "the stone bridge held by Colonel Brown now became all important; its loss was the loss of my line of retreat..."[230]

Brown pulled in his skirmish line to strengthen the center of the battle line, and covered all commanding points as best as he could, given the size of his force. Lieb and the 159th Ohio were ordered by Brown to pull back from the battle line to the bridge and establish a new battle line on the east side of the river. Here they would protect the rear of Brown's force from Confederates who might cross the river upstream or downstream and prevent their route of retreat from being cut off. One company from the 149th Ohio replaced Lieb's regiment. By this time, Wallace's force around Monocacy Junction was in full retreat to the Baltimore Pike.[231]

When Tyler left the reserves, Gilpin resumed command and continued the march to the Stone Bridge. The day was excessively hot, and the march was halted a number of times to let the men fill their canteens and rest. The final delay came within one-fourth mile of the bridge. Sergeant William James of the 11th Maryland wrote that there were, "only two things that I cared for-water, and a shady place [to] lie down in." The reserves had spent about a half hour resting when Brown's force was attacked. Tyler then sent Lieutenant Goldsborough of his staff to order the reserves to retire down the Baltimore Pike toward New Market, Md. He apparently had decided not to use the largely green force. The 11th Maryland had not been engaged the entire day, although they were exposed for a time to artillery fire.[232]

230 *OR*, 37, s. 1, pt. 1, p. 197, 217, 222; Goldsborough, p. 25; Wallace, Vol. II, p. 787-788
231 Goldsborough, p. 24-25; *OR*, 37, s. 1, pt. 1, p. 218, 222
232 James, "Blue and Gray: A Baltimore Volunteer of 1864," *Maryland Historical Magazine*, Vol. XXXVI, March 1941, p. 27-28; Goldsborough, p. 25; *OR*, 37, s. 1, pt. 1, p. 214

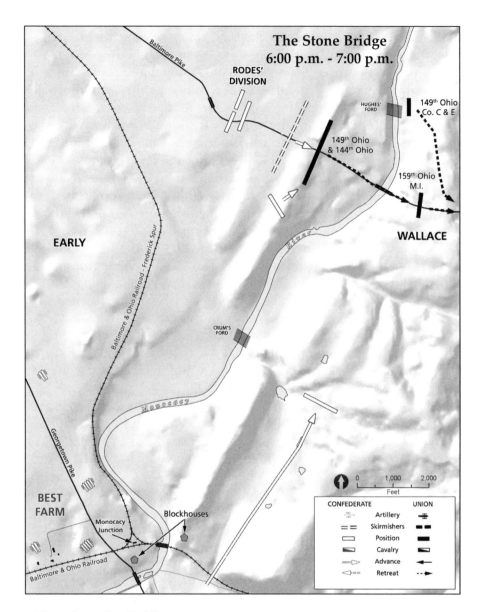

The Stone Bridge
6:00 p.m. - 7:00 p.m.

RODES'
DIVISION

HUGHES'
FORD

149th Ohio
Co. C & E

149th Ohio
& 144th Ohio

159th Ohio
M.I.

EARLY

WALLACE

Baltimore Pike

Baltimore & Ohio Railroad - Frederick Spur

River

CRUM'S
FORD

Monocacy

Georgetown Pike

BEST
FARM

Monocacy
Junction

Blockhouses

Baltimore & Ohio Railroad

0   1,000   2,000
Feet

CONFEDERATE		UNION
	Artillery	
	Skirmishers	
	Position	
	Cavalry	
	Advance	
	Retreat	

Abandon the Bridge

As Lieb made his way to the east side of the river about 6:00 p.m. to set up the new defensive line, Rodes launched an attack in force from the west, aimed at capturing the Stone Bridge. A small Confederate force had managed to take up position in woods on the eastern bank and had fired at Lieb's regiment as they attempted to cross the bridge. At the same time, Brown's entire line was attacked and the left flank was turned and forced back. Tyler ordered Brown's men to

125

fall back. Meanwhile, word reached the Union soldiers that the Confederates were at their rear, attempting to cut off their line of retreat. This information caused the retreat to break down into confusion and panic, with regiments crowding on the bridge as they attempted to flee to safety.

Lieb had remained on the western bank and assisted with the withdrawal. The Confederate artillery aimed at the bridge and fired several shots. One shell scored a direct hit, creating even more panic. Brown successfully rallied several of the men on the western side of the river, in an orchard overlooking the bridge. He directed them to fire at the Confederates who were pressing from the west and at those in the woods and wheat field southwest of the bridge. This action stalled the Confederate advance for a time and enabled a portion of Brown's command to withdrawal to safety. The Confederates positioned in the woods on the eastern bank then opened fire on the Union left flank and moved toward the bridge. Brown again returned fire and stopped the Confederate advance in this area.[233]

While Brown's force continued to withdraw across the bridge, reports came in via civilians that Wallace had passed through the area nearly two hours earlier. This information, and the renewed firing on the flank by the Confederates, panicked the Union troops, who believed they were surrounded. Many soldiers, fearing capture, broke and threw their weapons and accouterments away while attempting to escape to safety. Private Samuel McClain of the 144th Ohio National Guard stated that, "Our men are giting cut all to pieces. Every man must save themselves." By this time, the troops at Hughes Ford had retreated. Brown reached New Market at about 8:00 p.m. with roughly 300 men from his command, less than half the total number before the battle began. Rodes' division bivouacked for the night about a mile east of Frederick on the western side of the river.[234]

Lieb's Escape

When the Confederates attacked, Lieb remained on the western side of the bridge and directed the fleeing soldiers to safety. As Confederates closed in from the west and east, Lieb determined that it was time to retreat or he risked being captured. He decided to ride

233 *OR*, 37, s. 1, pt. 1, p. 218, 222; Goldsborough, p. 25
234 *OR*, 37, s. 1, pt. 1, p. 218; Samuel McClain, 144th OH, to Lucinda, July 9, 1864, MS-640, Samuel McClain Papers, Center for Archival Collections, BGSU; CPT Cary Whitaker, 43rd NC, Diary, July 9, 1864, BR 662, Brock Collection, Huntington Library, San Marino, CA (HL)

north and cross at Hughes Ford, but before he reached the ford, the Confederates cut off this route of retreat. Lieb had to ride down a very steep bluff, but still managed to cross the river to safety. He made his way back to where he had left his command, but found they had gone and the Confederates had taken possession of the area. Lieb made his way back toward Baltimore with a couple of 8th Illinois cavalrymen he met on the road. He finally located his command at Ridgeville, near Mount Airy, Md.[235]

Tyler's Escape

During the 6:00 p.m. attack, Tyler was on the east side of the river on a hill overlooking the bridge. He was informed that Confederate cavalry was a mile down the road in his rear at Bartonsville, Md. With Captain Francis Webb, Lieutenant Edward Goldsborough and a few orderlies from his staff, Tyler immediately rode off to investigate the report. They reached the home of N.O. Clines just as a group of Confederates discovered them, opened fire and gave chase. Cut off from his retreating force, Tyler and his group had to ride toward Hughes Ford and on to Liberty Road. They were unable to lose their pursuers and rode into Mount Pleasant where they encountered a squad of Confederate cavalry plundering stores. The Confederates opened fire and the group fled again. Tyler and his two aids were separated from the orderlies, who were either wounded or captured. By this time, their horses were exhausted and the Confederates were closing in. They had just turned into the woods, hoping to hide from there pursuers, when Webb's horse fell and he was thrown under it. Tyler and Goldsborough dismounted to help Webb and sent the horses off. They hid in the bushes while the Confederates followed the horses and captured them.[236]

Tyler and Goldsborough helped Webb to the house of Ephriam Creager, who cared for the captain while Tyler and Goldsborough remained hidden in the woods. They stayed there until Monday, July 11, when a squad of Union cavalry rescued them and Webb. They were brought into Frederick, which had been reoccupied by Union cavalry from Harpers Ferry, and with an escort of cavalry, they traveled down the Baltimore Pike toward Baltimore. They then rejoined their command at the Relay House near Ellicott's Mills, Md.[237]

---

235 *OR*, 37, s. 1, pt. 1, p. 222
236 *OR*, 37, s. 1, pt. 1, p. 215; Goldsborough, p. 25-27
237 *OR*, 37, s. 1, pt. 1, p. 215; Goldsborough, p. 27

CHAPTER EIGHT

BACK TO BALTIMORE

At about 5:00 p.m. on July 9, 1864, Confederate forces were able to weaken the Union right flank. An intense artillery barrage forced the 110th Ohio Infantry Regiment, which was posted near the Monocacy River and the Georgetown Pike, to pull back from its position and seek cover. This movement provided some relief from the bombardment, but created an opportunity for Confederate infantry to turn the flank. The 110th Ohio and other regiments on the right flank were gradually forced back toward Gambrill Mill. As Confederate Major General John Gordon's division overwhelmed the Union position on the Thomas Farm, Union commander Major General Lew Wallace ordered a general withdrawal toward Baltimore.

Wallace's order was passed down the line to each of the regiments. As they broke contact with Gordon's division and made their way to the Baltimore Pike, any chance for an organized withdrawal quickly disintegrated. Private Alfred Roe, 9th New York Heavy Artillery Regiment, wrote, "The lines were thrown into great confusion. The advancing Confederates who, in great numbers, are bearing down upon us." Colonel William Emerson, 151st New York Infantry Regiment, wrote in his official report, "[W]e were ordered to retire to the Baltimore pike. In doing so the command fell into considerable confusion after crossing the railroad."[238]

Gordon's division came from the Thomas Farm, while Confederate Major General Stephen Ramseur's division crossed the railroad bridge behind Union Lieutenant George E. Davis' detachment at the junction. Lowry's Artillery Battery, which was positioned on the Best Farm, rejoined Gordon's division as soon as the ford near the burned covered bridge was cleared. With the assistance of one section (two guns) of artillery, the infantry pursued the Union regiments for roughly two miles. Lieutenant Colonel Aaron W. Ebright, 126th Ohio Infantry

---

238 Alfred S. Roe, *The Ninth New York Heavy Artillery Worcester* (MA, 1899), p. 132-133; U.S. War Department, *The War of the Rebellion: A Compilation of the Official Records of the Union and Confederate Armies* (Washington, 1880-1901), 37, Series 1, pt. 1, p. 205 (hereinafter cited as *OR* with references to volume, series, part and page)

Regiment, mentioned in his official report that, "the enemy followed us for some miles, annoying us with shot and shell."

There were also Confederate cavalry patrols along the roads taken by Union soldiers. The retreating soldiers made their way to the town of Monrovia, six miles to the east. Private Lewis H. Fuller, 106th New York Infantry Regiment, wrote, "It was every man for himself for the first eight miles." Private Daniel Long, 151st New York Infantry Regiment, wrote a letter to his wife telling her, "…we had to fall back, and in confusion. I got separated from the rest. They came very near surrounding us and I think they must have taken a great many men prisoners." In fact, the Confederates took 600 Union prisoners.[239]

One of the last regiments to receive the order to retreat was the 10th Vermont, which was located on the extreme left of the battle line, at the crossroads of Baker Valley Road and the Georgetown Pike. By the time the regiment fell back toward Gambrill Mill, it had to cross in front of the new Confederate line. This placed the soldiers in the open and under constant fire as they crossed the fields. After a short distance, they discovered the escape route toward the Baltimore Pike was cut off. The only means of retreat left to them was southeast down the B&O Railroad tracks.[240]

Heroic Actions

When the Union artillery had exhausted its ammunition, Brigadier General James Ricketts ordered them to retire from the battlefield. While withdrawing, Orderly Sergeant Marian A. Brian, who was the acting Lieutenant and Chief of Caissons, noticed the 24-pounder brass howitzer and the 12-pounder brass mountain howitzer, located at the blockhouse on the eastern bank of the Monocacy River, had been deserted. He took a team of horses from one of the battery wagons—which he then burned—and, while under Confederate artillery and small arms fire, hitched the team of horses to the limber of the 24-pounder and removed it from the battlefield.

---

239 LTC J. Floyd King to MAJ J. Stoddard Johnston, July 22, 1864, Box 34, James Eldridge Collection, Huntington Library, San Marino, CA (HL); Lewis Fuller, Diary, July 9, 1864, 106th New York File, Monocacy National Battlefield Archives (MNBA); Daniel Long to His Wife, July 10, 1864, 151st New York File, MNBA

240 George G. Benedict, *Vermont in the Civil War: A History Of The Part Taken By The Vermont Soldiers And Sailors In The War For The Union 1861-5*, Vol. 2 (Burlington, VT: The Free Press Association, 1888), p. 314-316; Edwin M. Haynes, *A History of the Tenth Regiment Vermont Volunteers* (Lewiston, ME: The Tenth Vermont Regimental Association, 1870), p. 195

The 12-pounder was also retrieved after it was discarded by some Union soldiers. They had tried to carry it to safety, but quickly sought to lighten their load while retreating. Brian brought up the other battery wagon, and with the assistance of three other soldiers from the Alexander's Baltimore Battery, lifted the 12-pounder from its trunion-bed and heaved it over the tailgate into the wagon. His alertness and ingenuity successfully prevented two artillery pieces from falling into Confederate hands.[241]

There were also two acts of gallantry by Union soldiers during the battle that received special recognition. Lieutenant George E. Davis, Company D, 10th Vermont Infantry Regiment, was detached with other men from his regiment and sent across the river to defend the bridges at the junction. As the battle progressed, he found himself in command and successfully held the junction against Confederate Major General Stephen Ramseur's division until compelled to retreat at the end of the day. For his actions, he was awarded the Medal of Honor on May 27, 1892. The citation reads: "While in command of a small force, held the approaches to the two bridges against repeated assaults of superior numbers, thereby materially delaying Early's advance on Washington."

A second Medal of Honor was awarded to Corporal Alexander Scott, also from the same company. Shortly after the Union broke contact with the Confederates on the Thomas Farm, confusion had spread through the ranks as soldiers were separated from their regiments and closely pursued. The Vermont flag bearer, Corporal Edwin Parker, who feared that he might not escape, persuaded Scott to take the flag. Scott then encountered the National flag bearer, Sergeant William Mahoney, who was suffering from exhaustion. Fearing the National flag also might be captured, he urged Scott to take it. Scott carried both flags to safety and kept them several days until they could be returned to their proper caretakers. Scott received his medal on September 28, 1897. The citation reads: "Under a very heavy fire of the enemy saved the National flag of his regiment from capture."[242]

While in Baltimore, many soldiers were envious of Scott and wished to share in the distinction of carrying the regiment's National and State flags. One of Scott's comrades, Corporal Augustus Crown

---

241 G. Leonard Hoffman to MG Lew Wallace, April 25, 1896, Lew Wallace Collection, Indiana Historical Society (IHS)

242 Haynes, p. 195; U.S. Army Center of Military History, Medal of Honor, Full Text of Civil War Citations; available from http://www.history.army.mil; Internet; accessed 23 January 2009

admitted that he would have liked Scott to give him one of the flags, but he did not dare express his wish. There was no question Scott had earned the distinctive right to carry both flags.[243]

There were two other soldiers mentioned in the official records for their heroic deeds with flags. Corporal William R. Moyer, 110th Ohio Infantry Regiment, heroically saved the colors of his regiment when the color sergeant was mortally wounded and the flag was left on the battlefield. Similarly, Corporal James Love of the 126th Ohio Infantry Regiment noticed the color bearer of another regiment

Corp. Alexander Scott

had fallen, so he seized the flag and boldly waved it a few times before he, too, was mortally wounded.[244]

Casualties

The Battle of Monocacy was a hard fought engagement that resulted in many casualties on both sides. Gordon stated that, although short, "The Battle of Monocacy was one of the severest ever fought by my troops." The final attack made by Gordon's division at 3:30 p.m. took less than two hours, but they suffered 698 (wounded, killed, captured, or missing) of the estimated 900 total Confederate casualties for the day. His three brigades (Evans, York and Terry) had 419, 163 and 116 casualties, respectively.[245]

During Gordon's attack, Lieutenant James Mincy, 61st Georgia Infantry Regiment, took his battalion's battle flag after the fifth consecutive flag bearer had been shot down. Soon after, he shared the same fate. A few other notable Confederates killed that day were the 61st Georgia Regiment's Colonel John Lamar and Lieutenant Colonel David

243 Haynes, p. 195

244 *OR*, 37, s. 1, pt. 1, p. 209, 212

245 *OR*, 37, s. 1, pt. 1, p. 352; MG John Gordon to Robert E. Lee, February 6, 1868, Lee Headquarter Papers, Virginia Historical Society (VHS); MG John B. Gordon, Report of Operations from June 28-July 9, 1864, Ni51, John Page Nicholson Collection, HL

Van Valkenburg, and the 17th Virginia Cavalry Regiment's Lieutenant Colonel William Tavenner. Brigadier Generals Clement Evans and John McCausland, Captain Eugene Gordon (Evans' adjutant and brother to John Gordon) and Lieutenant Colonel John T. Hodges, 9th Louisiana Infantry Regiment, were wounded. These were but a handful of the men in Gordon's division who failed to escape the battle unscathed.[246]

As the battle concluded on the Best Farm, Lieutenant George W. Hobson, Kirkpatrick's Confederate Artillery Battery, was shot from his horse while talking to Sergeant John H. Berkeley about two artillerymen (Privates Alexander Gardner and Joseph Page) who had been killed a few minutes earlier. Hobson was telling Berkeley, "Those poor boys must be buried and their graves marked, if I have to go back." These were his last words; while in mid-sentence he was struck by a bullet and died moments later. Chaplain Thomas W. Gilmer took the bodies of the three men to Mount Olivet Cemetery and had them buried.[247]

Union soldiers also suffered badly. Although they had a total of 1,294 casualties, roughly 600 of those were captured, leaving about 700 men wounded or killed. Corporal Roderick Clark, 14th New Jersey Infantry Regiment, wrote about being wounded: "I was hit in the left ankle by a minie-ball, completely crushing the joint. I was struck with another minie-ball under the shoulder blade…. I don't know how long I lay unconscious, but when I came to the Rebels were all around me."[248]

The 14th New Jersey Infantry Regiment had more men wounded and killed during the battle than any other regiment. Major Peter Vredenburgh of the 14th New Jersey sent a letter to his mother telling her, "I never saw such accurate firing every one of our Captains was killed or wounded except one & he did not play up or he would have been too. Col. Hall was wounded in the arm." The regiment had more than 140 casualties; more than 110 of these were wounded or killed.[249]

---

246 G. W. Nichols, *A Soldier's Story of his Regiment (61ˢᵗ Georgia) and incidentally of the Lawton-Gordon-Evans brigade* (Jessup, GA: 1898), p. 172-173; *OR*, 37, s. 1, pt. 1, p. 88, 352

247 William H. Runge, ed. *Four Years in The Confederate Artillery: The Diary of Henry Robinson Berkeley* (Chapel Hill: Univ. of North Carolina Press, 1961), p. 85-86

248 *OR* 37, s. 1, pt. 1, p. 202; "Monocacy, Terrible Experience of a 14th N.J. Boy in that Battle," *National Tribune*, April 15, 1886

249 MAJ Peter Vredenburgh, 14th NJ, to His Mother, July 12, 1864, Collection 1, Folder 3, Peter Vredenburgh Papers, Monmouth County Historical Association Library & Archives, Freehold, NJ (MCHALA); Brett Spaulding, 1/31/2007, Casualty List, MNBA

Colonel William Seward, Jr., commander of the 9th New York Heavy Artillery Regiment and son of Secretary of State William H. Seward, was hurt early in the day when his wounded horse fell on him. At the end of the day, he was unable to march off the battlefield with his men. Fortunately, he found a mule, used a silk handkerchief as a bridle, and thus was able to ride off to safety. Lieutenant Colonel Edward P. Taft, also of the 9th New York Heavy Artillery, was less fortunate; as the right flank was pushed back, his men noticed Taft, who had been wounded in the left leg, had been left behind. A group of men were ordered to retrieve him, but before they could reach him, he was swept up in the Confederate line. Taft spent the night on the battlefield as a prisoner and was taken to a hospital in Frederick the next day.[250]

Treat the Wounded

At the conclusion of the battle, care for the dead and wounded began immediately. Union and Confederate medical personal, along with local citizens, provided aid to the wounded of both armies without discrimination. Throughout the night, surgeons and stewards worked feverishly. Confederate hospital steward Henry Beverige, 25th Virginia Infantry Regiment, wrote that he was "up nearly all night with Dr. Henkel at the Hospital sending our wounded to F. City." Union Surgeon William A. Brown, 149th Ohio National Guard, refused to abandon his wounded men at Stone Bridge and was left behind during the retreat to continue to provide aid to them.[251]

Civilians such as the Worthingtons did their best to help the wounded. At one point, Mr. Worthington comforted a mortally wounded Union soldier in the front yard of his home, while in the back yard his wife did the same for a mortally wounded Confederate. Captain Chauncey Harris, 14th New Jersey Regiment, was severely wounded in the shoulder and knee and taken to Edward Baker's farm, about one mile south of the battlefield. Baker's daughter Clementine cared for Chauncey, and after several weeks he recuperated, they fell in love and were married less than a year later.[252]

After being wounded, a soldier named Mincy of the 61st Georgia Infantry Regiment had a Yankee doctor tend his wound. He told a

---

250 Roe, p. 132-133
251 Henry Beverige, 25th VA, Diary, July 10, 1864, Duke University Library (DUL); *OR*, 37, s. 1, pt. 1, p. 218-219
252 Glenn Worthington, *Fighting For Time* (Shippensburg, PA: White Mane, 1985), p. 161-162

friend that the doctor ran a silk handkerchief through the wound and treated him very kindly. Clark of the 14th New Jersey Infantry Regiment recalled the events as he lay wounded on the battlefield:

> All through the night doctors of both sides and their assistants called on me frequently. The Rebel doctor gave me a drink of liquor, but the Union doctor had only a little for his own regiment. This same rebel doctor, with two stretcher bearers, came after me, and put me in the ambulance with two wounded Rebels and started us for Frederick City.

As a result of the battle of Antietam, a number of hospitals had been established in Frederick and were able to handle the arriving wounded. Lieutenant Enoch Cowart, 14th New Jersey Infantry Regiment, mentioned in a letter to his cousin, "These immense hospitals have every convenience for the sick and the kindness and generosity of the Ladies of Frederick is proverbial." Once in the hospital, Private Josiah Lewis Hill, 110th Ohio Infantry Regiment, wrote, "Safe in hospital at last and in good bed with kind people to take care of us."[253]

After liberating Frederick on July 10, Lieutenant Colonel William Blakely, 14th Pennsylvania Cavalry Regiment, detailed a burial party that took two days to inter the dead from the battle. Medical Inspector G.K. Johnson arrived on the 10th and supervised the burial of 117 soldiers on the battlefield and four soldiers in the surrounding area. While this took place, 189 wounded Union soldiers were collected on the 10th and 11th and taken to the general hospital in Frederick, and an additional 15 men were found in the nearby town of New Market. The Confederates left 405 soldiers on the battlefield and about 30 men in various country houses. Most of the seriously wounded could not be carried away with the army as it made its way toward Washington.[254]

Once the Confederates could be moved, they were sent on trains to the hospital in Baltimore or taken to the prisons at Point Lookout, Fort McHenry, Fort Delaware, Elmira or Johnson Island. The major-

---

253 Nichols, p. 172; "Monocacy, Terrible Experience of a 14th N.J. Boy in that Battle," *National Tribune*, April 15, 1886; Hill, ed. "A Civil War Diary kept by Josiah Lewis Hill from August 22, 1862 to July 1, 1865 and a History of the 110th Ohio Voluntary Infantry," MNBA; Enoch Cowart, 14th NJ, to Mary Ann Backus, August 10, 1864, Box 1, Folder 1, Cowart Family Papers, MCHALA

254 *OR*, 37, s. 1, pt. 1, p. 180, 203-204; *OR*, 37, s. 1, pt. 2, p. 256; Samuel Clarke Farrar, *The Twenty-Second Pennsylvania Cavalry and the Ringgold Battalion 1861-1865* (Pittsburgh, PA: The Twenty-Second Pennsylvania Ringgold Cavalry Association, 1911), p. 270-271

ity of Union captives were sent to Danville Prison in Virginia. Lieutenant Charles Thompson Stuart, 26th Georgia Infantry Regiment, wrote, "Ten [d]ays after, I, with a hundred or more, was shipped to the General Hospital at Baltimore, my old home, in hot iron prison cars, without water and with very little ventilation."

The exchange of Confederate prisoners taken at Monocacy for Union prisoners began in September and continued until March. Those prisoners who were not exchanged and survived their incarceration were paroled or released between May and July 1865. Union and Confederate soldiers who died in the hospitals at Frederick and whose remains were not retrieved by family or friends were buried in Mount Olivet Cemetery. Union soldiers remained in the cemetery until 1866 when they were removed and reburied at Antietam National Cemetery. Confederate soldiers buried on the battlefield were placed in a mass grave at Mount Olivet Cemetery some time in 1870.[255]

Union Cavalry

On July 9, the 8th Illinois Cavalry Regiment was posted on the extreme left flank of the Union line, near Baker Valley Road, when the retreat was ordered. The commander, Lieutenant Colonel David Clendenin, had 80 men with him while the rest of his command was spread out down the Monocacy River and Georgetown Pike. One squadron had been ordered to destroy all bridges that the Confederates could use to cross the Monocacy River, while scouts patrolled the Georgetown Pike as far as the town of Urbana, about three miles south of the battlefield. Another 50 cavalrymen patrolled between Urbana and Buckeystown Pike.[256]

When Clendenin received the order to retreat, he withdrew his small force down the Georgetown Pike toward Washington. While retreating, 35 cavalrymen from Major General Julius Stahel's force, who had been out on patrol from Harpers Ferry, were absorbed into Clendenin's ranks. Confederate Brigadier General John McCausland's

---

255 Charles Thompson Stuart, "Autobiographical sketch of the war service of Charles Thompson Stuart, Lieutenant, Company H, 26th Regiment, Georgia Volunteers," Unpublished Manuscript, U.S. Army Military History Institute (USAMHI); Brett Spaulding, 1/31/2007, Casualty List, MNBA; Steven R. Stotelmyer, *The Bivouacs of the Dead*, (Baltimore, MD: Toomey Press, 1997), p. 47; R.A. Brock, ed. *Southern Historical Society Papers*, Vol. XXXVIII (Richmond, VA: The Society, 1910; Reprint, New York: Kraus Reprint Company, 1977), p. 288

256 *OR*, 37, s. 1, pt. 1, p. 220-221

**Flag of the Nighthawk Rangers,
Company F, 17ᵗʰ Virginia Cavalry Regiment**

cavalry brigade pursued the retreating cavalrymen with the 17ᵗʰ Virginia Cavalry Regiment under Major Frederick C. Smith, who had taken command earlier in the afternoon when Lieutenant Colonel William Tavenner was killed on the Thomas Farm.[257]

The 17ᵗʰ Virginia pressed Clendenin's force very closely and made several charges at them. When they reached the town of Urbana, a disastrous attack was made. Smith led his regiment on a charge into the ranks of the 8ᵗʰ Illinois. Both sides took losses in the charge, and Confederate Private James Mills, the bearer of Company F's flag, was shot in the shoulder. He fell from his horse and had the flag wrestled away by some Union cavalrymen. Mills was left on the battlefield and the Virginian's were forced to fall back without their flag. Union Lieutenant John A. Kinley was killed; he was the only soldier from the 8ᵗʰ Illinois lost that day. Smith quickly regrouped his men and charged again. This time, as he rode forward with saber in hand, he was mortally wounded. The charge lost its momentum and the Confederate cavalrymen once again fell back. Corporal Silas Wesson of the 8ᵗʰ Illinois wrote in his diary, "we got the rebel flag and killed the Maj. commanding."[258]

After the 17ᵗʰ Virginia fell back, Clendenin ordered Stahel's men to keep the road clear to his rear, and dismounted his men as skirmishers, making it appear as if he was reinforced. The Virginians

---

257 *OR*, 37, s. 1, pt. 1, p. 214, 215; George Hyland, Diary, July 9, 1864, 8ᵗʰ Illinois Cavalry File, MNBA

observed this and dismounted to engage the Union cavalrymen on foot. To keep their horses out of danger, they were sent to the rear. In doing so, they inadvertently blocked the road and prevented the rest of McCausland's brigade from moving forward. Clendenin took advantage of the situation and immediately recalled his men to their horses, and left the Confederates behind. After moving all night, Clendenin joined Wallace at Monrovia.[259]

Back to Baltimore

During the retreat, Colonel William Henry, commander of the 10th Vermont Infantry Regiment, led a group of roughly 150 soldiers over land to Monrovia, where more than one thousand troops from the 6th Maryland, 67th Pennsylvania and part of the 122nd Ohio Infantry regiments were located. They were the last of the 3rd Division, VI Corps troops to arrive in Baltimore and did not arrive in time to take part in the battle. Henry loaded empty railroad cars with his troops and moved to the intersection of the railroad and the Baltimore Pike west of Monrovia. At this location, outposts were established as they waited for Wallace and the rest of the army.[260]

Wallace arrived after dark, and the rest of his force continued to report throughout the night. Colonel Allison L. Brown, commander of the 149th Ohio National Guard, arrived with 300 men from the Stone Bridge at about 8:00 p.m. The portion of the 122nd Ohio Infantry Regiment that took part in the battle arrived at New Market about 9:00 p.m., where it rejoined the rest of its regiment. All of the regiments and separated soldiers did their best not to be captured by Confederate cavalry patrols. Private Alfred Roe, 9th New York Heavy Artillery, wrote, "If the men knew enough to keep off the traveled ways, in the woods and fields, they generally managed to escape the foe." Roe was captured and remained a prisoner until the end of the war. Ser-

---

258 *OR*, 37, s. 1, pt. 1, p. 220-221; Silas D. Wesson, 8th IL Cavalry, Diary, July 10, 1864, *Civil War Times Illustrated* Collection, U.S. Army Military History Institute (USAMHI); Addison A. Smith, "The Story of The Life and Trials of A Confederate Soldier and The Great Loop He Made In Three Years, Including the Original Narrative and War Time Letters of Lieutenant Addison Austin Smith, Company G 17th Regiment of Virginia Cavalry, CSA," Unpublished Manuscript, Civil War Materials, Public Library, Jackson County, WV, p. 26; Daisy C. Neptune, "Flag of the Nighthawk Rangers," *Confederate Veteran*, Vol. XL, 1932, p. 292

259 *OR*, 37, s. 1, pt. 1, p. 220-221; Hyland, Diary, July 9, 1864, MNBA; Wesson, Diary, July 10, 1864, USAMHI

260 Benedict, p. 314-316; *OR*, XXXVII, s. 1, pt. 2, p. 139; William E. Bain, ed. *The B&O in the Civil War* (Denver, CO: Sage Books, 1966), p. 122-123

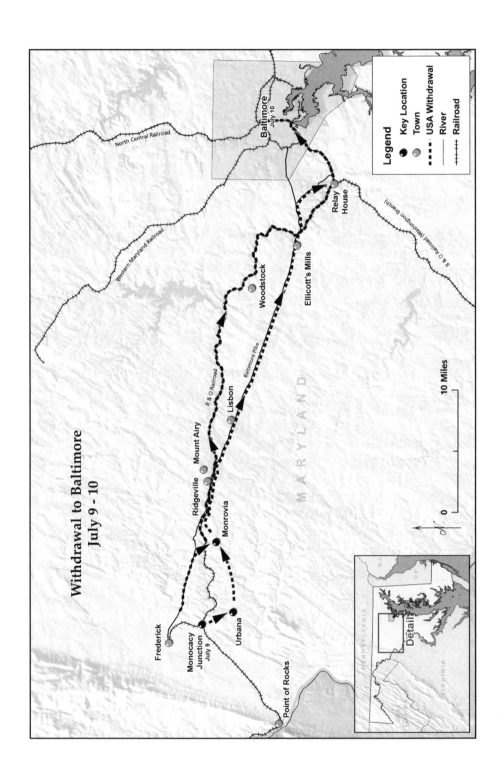

Withdrawal to Baltimore
July 9 - 10

Legend
Key Location
Town
USA Withdrawal
River
Railroad

MARYLAND

Frederick
Monocacy Junction
July 9
Urbana
Point of Rocks
Monrovia
Ridgeville
Mount Airy
Lisbon
Woodstock
Ellicott's Mills
Relay House
Baltimore
July 10

North Central Railroad
Western Maryland Railroad
B & O Railroad
Baltimore Pike
B & O Railroad (Washington Branch)

PENNSYLVANIA
VIRGINIA
Detail

N

0   10 Miles

geant George Blotcher, 87th Pennsylvania Infantry Regiment, recorded in his diary, "I took the Baltimore & Ohio Railroad track during the night in company with others but during the night, after been weary and tired, crept into a large hay heap where I slept till the next morning when the sun was bright."[261]

Blotcher and the few soldiers he encountered did not link up with their regiments at Monrovia, but continued to move east along the railroad. On July 11, they found a hand car at Woodstock, Md., that they used to move east to the Relay House on the B&O Railroad near Ellicott's Mills, Md., where they arrived at midnight. Some soldiers, like Long of the 151st New York Infantry Regiment, remained hidden until the Confederates had left the area. On the 12th, Long reported to the Provost Marshal in Frederick.[262]

After the battle, Wallace sent two messages. The first was to John Garrett, president of the B&O Railroad, and addressed Wallace's need to take care of his army and get them back to Baltimore. He told Garrett, "I did as I promised. Held the bridge to the last. They overwhelmed me with numbers. My troops fought splendidly. Losses fearful. Send me cars enough to Ellicott's Mills to take up my retreating columns. Don't fail me."[263]

The second message was sent to Chief of Staff Major General Henry Halleck, informing him, "I am retreating with a foot-sore, battered, and half-demoralized column. Forces of the enemy at least 20,000. They do not seem to be pursuing. You will have to use every exertion to save Baltimore and Washington."[264]

At Monrovia, Wallace ordered Clendenin to provide the rear guard, and attached two artillery pieces—with a limited amount of ammunition—from Alexander's Baltimore Battery to assist them. When Captain Edward H. Lieb, acting commander of the 159th Ohio National Guard (mounted infantry), reported to Clendenin at Ridgeville, Md., he was ordered to have his men take up the extreme right of the rear guard. The train at Monrovia was loaded with about 200 wounded and an unspecified number of stragglers, and was sent to Baltimore where it arrived at about 5:00 a.m. on the morning of July 10.[265]

261 Roe, *The Ninth New York Heavy Artillery*, p.134; *OR*, 37, s. 1, pt. 1, p. 198, 211, 218
262 SGT George Blotcher, 87th PA, Diary, July 9-11, 1864, Historical Society of York County, York, PA (HSYC); Daniel Long to His Wife, July 12, 1864, 151st New York File, MNBA
263 *OR*, 37, s. 1, pt. 2, p. 139
264 *OR*, 37, s. 1, pt. 2, p. 145
265 *OR*, 37, s. 1, pt. 1, p. 221, 224; *OR*, 37, s. 1, pt. 2, p. 160, 161

During the night, Wallace's army marched down the Baltimore Pike toward Baltimore, while the two and a half regiments that missed the battle provided the rear guard for the weary regiments. While in route, Wallace received a message from Halleck stating, "[I am] directed by the President to say that you rally your forces and make every possible effort to retard the enemy's march on Baltimore." The army marched through Ridgeville and bivouacked for the night between 1:00 and 2:00 a.m. The soldiers lay down on the sides of the road while the men from the regiments that had not fought stood guard. Wallace sent a message at 4:00 a.m. on the 10th for Halleck, informing him "I have been defeated; the enemy are not pursuing me, from which I infer they are marching on Washington." The march to Baltimore was resumed just before first light.[266]

The army marched through Lisbon, Md., and began to arrive at Ellicott's Mills around noon on July 10, after traveling roughly 25 miles. Following orders from Halleck, Wallace had Ricketts' division remain at Ellicott's Mills to protect Baltimore from a possible attack from the Confederate army. He also sent the 10th Vermont and another regiment to the Relay House and had Alexander's Baltimore Battery and Clendenin's cavalry report to Ricketts. Cavalry patrols were sent out on various roads, where they fought a few small engagements with Confederate cavalry from Brigadier General Bradley Johnson's division, who were moving toward Point Lookout.[267]

On July 11, soldiers continued to arrive in Ellicott's Mills throughout the day. With the Confederate threat of attack diminished, Wallace ordered Ricketts to board the three locomotives and 90 large cars that Garrett had sent to Ellicott's Mills at Wallace's request. The regiments left between 4:00 and 6:00 p.m. and did not arrive in Baltimore until late in the evening. Once the cars were offloaded, the regiments were ordered to camp near the railroad at the Mount Clare Station. Lieb's command brought up the rear guard on the Baltimore Pike and arrived in the city about 7:00 p.m., where he was then ordered to Camp Carroll. Wallace's troops from the VIII Army Corps were ordered to report for duty at various forts in Baltimore.[268]

266 *OR*, 37, s. 1, pt. 1, p. 222, 224; *OR*, 37, s. 1, pt. 2, p. 145; LT James Read, 10th VT, Diary, July 9 & 10, 1864, James B. Ricketts Collection, Manassas National Battlefield Park Archives (MNBPA); Fuller, Diary, July 10, 1864, MNBA

267 *OR*, 37, s. 1, pt. 1, p. 198, 204, 208, 222; *OR*, 51, s. 1, pt. 1, p. 1177; *OR*, 37, s. 1, pt. 2, p. 213; Fuller, Diary, July 10, 1864, MNBA; Read, Diary, July 10, 1864, MNBPA; Vredenburgh to His Mother, July 12, 1864, MCHALA

268 Fuller, Diary, July 11-12, 1864, MNBA; *OR*, 37, s. 1, pt. 1, p. 204, 222; *OR*, 37, s. 1, pt. 2, p. 217, 160; Read, Diary, July 11, 1864, MNBPA

Late on July 11, Wallace directed Ricketts to place six of his regiments at various defensive positions within the city. The following morning, one regiment was sent to Fort Marshall, located east of Baltimore in the Highlandtown area and another was sent to Bel Air Market. A third was positioned on Baltimore Street between Eutaw and Canal streets, while a fourth was sent to Green Street between Columbia and Franklin streets. The fifth and sixth regiments went to Franklin and Monument streets, with both positioned between Eutaw and Holliday streets. The 9th New York Heavy Artillery was sent to Washington to man the heavy artillery in the forts around the city. They were originally ordered on the evening of July 8, but by the time the order reached Baltimore, they had been sent to Monocacy Junction and were engaging the Confederates. The rest of Ricketts' division remained in camp near the railroad. Ricketts received orders from Wallace and moved his division to Druid Hill Park at 6:00 a.m. on July 13.[269]

Wallace

On July 11, while in Baltimore, Wallace received General Order No. 228 from Secretary of War Edwin M. Stanton. He was not commended for a job well done, but informed that Major General Edward O.C. Ord would replace him as commander of the VIII Army Corps and all troops in the Middle Department. Wallace asked Stanton for clarification and was told that he would report to Ord, and that Wallace would remain in charge of the administration of the Middle Department. Though Ord had left Washington for Baltimore that day, he was now in command of all military operations and movements.[270]

At 11:00 p.m. on July 13, Ord received a message from Halleck ordering him to move his command to Washington by railroad, under the direction of General Grant. Ord responded by informing Halleck that he would leave the following morning as soon as he was able to assemble his command. The troops in Baltimore, including Ricketts' division, were spread out to guard against any possible Confederate cavalry attack. On the morning of the 14th, Ord sent the troops to the B&O Railroad Mount Clare Station. Brigadier General Erastus Tyler was replaced by Brigadier General John R. Kenly as brigade commander of the VIII Corps troops. Ord based his decision on Tyler's

269 *OR*, 37, s. 1, pt. 1, p. 204; *OR*, 37, s. 1, pt. 2, p. 119, 146, 216; Fuller, Diary, July 12 & 13, 1864, MNBA; Read, Diary, July 12 & 13, 1864, MNBPA; Cowart to Backus, August 10, 1864, MCHALA
270 *OR*, 37, s. 1, pt. 2, p. 214-215

LOC

Maj. Gen. Edward O.C. Ord

poor physical condition after the battle. The VIII Corps troops and the men of Ricketts' division arrived in Washington after dusk. They would join Major General Horatio Wright, commander of the VI Corps, on the evening of July 17 at Clark's Gap near Leesburg, Va. Wright commanded the pursuit of Early, who had recrossed the Potomac River after failing to enter Washington.[271]

As the Confederate army retreated back to Virginia and the threat to Washington was averted, attention again shifted to the Battle of Monocacy and Wallace. Articles in various newspapers during and after the crisis highlighted the battle and Wallace's actions. As time passed, more people began to realize the significance of what Wallace had accomplished on the banks of the Monocacy River. According to an article in the July 11 edition of the *New York Daily Tribune*, "Gen. Wallace had done promptly and thoroughly all that lay in his power – and in this war that is a high eulogy to bestow on a General." The *Baltimore American* wrote on July 18, "[T]he country does not yet know how much it owes the gallant men who fought that battle." On July 22, The *New York Times* ran an article that read, "Gen. Wallace showed a more thorough appreciation of what the emergency demanded…and did more practical service than any other military officer north of the Potomac."[272]

Wallace sent a message on July 18 to Garrett and Garrett's Master of Transportation William P. Smith thanking them for all the assistance they rendered him during the crises:

> I avail myself of the first leisure moment to express to you and Mr. W. P. Smith my most sincere acknowledgements for the very great services rendered to me and my little army before and after the battle

271 *OR*, 37, s. 1, pt. 2, p. 295, 328; *OR*, 37, s. 1, pt. 1, p. 268-269; Read, Diary, July 14, 1864, MNBPA

272 "The Raid," *New York Daily Tribune*, July 11, 1864; "The Monocacy Battle," *Baltimore American*, July 18, 1864; "Gen. Wallace On Future Incursions," *New York Times*, July 22, 1864

of Monocacy. To sum it all up in a few words, I say frankly that without your road, under your energetic and zealous management, it would have been impossible for me to have maintained my position five minutes in presence of the force that attacked me on that occasion. Therefore, please accept my thanks, and believe me most truly and gratefully, your friend and servant.[273]

Stanton met with Wallace on July 23 and told him the battle, "was timely, well-delivered, well-managed, and saved Washington City." Five days later on July 28, General Orders No. 237 was issued. The order reinstated Wallace as commander of the VIII Army Corps and all troops serving in the Middle Department. Ord was reassigned to command the XVIII Army Corps.[274]

When Wallace gathered all available forces at Monocacy Junction, he left Baltimore virtually undefended. Confederate cavalry operating in the area threatened the city, which was his responsibility. The railroad could be utilized to remove wounded troops and an army that was in no condition to conduct additional delaying actions. The move to Baltimore allowed Wallace to organize and resupply his forces, and if needed, he could use the railroad to reinforce Washington.

At the Battle of Monocacy, Early failed to capitalize on his superior numbers and engage more men. He expected to engage inexperienced soldiers, and as a result, only a fraction of his force was engaged. Early also wanted to conserve his army for the march on Washington. A lapse in communication led to the Confederate ranks receiving inaccurate information about who they were fighting, and continued to feed the false notion that the Union troops were comprised of inexperienced soldiers. Thus, Wallace, though outnumbered, was able to delay the Confederates for an entire day. Would it be enough time for reinforcements to reach Washington and save the capital?

---

273 *OR*, 37, s. 1, pt. 2, p. 381
274 *OR*, 37, s. 1, pt. 2, p. 489; MG Lew Wallace to Benson Lossing, July 24, 1864, Lew Wallace Papers, IHS

Chapter Nine

AN IMPOSSIBLE MISSION

Confederate Major General Jubal Early's Corps left the Richmond area on June 12, joined forces with Confederate Major General John Breckinridge at Lynchburg, Va., and drove Union Major General David Hunter out of the Shenandoah Valley. With Hunter's retreat to the Ohio River, the route to Maryland was virtually undefended. Early's army marched down the Shenandoah Valley, arriving in Staunton, Va., on June 26. Here Early received a message from General Robert E. Lee informing him that an effort should be made to release the prisoners held at the Union prison camp located at Point Lookout. After two days of refitting, the army resumed its march to Maryland. On June 28, Early sent a message to Lee stating:

> I therefore decided it – but to turn down the valley and proceed according to your instructions to threaten Washington and if I find an opportunity – to take it. ... I will send a select body of the cavalry to cut the railroads between Washington and Harrisburg and Baltimore and Philadelphia while I am moving on Washington. I shall also make an effort to release our prisoners at Point Lookout...[275]

The Point Lookout Mission was a joint operation that required a cavalry detachment to cooperate with the Confederate Marine Corps and Navy. Confederate intelligence revealed that a black, dismounted cavalry regiment from Massachusetts guarded the prison. Lee believed the discipline in command would be poor and the guards could be easily overpowered. In July, there were between 12,800 and 14,500 Confederate prisoners held in the prison. Once they were liberated, they could be organized, armed and

---

275 Jubal Early to Robert E. Lee, June 28, 1864, CW 100, Huntington Library, San Marino, CA; U.S. War Department, *The War of the Rebellion: A Compilation of the Official Records of the Union and Confederate Armies* (Washington, 1880-1901), Vol. 37, Series 1, Part 1, p. 766-768 (hereinafter cited as *OR* with references to volume, series, part and page)

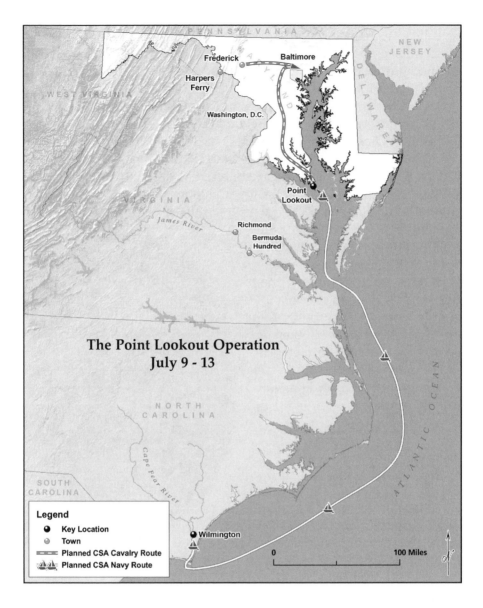

The Point Lookout Operation
July 9 - 13

Legend
●   Key Location
◔   Town
═══ Planned CSA Cavalry Route
⚓⚓⚓ Planned CSA Navy Route

0   100 Miles

marched to Washington where they would reinforce Early, who would attempt to capture the Union capital.[276]

By July 6, the balance of Early's army crossed the Potomac River into Maryland at Boteler's Ford near Sharpsburg. A special courier, Captain Robert E. Lee (General Lee's son), arrived that day with a message from his father informing Early an attempt would be made

---

276 Magnus S. Thompson, "Plan To Release Our Men At Point Lookout," *Confederate Veteran*, Vol. XX, February 1912, p. 69; *OR*, 37, s. 1, pt. 1, p. 767; *OR*, 7, s. 2, p. 502, 1243

on July 12 to release the prisoners from Point Lookout, and that his cavalry detachment should make every effort to unite with them. Early was not informed that the effort would be made by sea, and Lee stated that he had not been advised of the details of the operation.[277]

On the evening of July 8, recently promoted Brigadier General Bradley Johnson was given command of the Point Lookout operation. Johnson had been promoted only days before, on June 28, and given command of the late Brigadier General William E. Jones' brigade. Jones had been killed at the Battle of Piedmont, Va., on June 5. Johnson was a Frederick, Md., native, and the grand nephew of the state's first governor, Thomas Johnson. The mission that Early assigned Johnson required him to disrupt the communication and railroad lines north of Baltimore and between Washington and Baltimore, then ride south and aid in overwhelming the Union garrison guarding the prisoners. He would then organize and arm the former prisoners and march them to Washington. Johnson later said he told Early:

LOC

> [T]he march laid out for me was utterly impossible for man or horse to accomplish; it gave me four days, not ninety-six hours, to compass near three hundred miles, not counting for time lost in destroying bridges and railroads, but that I would do what was possible for men to do.[278]

Brig. Gen. Bradley T. Johnson

277 Jubal Early, *Narrative of the War Between the States* (Wilmington, NC: Broadfoot, 1989), p. 385; William A. Tidwell, James O. Hall and David Winfred Gaddy, *Come Retribution: The Confederate Secret Service and the Assassination of Lincoln* (Jackson, MS: Univ. Press of Mississippi, 1988), p. 146

278 Daniel C. Toomey, *The Civil War In Maryland* (Baltimore, MD: Toomey Press, 2004), p. 124; Bradley Johnson, "My Ride Around Baltimore In Eighteen Hundred and Sixty-Four," *Journal of the United States Cavalry Association,* Vol. II, (Fort Leavenworth, Kansas: 1889), p. 252-253; Douglas Southall Freeman, *Lee's Lieutenants: A Study in Command* (NY: Simon and Shuster, 1998), p. 564; Early, p. 385; Scott Sheads and Daniel Toomey, *Baltimore During The Civil War* (Baltimore, MD: Toomey Press, 1997), p. 72

The supposed secret naval portion of the operation, details of which had not been given to Early, was assigned to Commander John Taylor Wood, an 1853 graduate of the United States Naval Academy, nephew of Confederate President Jefferson Davis and grandson of former United States President Zachary Taylor. He was an officer aboard the CSS *Virginia*, formerly the Union frigate USS *Merrimack*, during the famous ironclad battle with the USS *Monitor*, and led a number of successful raids against Union ships. For the attempt on Point Lookout, Wood would command two blockade runners confis-

cated by the Confederate government: *Let-Her-B* and *Florie*. They were loaded at Wilmington, N.C., with several field pieces and 2,000 arms for the prisoners. Initially, there was a problem securing an adequate number of arms for the operation, but it was rectified on July 9, and the ships were prepared to sail. A battalion of marines under Brigadier General George Washington Custis Lee was divided into two detachments for each ship. Once on land, they would help equip and reorganize the liberated prisoners. On the night of July 9, the steamers sailed down the inlet and waited for the tide to enable them to cross the bar and put out to sea.[279]

U.S. Naval Historical Center

Commander John T. Wood

Point Lookout Defense

Point Lookout was located on the southern peninsula of Maryland where the Chesapeake Bay and the Potomac River converge, and was the largest prison in the north. Established in 1863, after the Battle of Gettysburg (July 1-3), it was a converted military hospital that was to

---

279 Richard R. Duncan, "Maryland's Reaction To Early's Raid In 1864: A Summer Of Bitterness," *Maryland Historical Magazine* (Fall 1969), p. 264; COL George Harper to CPT Parker, AAG, July 31, 1864, RG 108, E112, NARA, Washington D.C.; *OR*, 40, s. 1, pt. 3, p. 757; Royce Gordon Shingleton, *John Taylor Wood: Sea Ghost of the Confederacy* (Athens, GA: Univ. of Georgia Press, 1979), p. 2-5; U.S. Naval War Records Office, *Official Records of the Union and Confederate Navies in the War of the Rebellion, Washington, 1894-1922*, Vol. 5, Series 2, p. 467 (hereinafter cited as *ORN* with references to volume, series and page); Ralph Donnelly, *The Confederate States Marine Corps: The Rebel Leathernecks* (Shippensburg, PA: White Mane, 1989), p. 110-111

accommodate 10,000 prisoners, but it actually held anywhere from 12,000 to 20,000 men at a time. The peninsula was an ideal location for a prison. The bay and river allowed easy access for ships delivering supplies or prisoners. Prisoners would have few options for escape, with the bay and river too wide to swim and all the roads leading farther into northern territory. Like all Civil War prisons, Point Lookout had deplorable conditions, with the soldiers suffering from exposure, disease and poor sanitation. Lee believed freeing the prisoners would greatly benefit the campaign, nearly doubling the size of Early's army.

Apparently, the Union authorities suspected something, because as early as July 5, patrols were increased along the roads to Point Lookout. A lieutenant and 10 men were sent to the vicinity of Upper Marlboro, Md., to watch the roads, and were specifically ordered to look for small bodies of Confederate cavalry moving south. The balance of their company was sent to Port Tobacco, Md., and likewise told to keep a sharp eye to ensure the telegraph lines were not cut. From Port Tobacco, another small detachment was to ride to Point Lookout with the same orders.[280]

As a result of Early's movement into western Maryland, Secretary of War Edwin M. Stanton annexed Point Lookout to the Department of Washington and ordered Brigadier General James Barnes to take command. Barnes left Washington by steamship and arrived on July 6. Stanton telegraphed Barnes on July 7 telling him, "You cannot be too vigilant, as the enemy is now operating in Maryland in large force." He sent a second telegraph informing Barnes, "The Navy will furnish any additional force of gun-boats you may require for protection. Report your wishes." Barnes met with the captains of the five-gun sailing schooner USS *William Bacon* and five-gun steam schooner USS *Currituck*, both stationed at Point Lookout, and made arrangements with them for additional naval support if it became necessary.[281]

On the night of July 7, Barnes determined that support was warranted. The two- and six-gun steam tugs USS *Resolute* and USS *Fuchsia*, respectively, were ordered to report for duty. Extra pickets were placed in front of the prison, and the entire command was ordered to be ready to move at a moment's notice. At Bermuda Hundred, Va., Major General Benjamin F. Butler learned from a Confederate deserter that an attack on Point Lookout and freeing of the prisoners was one of Early's objectives. This report was forwarded to Barnes on July 8, confirming his and Stanton's concerns of a possible attack. Also on

280 *OR*, 37, s. 1, pt. 2, p. 62
281 *OR*, 40, s. 1, pt. 3, p. 30, 58, 71, 90; *ORN*, 1, s. 2, p. 69, 240

the 8th, Secretary of the Navy Gideon Welles ordered Commander F.A. Parker, the Potomac Flotilla commander, to take additional precautions in covering the prison with his gunboats. Parker responded by sending a third gunboat to protect the prison. Later that night, 250 Confederate prisoners were transferred to Elmira Prison in New York, accompanied by 341 guards. The loss of these guards, along with the 36th United States Colored Troops, which had left on June 30, left the garrison that remained at the prison greatly depleted.[282]

Barnes' garrison and five gunboats were ready and waiting for a Confederate attack. The entire Potomac Flotilla and the North Atlantic Blockading Squadron were also on alert. On July 10, orders were issued that sent USS *Currituck* to the Havre de Grace Bridge, USS *Fuchsia* to the Bush River Bridge, and USS *Resolute* up the bay, no doubt because Bradley Johnson's cavalry was operating in the area. The 20-gun frigate USS *Minnesota* was sent from the North Atlantic Blockading Squadron to take their place at Point Lookout, along with the 10-gun side-wheel steam schooner USS *Massasoit* and gunboat USS *Saco* from the naval yard in Boston, Mass. The 11-gun steamer USS *R. R. Cuyler* also was sent to the prison, and arrived there on July 12, followed by *Massosoit* and *Saco* on the 13th, and *Minnesota* on the 14th. Later that day, the 10-gun side-wheel steam schooner USS *Mackinaw* was the last to arrive.[283]

The Mission Begins

At sunrise on July 9, Johnson's Brigade (a total of about 1,500 men from the 8th, 21st and 22nd Virginia Cavalry regiments; the 34th and 36th Virginia Cavalry battalions; the 1st Maryland Cavalry Regiment; and the 2nd Maryland Cavalry Battalion), along with a battery of horse artillery, moved east from Middletown to Worman's Mill, Md., two miles north of Frederick on Old Liberty Road. The brigade took up a position and watched the army's left flank under Major General Robert Rodes engage the Union defenders at the Stone Bridge on the Baltimore Pike. As soon as Johnson believed the battle was well in hand, he began to execute his orders, moving the brigade eastward down Old Liberty Road.[284]

282 *OR*, 40, s. 1, pt. 3, p. 90-91, 275; *ORN*, 5, s. 1, p. 458, *ORN*, 1, s. 2, p. 89, 191

283 *OR*, 40, s. 1, pt. 3, p. 174, 206, 251-252; *ORN*, 5, s. 1, p. 458-460, 464; *ORN*, 10, s. 1, p. 260; *ORN*, 1, s. 2, p. 138, 145, 188, 196, 130-131

284 J. Kelley Bennette, 8th Virginia Cavalry, Diary, July 9, 1864, Collection 886, Univ. of North Carolina (UNC); Toomey, p. 124; Johnson, "My Ride...," p. 253; Early, p. 386

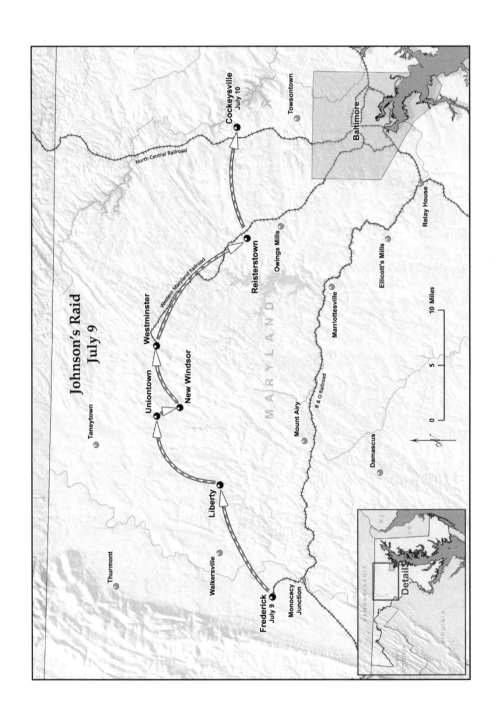

Johnson's Raid
July 9

Hospital Steward J. Kelley Bennette, 8th Virginia Cavalry Regiment, described the movements of the brigade during the mission: "We paid no respect whatever to roads; if they did not lead exactly as we wished to go we very unceremoniously left them to go their way alone while we made a road of our own thro' the fields."[285]

They moved through Liberty and Uniontown, and rested a short time until nightfall within sight of New Windsor, about 20 miles northeast of Frederick. Although the stores had already closed for the evening, when the Confederate cavalry arrived, the shopkeepers were forced to reopen and accept

LOC

Maj. Harry Gilmor

Confederate script as payment for items such as boots, shoes and clothes. The Confederates also burned the railroad station and a bridge before they left.[286]

While at New Windsor, Johnson detailed native Marylander Major Harry Gilmor as the advance guard of the brigade. With 20 men, Gilmor rode seven miles east to the larger town of Westminster with orders to cut the telegraph lines. Approaching the town, Gilmor learned there was a large Union cavalry force there, so he ordered sabers drawn, closed up the column and charged. The Union soldiers were taken completely by surprise and were only able to fire a couple of shots while retreating from the town.[287]

After the area was secured, a courier arrived with orders for Gilmor to issue a levy for 1,500 shoes, boots and suits. The demand required

285 Bennette, Diary, July 9, 1864, UNC

286 Toomey, p. 125; "Seventy-Fifth Anniversary of Harry Gilmor's Colorful Raid," *The Sunday Sun*, Baltimore, July 9, 1939; Duncan, "Maryland's Reaction To Early's Raid In 1864," p. 265; Bennette, Diary, July 9, 1864, UNC

287 Harry Gilmor, *Four Years In The Saddle* (NY: Harpers & Brothers, 1866), p. 190

the town to provide the supplies before Johnson arrived with the rest of the army. Between 10:00 and 11:00 p.m., the brigade moved into Westminster and stayed for about an hour. Mayor Jacob Grove could not convene the town council before Johnson's arrival, and was unable to meet the demand. Gilmor came to the town's aid and persuaded Johnson to forget the matter. A section of the branch line from the B&O Railroad was also destroyed during the Confederate occupation.[288]

After riding through the night, the cavalrymen rested for about two hours on the morning of July 10. Gilmor's advance guard passed through Reisterstown, 13 miles southeast of Westminster, around 8:00 a.m., and commandeered about 40 horses. They proceeded east to Cockeysville, 14 miles north of Baltimore, where they began burning two bridges of the North Central Railroad and the turnpike bridge. As Johnson and the rest of his brigade entered the town, they assisted with the destruction.[289]

Bracing for Attack

As Johnson's Brigade moved east destroying railroad bridges and cutting telegraph lines, alarm swept through the Baltimore and Annapolis areas. The Maryland Constitutional Convention in session at Annapolis was adjourned, and hasty defenses were prepared around the city. The War Department requested that gunboats be sent to important railroad bridges over the Susquehanna, Gunpowder and Bush rivers north of Baltimore, and 100 veterans were dispatched to guard the Havre de Grace Ferry across the Susquehanna. There was such a panic that a call for 100-days volunteers was raised. Unable to recruit volunteers for the normal 100 days, the term of service was lowered to just 30 days. With this change, a regiment was raised in Wilmington, Del., and designated the 7th Delaware Regiment. Under the command of Captain Thomas Hugh Stirling, 55 volunteers were organized into a company and rushed to defend the Philadelphia, Wilmington and Baltimore Railroad over the Gunpowder River. They reinforced a detachment of 32 soldiers from 159th Ohio National Guard's Company

---

288 Bennette, Diary, July 9, 1864, UNC; Toomey, p. 125; Duncan, "Maryland's Reaction To Early's Raid In 1864," p. 265

289 Toomey, p. 125; Bennette, Diary, July 10, 1864, UNC; R.A. Brock, ed. *Southern Historical Society Papers,* Vol. XXII (Richmond, VA: The Society, 1894; Reprint, New York: Kraus Reprint Company, 1977), p. 298; Bradley T. Johnson to General John R. Kenly, July 10, 1864, Bradley T. Johnson Papers, Duke University Library (DUL); *OR,* 37, s. 1, pt. 2, p. 174, 180

F around 3:00 a.m. on July 10. Stirling's men were positioned on the north side of the bridge, while Lieutenant Robert Price's men of the 159th Ohio were positioned on the south side.[290]

Extra precautions were taken to protect Baltimore against the Confederates operating in the area. The city streets were barricaded to prevent a cavalry charge from easily penetrating into the city, and citizens were armed as a last line of defense. Passes were required for persons leaving or entering the city, and ships were required to obtain permits from military authorities to leave port. Chief of Staff Major General Henry W. Halleck requested all convalescents fit for duty be sent from Philadelphia, Pa., to Baltimore to help in the defense.[291]

On July 12, Major General Edward O.C. Ord, who had replaced Major General Lew Wallace as commander of the VIII Army Corps and all troops in the Middle Department, requested cavalry and either artillery field batteries or siege howitzers to protect Baltimore from the Confederates. The city's defensive force stood at 500 blacks, 200 sailors, 3,000 militia and a body of armed citizens. The only troops considered suitable to take the field were the veterans of Brigadier General James Ricketts' division. They had just fought the Battle of Monocacy and were reduced to an aggregate force of 2,488 men.[292]

Weigh Anchor

The Confederate naval portion of the operation, under Commander John T. Wood, reached Fort Fisher at the mouth of the Cape Fear River in North Carolina and waited for word that Early was moving against Washington. Before the tides changed and Wood set out to sea, he received a telegram from Jefferson Davis, in which the Confederate President wrote:

> The object and destination of the expedition have somehow become so generally known that I fear your operations will meet unexpected obstacles. General R. E. Lee has communicated with you and left your action to your discretion. I suggest calm consideration and full comparison of views with Generals G.W.C. Lee, and others with whom you may choose to advise.

---

290 Duncan, "Maryland's Reaction To Early's Raid In 1864," p. 265; "Seventy-Fifth Anniversary of Harry Gilmor's Colorful Raid," *The Sunday Sun*, Baltimore, July 9, 1939; *OR*, 37, s. 1, pt. 1, p. 225, 229-230; *OR*, 37, s. 1, pt. 2, p. 185, 189, 193; *ORN*, 5, s. 1, p. 459
291 *OR*, 37, s. 1, pt. 2, p. 180, 188, 248, 323
292 *OR*, 37, s. 1, pt. 2, p. 214, 248; *OR*, 40, s. 1, pt. 3, p. 207

Wood cancelled the naval portion of the mission, but it was impossible, of course, to inform Early or Johnson of the decision. *Let-Her-B* and *Florie* were released from government service and returned to their captains on July 18.[293]

Gilmor's Raid

At Cockeysville on July 10, Gilmor was detached around 12:00 p.m. with about 135 men from the 1st Maryland Cavalry Regiment and the 2nd Maryland Cavalry Battalion. They were ordered to destroy the railroad bridge over the Gunpowder River and disrupt communication with the north. Headed for the Gunpowder Bridge, Gilmor detoured several miles to the south with a few officers and men to stop at his family home, "Glen Ellen," in Towsontown, only a few miles north of Baltimore. This was the first time Gilmor had seen his family since being captured and imprisoned at Fort McHenry from September 1862 to February 1863. The detachment left later that evening and rode northeast through Timonium, over York Road and the Philadelphia Pike, toward the bridge.[294]

They proceeded down Bel Air and Harford roads, cutting the telegraph lines. Near Kingsville, about 10 miles north east of Baltimore, they came to the home of Ishmael Day. Day was a local farmer who had the Union flag flying in his yard. Sergeant Eugene Fields and another soldier in Gilmor's command demanded that Day take the flag down, but he refused. Fields dismounted and attempted to lower the flag, but the farmer shot him in the face and chest with buckshot. Fields was mortally wounded, and Day fled into the woods, escaping the pursuing Confederates. In retaliation for killing Fields, Day's house, barn and other buildings were burned. In August, Wallace sent an officer to assess the damage and collect a sum equal to the damage from the surrounding residents. Individuals who had an assessment levied against them appealed to President Abraham Lincoln, and the cases were dropped.[295]

---

293 Thompson, "Plan To Release Our Men At Point Lookout," *Confederate Veteran*, Vol. XX, February 1912, p. 69-70; Toomey, p. 124; Duncan, "Maryland's Reaction To Early's Raid In 1864," p. 264; *OR*, 40, s. 1, pt. 3, p. 761; Tidwell, Hall and Gaddy, p. 148; Donnelly, p. 113, 114

294 Duncan, "Maryland's Reaction To Early's Raid In 1864," p. 265; Johnson, "My Ride...," p. 253-254; MAJ Harry Gilmor, Report, July 28, 1864, MS 1287, Harry Gilmor Papers, Maryland Historical Society (MHS); *OR*, 37, s. 1, pt. 2, p. 192-193

Gilmor next struck Magnolia Junction, about a mile northeast of the Gunpowder Bridge, at roughly 4:30 a.m. on July 11. The station was captured, and the telegraph lines were cut. He then waited for a train to arrive. The 8:30 a.m. passenger train from Baltimore to Philadelphia was stopped around 9:30 a.m. Confederate Captain Bailey and 20 men fired a volley into the engine, causing the engineer to stop the train. Before fleeing to safety, the engineer disabled the engine. While the passengers and baggage were unloaded and searched, Gilmor learned from two female southern sympathizers that Union Major General William B. Franklin was aboard. (In his memoirs, Gilmor denied that the women told him anything). Franklin, who was dressed in civilian clothing, was returning home to recuperate from a severe leg wound received at the Battle of Sabine Crossroads at Mansfield, La., on April 8. Most of the soldiers captured on the train were paroled, but a few, including Franklin, were taken prisoner. A horse and buggy was seized to

Maj. Gen. William B. Franklin

transport the prisoners. After the Confederate raid, Wallace issued an order to arrest the women who gave up Franklin, but they were not found.[296]

295 Toomey, p. 127; "Seventy-Fifth Anniversary of Harry Gilmor's Colorful Raid," *The Sunday Sun*, Baltimore, July 9, 1939; "Developments," *Philadelphia Inquirer*, July 12, 1864; Gilmor, p. 193; Gilmor, Report, July 28, 1864, MHS; *Baltimore Sun*, August 24, 1864

296 Duncan, "Maryland's Reaction To Early's Raid In 1864," p. 127-129; "The Escape Of Gen. Franklin," *New York Times*, July 15, 1864; "Developments," *Philadelphia Inquirer*, July 12, 1864; J. William Jones, *Southern Historical Society Papers*, Vol. 9, January to December 1881, (Millwood, NY: Kraus Reprint Co., 1977), p. 75; "Seventy-Fifth Anniversary of Harry Gilmor's Colorful Raid," *The Sunday Sun*, Baltimore, July 9, 1939; *OR*, 37, s. 1, pt. 2, p. 220; Gilmor, p. 194; LTC John Wooley to Col., Lew Wallace Collection, Indiana Historical Society (IHS)

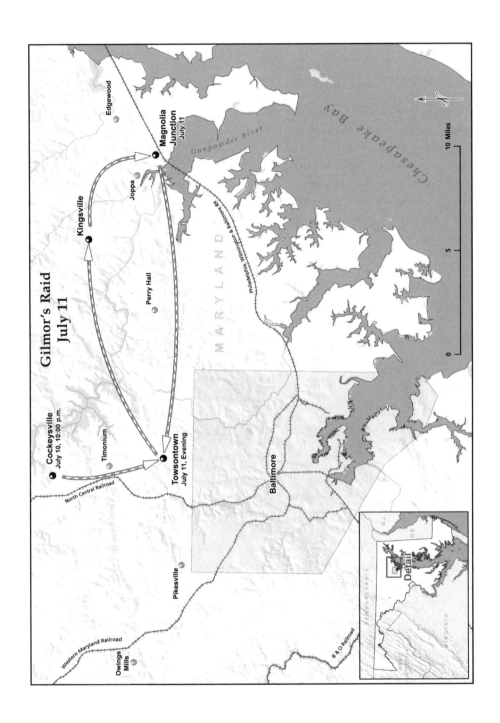

Gilmor's Raid
July 11

Cockeysville
July 10, 10:00 p.m.

Timonium

North Central Railroad

Towsontown
July 11, Evening

Kingsville

Perry Hall

Joppa

Edgewood

Magnolia
Junction
July 11

Gunpowder River

Philadelphia, Wilmington & Baltimore RR

Chesapeake Bay

MARYLAND

Baltimore

Pikesville

Owings
Mills

Western Maryland Railroad

B & O Railroad

Detail

PENNSYLVANIA

VIRGINIA

0   5   10 Miles

While Gilmor waited for another train to arrive, he ordered the disabled train and the depot burned. Union soldiers assigned to guard the Gunpowder Bridge were given a chance to surrender. They refused, so Confederate sharpshooters attempted to drive them off the bridge. For some reason, the 10:00 a.m. express from Baltimore was not stopped on the south side of the bridge by the Union soldiers assigned to that area. Therefore, as the train approached them, the Confederates open fired and easily captured it. The engineer escaped but was unable to sabotage the engine. The (second) train was set on fire and backed over the bridge. The Union soldiers fled from its path and a few were compelled to jump into the Gunpowder River. The steamer USS *Juniata*, a sloop-of-war with 11 guns, was only 300 yards away and was assigned to help defend the bridge when the Confederates attacked; however, it took no part in the action because it could not muster enough power to get into position. USS *Teaser*, a two-gun steam tug, had been ordered to the bridge on July10, but when it arrived, the bridge was in flames and there were no Confederates in the area.[297]

The burning railroad cars fell into the river, destroying the bridge's draw span section, but not before the Union defenders managed to uncouple two cars and save them. Before Gilmor left Magnolia Junction, his men burned all the railroad property. Conductor T.R. Munshower stated that after he escaped, Gilmor's men burned three first-class cars, one second-class car, a baggage car, the engine Henry Clay, one freight car and a North Central engine that was on a siding. The only casualty resulting from all this action was the death of Fireman Abraham Ward. Union Captain Stirling was promoted to major for his gallant conduct during the engagement. The bridge took three days to repair, and telegraph communication was reestablished with Philadelphia on July 13.[298]

Gilmor's detachment left around 4:00 p.m. and advanced down York Road with the prisoners he had taken off the train at Magnolia Station. He had intended to enter Baltimore, but having learned of the defensive precautions the city had taken, they proceeded west to Towsontown instead. While en route, they received a report that

---

297 Duncan, "Maryland's Reaction To Early's Raid In 1864," p. 266; Toomey, p. 127-128; *OR*, 37, s. 1, pt. 2, p. 184, 214; Gilmor, p. 195-196; *ORN*, 5, s. 1, p. 460, 465; *ORN*, 1, s. 2, p. 116, 220

298 "Developments," *Philadelphia Inquirer*, July 12, 1864; Duncan, "Maryland's Reaction To Early's Raid In 1864," p. 266; *OR*, 37, s. 1, pt. 2, p. 247-248; *OR*, 37, s. 1, pt. 1, p. 229-230; Gilmor, p. 229; *OR*,40, s. 1, pt. 3, p. 226

Union cavalry was waiting for them there. Gilmor rushed in with a small squad of 10 men and left orders for the rest of the detachment to charge in if shots were heard. They found no Union cavalry.[299]

In Towsontown, Gilmor and his men were having a drink of ale at Ady's Hotel when they learned that 75 Union mounted volunteers were riding to intercept them. Gilmor detached Captain Nickolas Owings and 12 men to guard the prisoners. They were ordered to wait near the home of a Mr. Craddock between Owings Mills and Randallstown while Gilmor laid a trap for the Union troops. He sent Lieutenant William H. Kemp and 15 men from Company C to attack the advance guard and fall back, hoping to draw the unsuspecting volunteers into an ambush. The ruse worked; the surprised Union cavalrymen retreated, and some were chased as far as Govanstown, four miles outside of Baltimore.[300]

By this time, Gilmor and his entire detachment were suffering from extreme exhaustion. It was late on July 11, and they had had very little, if any, sleep since the operation began on the morning of July 9. Men were now falling asleep in their saddles. To prevent the horses from inadvertently wandering off, Gilmor rode in the rear; however, it wasn't long before he, too, fell asleep and was separated from his men. A Union picket stopped Gilmor, waking him. Luckily, it was dark and the picket could not see that he was a Confederate officer. Gilmor passed himself off as a Union cavalryman and was allowed to ride on. He found his men a short time later, all asleep along the roadside.[301]

Gilmor returned to Towsontown and made his way about 12 miles west to Owings Mills by way of the Reisterstown Road. He rendezvoused with the exhausted guard detail, only to find them asleep. Franklin and the rest of the prisoners had escaped. Gilmor was extremely upset that they had lost a prize like Franklin and immediately sent out a detail to search for him. Franklin remained undiscovered. He hid in a house about four miles from Baltimore until a detachment from the 8th Illinois Cavalry Regiment, under the command of Major John Waite, retrieved him on the evening of July 13.[302]

---

299 Gilmor, p. 197-200; MAJ Harry Gilmor, Report, July 28, 1864, Harry Gilmore Papers, Maryland Historical Society (MHS); Toomey, p. 129
300 Gilmor, p. 198-201; Gilmor, Report, July 28, 1864, MHS
301 Gilmor, p. 200-201
302 "Developments," *Philadelphia Inquirer*, July 12, 1864; *OR*, 37, s. 1, pt. 2, p. 302, 323; Gilmor, p. 202; Abner Hard, *History of the Eighth Cavalry Regiment Illinois Volunteers, During the Great Rebellion* (Aurora, IL, 1868), p. 302

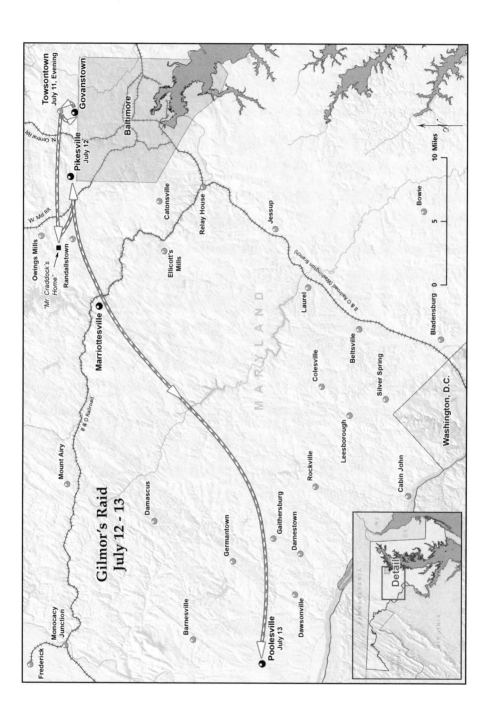

Gilmor's Raid
July 12 - 13

Towsontown
July 11, Evening

Govanstown

Pikesville
July 12

Baltimore

N. Central RR

W. Md RR

Owings Mills

"Mr. Craddock's
Home"

Randallstown

Marriottesville

Catonsville

Relay House

Ellicott's
Mills

Jessup

B & O Railroad (Washington Branch)

Laurel

Bladensburg

Bowie

MARYLAND

Beltsville

Colesville

Silver Spring

Leesborough

B & O Railroad

Mount Airy

Rockville

Cabin John

Washington, D.C.

Damascus

Germantown

Gaithersburg

Darnestown

Barnesville

Dawsonville

Poolesville
July 13

Frederick

Monocacy
Junction

PENNSYLVANIA

MD

Detail

VIRGINIA

0   5   10 Miles

159

July 12 was spent operating around Pikesville, northwest of Baltimore. A squad of 10 men was sent within four miles of Baltimore, while the rest of the detachment stayed at the Seven-Mile House on the Reisterstown Road. That night, Gilmor's detachment was reported crossing the B&O Railroad at Marriottesville, about 20 miles outside the city. After successfully carrying out his orders to disrupt the rail and telegraph communications north of Baltimore, Gilmor headed southwest toward Rockville, Md., to unite with Early. While en route, Gilmor learned Union cavalry occupied the town and Early was already moving toward Poolesville, Md. Gilmor changed direction and moved westward through Montgomery County, joining Early's army in Poolesville, only six miles from the Potomac River, at daybreak on the 14th.[303]

Johnson's Raid

After detaching Gilmor on July 10, Johnson's command spent several hours destroying one turnpike and two railroad bridges at Cockeysville, north of Baltimore. They continued on to Green Spring Valley and encamped at sunset about 12 miles northwest of Baltimore. The following morning, July 11, they were moving in a southerly direction when a 10-man squad from the 1st Maryland Cavalry Regiment (Confederate), commanded by Lieutenant Henry Blackistone, was detailed to burn Maryland Governor Augustus W. Bradford's home in Baltimore County. This was done in retaliation for Union Major General David Hunter's burning of former Virginia Governor John Letcher's residence in Lexington, Va., in June. Around 9:00 a.m., Mrs. Bradford was hastened from her house and permitted to take a few valuables and some clothing with her, as the first floor was set on fire. The brigade continued on to "Hayfields," the home of John Merryman, for lunch. Merryman had been a lieutenant in the Maryland militia in 1861 and had burned railroad bridges west of Baltimore to prevent Union soldiers from crossing into the state to reinforce Washington. Lincoln suspended the writ of habeas corpus in Maryland, and Merryman was imprisoned at Fort McHenry for a time. He was released on bond, and his case never came to trial.

Before leaving "Hayfields," Johnson sent a trusted friend, Colonel John C. Clarke, into Baltimore for information. Around mid-

---

303 "Seventy-Fifth Anniversary of Harry Gilmor's Colorful Raid," *The Sunday Sun*, Baltimore, July 9, 1939; Gilmor, Report, July 28, 1864, MHS; Gilmor, p. 203; *OR*, 37, s. 1, pt. 2, p. 318

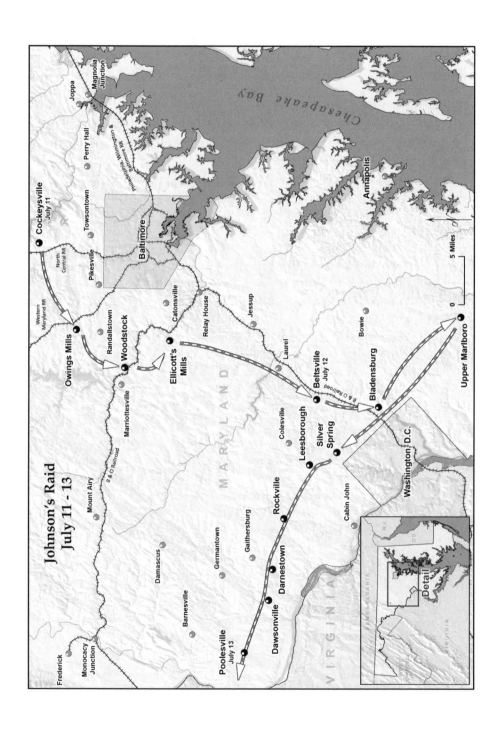

**Johnson's Raid
July 11 - 13**

Chesapeake Bay

Magnolia Junction

Joppa

Perry Hall

Cockeysville
July 11

Towsontown

Philadelphia, Wilmington & Baltimore RR

Annapolis

North Central RR

Pikesville

Baltimore

Western Maryland RR

Catonsville

Owings Mills

Randallstown

Relay House

Jessup

Woodstock

Bowie

Ellicott's Mills

Upper Marlboro

Marriottesville

M A R Y L A N D

Laurel

Beltsville
July 12

B & O Railroad

Bladensburg

B & O Railroad

Colesville

Silver Spring

Leesborough

Mount Airy

Rockville

Cabin John

Washington, D.C.

Damascus

Gaithersburg

Germantown

Darnestown

V I R G I N I A

Barnesville

Dawsonville

Frederick

Poolesville
July 13

Monocacy Junction

Detail

0   5 Miles

161

night on July 11, Johnson learned from two couriers sent by Colonel Clarke that the XIX and part of the VI Corps were at Locust Point, in south Baltimore, waiting to move by railroad to Washington. (Actually, the XIX and VI Corps were already arriving in Washington at the time). An officer and escort were sent to relay this information to Early, who had decided to delay the attack at Fort Stevens until the next morning, July 12.

That same day Johnson's men destroyed a portion of the railroad from Baltimore to Westminster and cut telegraph lines. They continued south, and while passing through Owings Mills at Painter's Mill Farm, they noticed freezers of ice cream being loaded on wagons for delivery to Baltimore. The ice cream was confiscated and issued to the troops for breakfast. It was scooped into just about anything that would hold it, including hats. Many had never seen anything like it; one soldier referred to it as "frozen mush," while some mountaineers from western Virginia thought the ice cream was "beer" and a little too cold to drink, so they put it in their canteens to melt. Johnson continued to ride south, stopping for lunch west of Baltimore at Doughregan Manor, the home of John Lee Carroll, who would be elected Maryland Governor in 1876. At Camp Bradford, four miles from Baltimore, 20 Union pickets were captured.[305]

Johnson continued to ride south, crossing the B&O Railroad north of Woodstock and passing within seven miles of the west side of Ellicott's Mills. Here, the railroad and telegraph lines were cut. The cavalry rode all day and camped at Triadelphia, about 20 miles southwest of Baltimore, between 9:00 and 10:00 p.m. Around midnight, there was word of Union cavalry camped nearby at Brookville. Johnson and his men hurried to try to intercept them, but they found the camp deserted. They spent the night at "The Caves," the home of John N. Carroll.[306]

On July 12 around 2:00 a.m., Johnson continued south along the railroad, reaching Beltsville, 15 miles northeast of Washington, around noon. Near Beltsville he burned two gondolas, 11 ballast cars, eight telegraph poles and the wooden portion of the Paint Branch iron rail-

304 Duncan, "Maryland's Reaction To Early's Raid In 1864," p. 266-267; Toomey, p. 126; "Developments," *Philadelphia Inquirer*, July 12, 1864; Bennette, Diary, July 10-11, 1864, UNC; Johnson, "My Ride...," *Journal of the United States Cavalry Association*, Vol. II, p. 254

305 Duncan, "Maryland's Reaction To Early's Raid In 1864," p. 268; Toomey, p. 125; *OR*, 37, s. 1, pt. 2, p. 212; Johnson, "My Ride...," p. 254-255; CPT Francis West Chamberlayne, Memoir, Chamberlalyne Family Papers, Virginia Historical Society (VHS); Bennette, Diary, July 11, 1864, UNC

306 Bennette, Diary, July 11, 1864, UNC; Toomey, p. 126; Johnson, "My Ride...," p. 256

road bridge. Overall, little damage was done to the bridge. Between Beltsville and Laurel, slightly to the northeast, a section of the B&O Railroad was torn up and a construction crew and camp train were captured. The camp train was burned along with three passenger cars, two dining cars, two house cars and one small four-wheel car. Johnson moved south and later that night attacked roughly 500 Union cavalrymen four miles north of Bladensburg. The Union troops were easily dispersed, and, with the help of an artillery piece, pursued back to the defenses of Washington at Fort Trotten. Several hundred government mules were also rounded up to provide mounts for the freed prisoners.[307]

By afternoon, Johnson resumed his ride southeast to Upper Marlboro. He did not have enough time to reach Point Lookout by evening, but believed that with fresh horses he could cover the remaining distance the next day. Johnson had not traveled far on the afternoon of July 12 before a courier delivered an order from Early recalling the brigade from the mission because the defenses at Fort Stevens had been reinforced and he decided against launching an all out attempt to capture the Union capital. Johnson reversed course, following the Washington Turnpike northwest as far as the Maryland Agricultural College, where he engaged in a brief skirmish with a Union patrol. From there, the adjutant of the 1st Maryland Cavalry Regiment, Captain George W. Booth, led the brigade west to Silver Spring. They traveled alongside the Washington defenses and were within artillery range, but were not fired upon, and occasionally drove in a Union picket. Booth reached Early's headquarters at Silver Spring after 9:00 p.m., while Johnson arrived with the last men of the brigade sometime after midnight. Johnson's brigade brought up the rear of the army while Colonel William L. Jackson's cavalry brigade provided the rear guard.[308]

On July 14, Union cavalry in Baltimore patrolled the surrounding area, while mounted citizens secured the roads leading to the city.

---

307 Bennette, Diary, July 12, 1864, UNC; Toomey, p. 126; George E. Pond, *The Shenandoah Valley in 1864* (NY: Charles Scribner's Sons, 1883), p. 61; MG Edward Ord to LG Ulysses Grant, July 12, 1864, Bradley T. Johnson Papers, Duke University Library (DUL); Johnson, "My Ride...," p. 256; *OR*, 37, s. 1, pt. 2, p. 234-235, 247-248; 38th Annual Report of the President and Directors to the Stockholders of the Baltimore and Ohio Railroad Co., For the Year Ending September 30, 1864, (Baltimore: J.B. Rose & Co.), p. 62

308 Early, p. 392; Bennette, Diary, July 12-13, 1864, UNC; Toomey, p. 126-127; Glen Worthington, *Fighting For Time* (Shippensburg, PA: White Mane, 1985), p. 281-282; Johnson, "My Ride...," p. 257; *OR*, 37, s. 1, pt. 2, p. 283

Citizens and ships no longer needed passes or permits to enter and/ or leave the city or port. Rumors of a rescue attempt at Point Lookout were brought to the attention of Union General Ulysses S. Grant, who clearly did not know the threat of attack had passed, yet seemed fairly unconcerned nonetheless. In a message sent to Major General Halleck, Grant mentioned "...a rumor in Baltimore that the enemy have sent to Point Lookout to rescue prisoners there. This can hardly be possible in view of the narrow outlet through which they would have to go in passing Washington with them. I call attention to the rumor, however, that you may direct the proper steps..."[309]

In September, with the approval of Wallace, a military commission in Baltimore tried and convicted four local civilians for assisting the Confederates during the July crises. Charles T. Cockey received the severest punishment—five years imprisonment and a fine of $1,000. Cockey was found guilty of guiding the Confederates through Owings Mills, Cockeysville and elsewhere in Baltimore County; leading them to where horses and other property could be seized; and provided them with other information and assistance. Dorsey Taylor was sentenced to one year hard labor at Dry Tortugas (he was actually sent to Clinton Prison) for "unauthorized communications and intercourse with the rebels." Both James Cullison and F. A. Carr were imprisoned for three months at Fort McHenry. Cullison was found guilty of "knowingly and wrongfully disposing of property of the United States, furnished and to be used for the military service." Carr was found guilty of working with the Confederates.[310]

Although Johnson and Gilmor had some success during their mission, crossing long distances, destroying rail and telegraph lines north of Baltimore and between Baltimore and Washington, and dealing with enemy forces left little time to attempt the release of prisoners from Point Lookout. Most important was the time needed to rest the men and their mounts. Johnson wrote, "It was physically impossible for men to make the ride in the time designated. I determined, however, to come as near it as possible." One inadvertent result of the operation was that it disrupted mail delivery south by Confederate agents operating in the north.[311]

309 *OR*, 37, s. 1, pt. 2, p. 323, 326, 301
310 *Baltimore Sun*, September 21 & 23, 1864
311 Worthington, p. 281; Johnson, "My Ride...," p. 256; *OR*, 40, s. 1, pt. 3, p. 769

CHAPTER TEN

TO THE GATES OF WASHINGTON

Confederate Lieutenant General Jubal Early provided the Confederacy with its first victory in the north at the Battle of Monocacy on July 9, 1864, and he also opened the road to Washington. After the battle, Early's army camped for the night and resumed the march down the Georgetown Pike the next morning. Brigadier General John Echols commanded Breckinridge's division and led the army's line of march, followed by divisions commanded by Major General John Gordon, Robert Rodes and Stephen Ramseur.

Breckinridge's division acted as the advance guard, and they moved at daylight. Ahead of them was Brigadier General John McCausland's cavalry brigade. Rodes' division, which camped at Frederick City, Md., left about 4:00 a.m. At the Monocacy River, the division crossed the ford near the burned remains of the covered bridge. Fording the river caused a delay, but once Rodes' division crossed, they fell in behind Gordon's division, which had left around 7:00 a.m. Ramseur's division provided the rear guard and remained at Monocacy Junction during the morning.

McCausland's brigade found the Georgetown Pike clear of Union forces until it reached the town of Gerrardsville, Md., about three miles north of Rockville. Here the Confederates encountered Union Major William Fry, 16th Pennsylvania Cavalry Regiment, commanding about 500 men of the Provisional Cavalry Regiment. Fry had left Washington in the morning and found Captain Albert Wells' squadron (Companies C and I, 8th Illinois Cavalry Regiment) at Rockville shortly after 11:00 a.m. Wells' squad had been cut off the previous day at the Battle of Monocacy and had fallen back toward Washington in an attempt to reconnect with their regiment. Wells' men fell in with Fry and a short time later engaged McCausland's brigade.[312]

---

312 U.S. War Department, *The War of the Rebellion: A Compilation of the Official Records of the Union and Confederate Armies* (Washington, 1880-1901), 37, Series 1, pt. 1, p. 236, 239, 248-249 (hereinafter cited as *OR*)

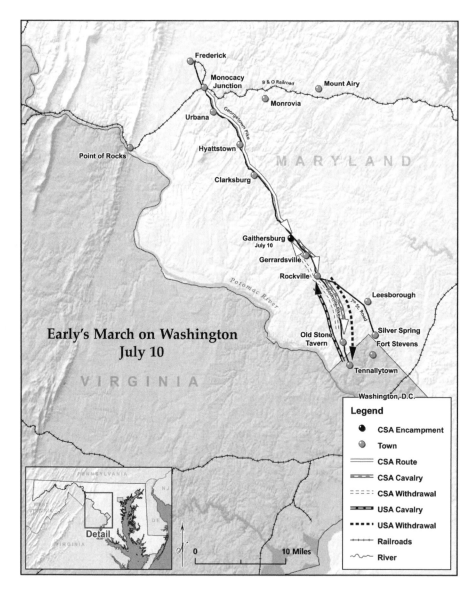

Early's March on Washington
July 10

Legend

●	CSA Encampment
◯	Town
═══	CSA Route
▭▭▭	CSA Cavalry
╌╌╌	CSA Withdrawal
▬▬▬	USA Cavalry
▰▰▰	USA Withdrawal
┼┼┼	Railroads
∿∿∿	River

Detail

0   10 Miles

As the engagement continued, Fry gradually withdrew his command back through Rockville and established a skirmish line about one mile south of the town. For about an hour, McCausland could not dislodge Fry, until a battery of artillery was brought up. Under the added fire power, Fry's force was gradually pushed back, and by 4:00 p.m., was within 2 miles of Tennallytown, Md. There he encountered infantry pickets defending Washington. Skirmishing continued until dark, when McCausland withdrew toward Rockville and Fry remained in position for the night.[313]

166

Destroy the Railroad

As the Confederate army moved south, work parties from Ramseur's division were detached to destroy the railroad bridge and buildings at Monocacy Junction. They burned the water station, sand house, agent and passenger houses, coal bins, platforms, telegraph office, telegraph lines and poles. In an attempt to destroy the bridge, they poured black powder into the castings and ignited it. The supply of powder was insufficient to do the job. Next, they tried firing solid artillery shot at the bridge. This attempt had limited success and managed to damage three spans, three towers, and many castings, and broke 17 suspension lines. It was three days before the bridge could be repaired and trains could once again use it.[314]

Ramseur's division left the junction around 12:00 p.m., and proceeded south down the pike toward Rockville. Union cavalrymen from Harpers Ferry, W.Va., under the command of Lieutenant Colonel William Blakely, 14th Pennsylvania Cavalry Regiment, entered Frederick and engaged Ramseur's rear guard. After driving the Confederates from the city, Blakely's cavalry forded the Monocacy River and harassed the Confederate division. After a few miles, Confederate artillery was engaged, forcing Blakely to fall back and return to Frederick. Ramseur continued toward Rockville and joined up with the rest of the Confederate army at about 1:00 a.m. on the morning of July 11. The army was camped around Gaithersburg, Md., with its headquarters at Summit Point.[315]

An Unforeseen Enemy

With the Union capital within the Confederate's grasp, a new factor began to take its toll on Early's men. This time it was the weather. The days were extremely hot and humid, and the road was very dusty.

---

313 *OR*, 37, s. 1, pt. 1, p. 249

314 38th Annual Report of the President and Directors to the Stockholders of the Baltimore and Ohio Railroad Co., For the Year Ending September 30, 1864, (Baltimore: J.B. Rose & Co.), p. 5, 58; Henry Kyd Douglas, *I Rode With Stonewall* (New York: Van Rees Press, 1941), p. 294

315 *OR*, 37, s. 1, pt. 2, p. 256; *OR*, 37, s. 1, pt. 1, p. 183, 203-204; Jedediah Hotchkiss, Diary, July 11, 1864, Manuscript Division, Library of Congress (LOC); Buckner M. Randolph, 49th VA, Diary, July 10, 1864, Randolph Sec. 10, Virginia Historical Society (VHS); CPT William Old, Early's Adjutant, Diary, July 11, 1864, Manuscript Division, LOC; Samuel Clarke Farrar, *The Twenty-Second Pennsylvania Cavalry and the Ringgold Battalion 1861-1865* (Pittsburgh, PA: The Twenty-Second Pennsylvania Ringgold Cavalry Association, 1911), p. 270; Douglas, p. 294

It was recorded in Georgetown that by 2:00 p.m. on July 10 the temperature had reached 92 degrees. This made the march tremendously difficult, and many of the soldiers began to collapse from exhaustion and sunstroke. Private George Q. Peyton, 13th Virginia Infantry Regiment, wrote:

> It was awful hot and the dust was about six inches deep. It was so fine that when you put your foot down, it moved away like water. More men broke down today than I ever saw before, and it felt like the hottest day that we had felt. We marched until 12K [midnight] and then lay down completely worn out.

The army covered a distance of about 20 miles and passed through the towns of Urbana, Hyattstown and Clarksburg before establishing camp about four miles north of Rockville. That evening, Generals John Breckinridge, John Echols, John Imboden and John Gordon had dinner two or three miles north of Rockville. As night set in, there was little relief from the heat. At 9:00 p.m., it was still 82 degrees. Early stated that, "the heat during the night had been very oppressive, and but little rest had been obtained."[316]

The next day, July 11, the heat continued to wear on Early's army. Lieutenant William Beavans, 43rd North Carolina Infantry Regiment, wrote that when the march commenced it was already "very warm," and that as the day wore on it had become "excessively hot & dusty." As the hours passed, the temperature continued to rise and grind away at the men. At 2:00 p.m., it had climbed to 90 degrees. Peyton wrote, "It was hotter than yesterday and I think at least half of the men fell out of the ranks and stopped by the wayside." First Sergeant Joseph Snider, 31st Virginia Infantry Regiment, wrote, "We had a very hot day and a great many of our brigade gave out. Near half of our Brigade straggled." Lieutenant W. Ashley, 69th North Carolina Infantry Regiment, described the day as the "hottest day we have experienced."[317]

On the morning of July 11, Fry's cavalry moved north on the Rockville Pike to re-engage the Confederates. Before he had gone far,

---

316 Jubal Early, *Narrative of the War Between the States Wilmington* (NC: Broadfoot, 1989), p. 389; *OR*, 37, s. 1, pt. 2, p. 199; Robert K. Krick, *Civil War Weather In Virginia* (Tuscaloosa: University of Alabama Press, 2007), p. 134; Walbrook D. Swank, ed. *Stonewall Jackson's Foot Cavalry: Company A, 13th Virginia Infantry* (Shippensburg, PA: Burd Street Press, 2000), p. 80

317 William Beavans, 43rd NC, Diary, July 11, 1864, No. 3244, Manuscript Department, University of North Carolina (UNC); Swank, p. 80-81; Frank Moore, ed. *The Rebellion Record: A Diary of American Events*, Vol. 10 (NY: D. Van Nostrand, 1869), p. 153; Krick, p. 134

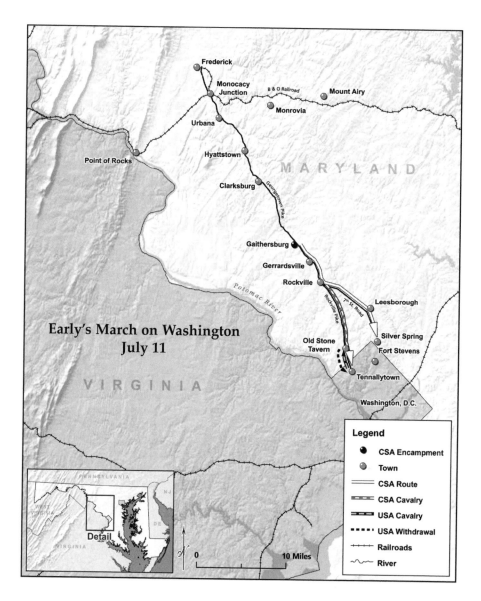

Early's March on Washington July 11

Legend

● CSA Encampment
● Town
— CSA Route
═ CSA Cavalry
═ USA Cavalry
▪▪▪▪ USA Withdrawal
+++ Railroads
〜 River

Frederick
Monocacy Junction
Mount Airy
Monrovia
Urbana
B & O Railroad
Point of Rocks
Hyattstown
MARYLAND
Clarksburg
Georgetown Pike
Gaithersburg
Gerrardsville
Rockville
Potomac River
Leesborough
Rockville Pike
7th St. Road
Old Stone Tavern
Silver Spring
Fort Stevens
VIRGINIA
Tennallytown
Washington, D.C.

Detail
PENNSYLVANIA
WEST VIRGINIA
VIRGINIA
N
J
DE
0   10 Miles

though, he was intercepted by Colonel Charles R. Lowell, Jr., commander of the 2nd Massachusetts Cavalry Regiment. Lowell's three squadrons and a fourth from the 8th Illinois Cavalry Regiment (Company G) along with Fry's men took on McCausland's brigade near Old Tavern, Md. As the fight intensified, Lowell was forced back to within two miles of Tennallytown, where a Union picket line was formed. He established a skirmish line on the Rockville Pike, and both sides continued the battle for the remainder of the day and into the next.[318]

Before McCausland moved down the Rockville Pike, Brigadier General John Imboden's cavalry brigade led the corps on its final leg to Washington. Rodes' division left around 3:30 a.m., moved through Rockville, took the 7th Street Road and passed through Leesborough before reaching Silver Spring, Md. The march was led by a brigade from Rodes' division, followed by an artillery battery. The rest of Rodes' division and the remaining battalion of artillery followed. Next in line was Ramseur's division, followed by another battalion of artillery. Behind them was Gordon's division, followed by the wagon train. Breckinridge's division, which was accompanied by Lieutenant Colonel J. Floyd King's battalion of artillery, brought up the rear.[319]

Aware of the hardship the heat was inflicting on his army, Early still urged his men on. Captain Cary Whitaker, 43rd North Carolina Infantry Regiment, recorded in his diary that Early told him: "Tell the men that [he] was very sorry to have to march them so hard but that now was the time, that they couldnt stop now but that if [we] succeeded in taking Washington they should be repaid for all this toil." As the army moved closer to Washington, Early wrote: "The day was so excessively hot, even at a very early hour in the morning and the dust so dense, that many of the men fell by the way, and it became necessary to slacken our pace."[320]

Prisoners also experienced the rigors of the march. They were marched in four ranks with a guard every 12 to 15 feet on both sides. Private John Roser, 110th Ohio Infantry Regiment, wrote of his captors: "[They] marched us very hard. 2 of our men died of Sun Stroke & heat. I tell you it was awful hot and dusty." When Sergeant Richard Waldrop, 21st Virginia Infantry Regiment, reached Washington, he wrote in his diary, "[W]e are now thundering at the gates of the 'National Capital' with I fear not much chance of success – This has been an awfully hot day & the road is lined with stragglers."[321]

Alarm in Washington

As the Confederates marched on Washington, the national capital was poorly defended. Army Chief of Staff Major General Henry Halleck wrote Lieutenant General Ulysses S. Grant on July 10:

318 *OR*, 37, s. 1, pt. 1, p. 236, 239, 240, 249-250; *OR*, 37, s. 1, pt. 2, p. 240
319 *OR*, 37, s. 1, pt. 2, p. 414, 594; Early, p. 389
320 *OR*, 37, s. 1, pt. 1, p. 348; CPT Cary Whitaker, 43rd NC, Diary, July 11, 1864, BR 662, Brock Collection, Huntington Library, San Marino, CA (HL)
321 Richard W. Waldrop, 21st VA, Diary, July 11, 1864, Manuscript Department, UNC; John Roser to His Wife Lucy, July 14, 1864, 110th Ohio File, Monocacy National Battlefield Archives (MNBA)

[W]e have no forces here for the field. All such forces were sent to you long ago. What we have here are raw militia, invalids, convalescents from the hospitals, a few dismounted batteries, and the dismounted and disorganized cavalry sent up from James River. One-half of the men cannot march at all.

The alarm in Washington had gradually increased since July 5, when reinforcements were sent from Washington to Harpers Ferry. On July 12, Union Major General Edward Ord reported, "The whole country is panic-stricken." War correspondent Sylvanus Cadwallader of the *Chicago Times* arrived in Washington from Petersburg, Va., on July 11 at about 10:00 a.m. and noticed, "[T]here was great alarm at the capital." As Early's army approached, Sergeant Major Joseph McMurran, 4th Virginia Infantry Regiment, took note: "[P]eople [were] much alarmed. Houses deserted & closed."[322]

As time passed, stories began to circulate regarding the size of the Confederate army. Eventually, on July 12, President Abraham Lincoln sent a message to Grant informing him, "[V]ague rumors have been reaching us for two or three days that Longstreet's corps is also on its way to this vicinity." This was only a rumor. The defenses around the capital were sound and could hold an attack at bay as long as there were enough men to man the fortifications. When Brigadier General Joseph R. West offered his services to Halleck on July 11, Halleck informed him, "[W]e have five times as many generals here as we want, but are greatly in need of privates. Any one volunteering in that capacity will be thankfully received." The same day, Halleck declined an offer by the quartermaster-general, Major General Montgomery C. Meigs, to use 2,700 civilians recruited from the quartermaster's depot to man the forts. Meigs then offered them to Major General Christopher C. Auger, commanding the Department of Washington, who accepted.[323]

Troops Needed

By July 1864, the vast numbers of soldiers protecting Washington had been sent to reinforce Grant's position in Virginia. This left roughly 25,000 men to defend the city, with about 13,000 of these north of the Potomac. The forts north of Washington were lightly manned, and over time their care had been neglected. The

---

322 *OR*, 37, s. 1, pt. 2, p. 59, 157, 248, 258; Benjamin P. Thomas, ed. *Three Years with Grant As Recalled by War Correspondent Sylvanus Cadwallader* (NY: Alfred A. Knopf, 1955), p. 226
323 *OR*, 37, s. 1, pt. 1, p. 196, 221

chance of a Confederate attack coming from this direction was thought to be extremely unlikely.[324]

On July 9, Major General John G. Barnard, chief engineer of the Washington defenses, sent a message to Halleck informing him, "[T]he militia regiments now garrisoning the forts scarcely know how to load or fire the guns." The conditions outside the forts faired no better. When Colonel William Hayward, commander of the 150th Ohio National Guard, learned of the Confederate movement toward Washington on July 8, he ordered "trees cut down and the ground cleared of everything that could afford a shelter for sharpshooters" from the Anacostia River to Fort Stevens. On the 11th, Cadwallader inspected the defenses and found the forts to be in "deplorable" condition. "The armament was insufficient, the ordnance supplies limited, and all of them so weakly manned as to make any protracted resistance impossible," he wrote. Major General Alexander McDowell McCook, commander of Northern Defenses, also examined the area and found the only troops north of Washington were small garrisons in the forts and small detachments of cavalry in the front. Also among the defenders was the 2nd Regiment District of Columbia Volunteers, 9th Veteran Reserve Corps and two batteries with two guns each.[325]

Washington was caught off guard and was unprepared for the advancing Confederates. On the evening of July 9, the quartermaster-general's office ordered the civilian clerks and workmen employed there to be organized and armed. The following day (July 10), a battalion of roughly 2,700 civilians was formed. About 250 men relieved guards from store houses, corrals, depots and public buildings. This enabled the invalid soldiers of the Veteran Reserve Corps guarding these locations to report to the forts. The Veteran Reserve Corps consisted of veteran soldiers who were no longer fit for field duty, but could serve in other capacities. By 9:00 a.m. on the 11th, 400 men of the quartermaster department reported for duty at Fort Stevens. Another 1,500 men arrived after 9:00 p.m. They were then sent to Fort Slocum and placed in the rifle pits.[326]

Five companies—276 men total—were held in reserve at the wood yard to defend public property. They were instructed twice daily in the manual of arms. Another two companies (150 men) were sent to Alexandria, Va., and put on picket duty. Approximately 2,800 sol-

324 *OR*, 37, s. 1, pt. 1, p. 231, 697
325 Thomas, p. 226-227; *OR*, 37, s. 1, pt. 1, p. 231, 245, 258; *OR*, 37, s. 1, pt. 2, p. 140
326 *OR*, 37, s. 1, pt. 1, p. 254-255, 257, 258-259, 261-262, 262-263

diers from hospitals, and convalescent and distribution camps were quickly organized into a Provisional Brigade, and marched to the front. They reported at Fort Stevens about 10:00 p.m., and were sent to Fort Slocum. The 2nd Regiment District of Columbia Volunteers were ordered from Edsall Station, Va., to Fort Stevens on July 10. They arrived at 9:00 a.m. the following morning and were positioned in the rifle pits between forts Stevens and Slocum. At 1:00 p.m., about 100 men from the regiment were sent to the skirmish line in front of Fort Stevens. The 25th New York Cavalry Regiment reported to Fort Stevens late on the 10th and went into camp behind the fort. The scramble was on to move all available men into position to defend against a Confederate attack.[327]

The Northern Defenses

As the Confederate army maneuvered toward Washington on July 11, the Union forts and rifle pits north of the capital were strengthened with all available troops. Approximately 1,175 quartermaster troops and a detachment from the Provisional Brigade occupied the entrenchments between forts Slocum and Totten. Between forts Slocum and Stevens were 550 men from the 12th Veteran Reserve Corps, an equal number from the 2nd Regiment District of Columbia Volunteers, and three companies of quartermaster troops totaling 221 men. One section from Battery L, 1st Ohio Independent Light Artillery, with 121 men and two guns, was also positioned in this area. The remaining troops from the Provision Brigade were placed in reserve to the rear of Fort Slocum.[328]

Fort Slocum was garrisoned by the 2nd Pennsylvania Heavy Artillery Regiment, 14th Michigan Independent Light Artillery Battery and 150th Ohio National Guard's Company G. When Meigs inspected the fort, he found the defense was not as strong as it should have been and ordered the Provisional Brigade to send all artillerymen from their ranks to bolster the garrison. A total of 105 men reported to the fort for artillery duty.

Fort Stevens was defended by the 13th Michigan Independent Light Artillery Battery (79 men), a detachment from the Provisional Brigade (52 men) and the 150th Ohio National Guard's Company K (78 men). Company K formed the picket line in front of the fort.

---

327 *OR*, 37, s. 1, pt. 1, p. 231-232, 262-263, 264; James C. Cannon, *Record of Service of Company K, 150th O.V.I. 1864* (Washington, D.C.: 1903), p. 14
328 *OR*, 37, s. 1, pt. 1, p. 235, 255-256, 259, 261-262

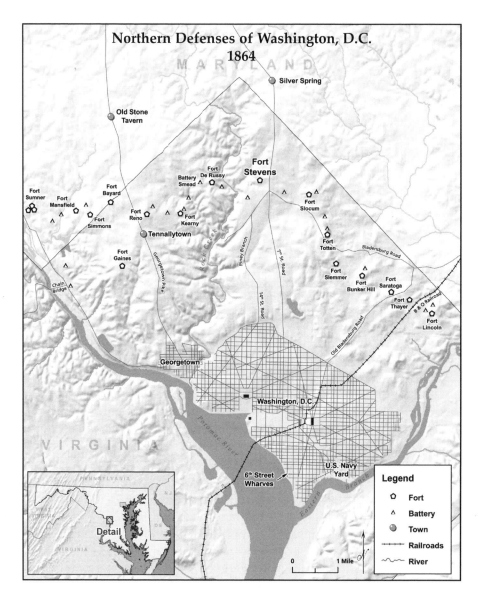

Northern Defenses of Washington, D.C. 1864

From Forts Stevens to De Russy, the rifle pits were manned by the 6th Veteran Reserve Corps, 157th Ohio National Guard (184 men), 9th Veteran Reserve Corps (350 men), 147th Ohio National Guard (465 men) and one section from the 1st Maine Light Artillery Battalion (112 men and two guns).[329]

Fort De Russy was garrisoned by Battery A, 1st Wisconsin Heavy Artillery Regiment, half of Battery L, 9th New York Heavy Artillery

---

329 *OR*, 37, s. 1, pt. 1, p. 235, 244, 245, 247, 256, 259

Regiment, and the 151st Ohio National Guard's companies C and G. Battery Smead was defended by half of Battery E, 9th New York Heavy Artillery Regiment and the 151st Ohio National Guard's Company I. Fort Kearny was manned by one company from the 9th New York Heavy Artillery Regiment and the 151st Ohio National Guard's Company K. Fort Reno was garrisoned by Company B, 9th New York Heavy Artillery Regiment, part of Battery I, 2nd United States Artillery Regiment and one company from the 151st Ohio National Guard. The 24th Veteran Reserve Corps was stationed at Fort Mansfield.

The rifle pits from forts Kearny, Reno and Simmons were manned by the 7th Veteran Reserve Corps, a Battery from the 9th New York Heavy Artillery, part of the 1st Veteran Reserve Corps, part of Battery I 2nd United States Artillery Regiment, and one company from the 151st Ohio National Guard. (The 147th, 150th, 151st and 157th Ohio National Guard regiments consisted of 100-days men.)[330]

Occupying the rifle pits were the 6th and 9th Veteran Reserve Corps between forts De Russy and Stevens, the 19th Veteran Reserve Corps from Fort De Russy to Battery Smead, the 1st Veteran Reserve Corps from Battery Smead to Fort Kearny, and the 22nd Veteran Reserve Corps in front of Fort Kearny.[331]

Grant Sends Reinforcements

Unaware of how the events at the Battle of Monocacy were unfolding for Union Major General Lew Wallace on July 9, Grant sent a message to Halleck informing him that he would send the XIX Corps (1st and 2nd divisions) to reinforce the Washington defenses if Halleck felt it was necessary. About 6,000 troops of the XIX Corps left New Orleans, La. on July 2 aboard ships destined for Petersburg. The remainder of the corps would leave shortly thereafter. The first troops were expected to arrive sometime between July 8 and 10. By the evening of the 9th none had arrived.

Grant also offered to send the remainder of the VI Corps (1st and 2nd divisions) if Early's army could be destroyed. At 11:00 p.m., Halleck responded that he felt reinforcements were necessary and that the VI Corps should be sent in addition to the XIX Corps. Before the reply was received, Grant decided to do just that.[332]

On the evening of July 9, the 1st and 2nd divisions, VI Corps, commanded by Major General Horatio Wright, were ordered from

---

330 *OR*, 37, s. 1, pt. 1, p. 239, 241, 344
331 *OR*, 37, s. 1, pt. 1, p. 344
332 *OR*, 37, s. 1, pt. 2, p. 7, 119, 133, 134, 136, 137

the Williams House, about five miles south of Petersburg, by way of Jerusalem Plank Road to City Point, Va. Approximately 11,000 soldiers strong, the divisions left around 11:00 p.m. and arrived early the next morning at City Point for transport to Washington. Wright departed at 10:00 a.m. on July 10 and the rest of his men left as transports were made ready. In all, the divisions took approximately 16 transports and left all wagons and artillery. Many of the returning regiments would soon be revisiting the defenses that they helped build.[333]

LOC

Maj. Gen. Horatio Wright

The voyage to Washington was relatively uneventful; however, soldiers on one ship containing the 121st New York and 96th Pennsylvania Infantry regiments began fighting among themselves shortly after leaving City Point. Apparently there was a dispute over the space assigned to them and a near riot ensued. One soldier was rescued from the water after he had been knocked off the ship. The officers quickly settled the dispute and the remainder of the trip was uneventful. A few of the transports that were still on the James River, such as the *S.R. Spaulding,* had been forced to anchor for the night due to fog. About 1:00 p.m. the steamer *Crescent,* which contained about 600 soldiers of the 153rd and part of the 114th New York Infantry regiments from the XIX Corps, arrived at Fort Monroe, Va., and were immediately ordered to Washington.[334]

333 *OR*, 37, s. 1, pt. 2, p. 134, 158, 159, 594-595; *OR*, 37, s. 1, pt. 1, p. 271, 273; COL Joseph W. Keifer, Official Report, Box OV1, Joseph Warren Keifer Collection, LOC

334 Augustus Buell, *The Cannoneer: Recollections of Service in the Army of the Potomac* (Washington, D.C.: The National Tribune, 1890), p. 267; *OR*, 37, s. 1, pt. 2, p. 159, 231, 283; MAJ Aldace F. Walker, 11th VT, to His Father, July 11, 1864, Vermont Historical Society (VTHS)

At the Gates

Union forces within the defenses of the city could see the clouds of dust stirred up by the troops and wagons of Early's army as it moved toward Silver Spring on the 11th. About 9:00 a.m., Imboden's cavalry brigade began to arrive outside Fort Stevens. The infantry and artillery followed, and the last troops arrived about 6:00 p.m. Now on the outskirts of the national capital, Captain Robert E. Park, 12th Alabama Infantry Regiment, wrote: "[I can] plainly see the dome of the Capitol."[335]

Most of Early's army was encamped along the 7th Street Road north of Fort Stevens. Rodes' division, which led the order of march, rested near the home of Postmaster General Montgomery Blair. Ramseur's division left at sunrise and stacked arms outside of Fort Stevens at 2:00 p.m. Gordon's division began its march about 5:00 a.m., came within sight of the Washington defenses at roughly 4:00 p.m., and camped on Francis Blair's property. Bringing up the rear guard, Breckinridge's division passed through Rockville around 11:00 a.m. and camped near Mr. Batchelor's home at about 6:00 in the evening. Early's headquarters was established a little north and east of Silver Spring at George Riggs' house.[336]

When Early's army reached the defenses on the afternoon of the 11th he noted, "The men [are] almost completely exhausted and not in a condition to make an attack." The divisions went into camp and stragglers filtered in throughout the afternoon and evening. Union troops from the forts welcomed the approaching Confederates with artillery fire. According to Private Isaac G. Bradwell, 31st Georgia Infantry Regiment, "The shells from these [guns] passed over our heads at a great altitude and burst far to our rear, doing no damage to anyone." Captain Park wrote that as his men rested they were, "eager to enter the city" and "full of surmises as to [their] next course of action."[337]

---

335 J. William Jones, *Southern Historical Society Papers*, Vol. 1 (Richmond, Virginia: 1876), p. 379; *OR*, 37, s. 1, pt. 2, p. 415; *OR*, 37, s. 1, pt. 1, p. 240

336 I.G. Bradwell, "Early's Demonstration Against Washington in 1864," *Confederate Veteran*, Vol. XXII, October 1914, p. 439; Hotchkiss, Diary, July 11, 1864, LOC; *OR*, 37, s. 1, pt. 2, p. 415; BG William Terry, Report, July 22, 1864, Chicago Historical Society (CHS); Joseph McMurran, 4th VA, Diary, July 11, 1864, Microfilm Reel Miscellaneous Nr 1316, Library of Virginia (LOV); Swank, p. 80-81; Beavans, Diary, July 11, 1864, UNC

337 *OR*, 37, s. 1, pt. 1, p. 348; Jones, *Southern Historical Society Papers*, Vol. 1, p. 379; COL Thomas Toon, 20th NC, Diary, July 11, 1864, Thomas Toon Papers, North Carolina State Archives (NCSA)

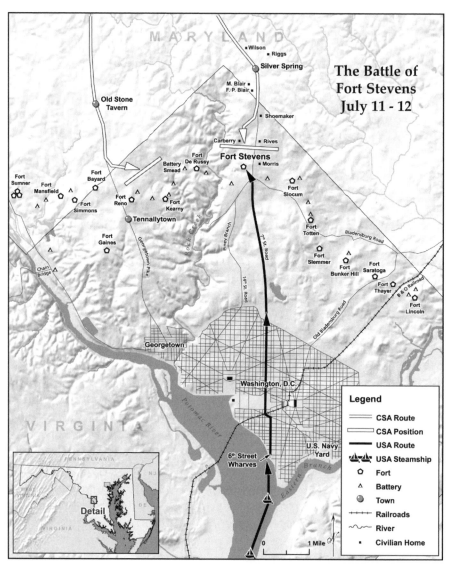

The Battle of
Fort Stevens
July 11 - 12

Legend

═══	CSA Route
▭	CSA Position
▬▬	USA Route
⛴	USA Steamship
⬠	Fort
∧	Battery
◉	Town
┼┼┼	Railroads
∿	River
▪	Civilian Home

The 150th Ohio National Guard's Company K formed the skirmish-line in front of Fort Stevens with pickets positioned on Francis P. Blair's farm in advance of the line. At 11:00 a.m., Imboden's cavalry brigade deployed as skirmishers and attacked the pickets. Between noon and 1:00 p.m., Confederate sharpshooters moved forward and gradually forced the pickets to fall back toward the defenses. Private William E. Leach was shot in the thigh and bowels, and died on the 13th. He was the company's only loss.[338]

---

338 Whitaker, 43rd NC, Diary, July 11, 1864, HL; Early, p. 389; *OR*, 37, s. 1, pt. 1, p. 245, 246

By 1:00 p.m., the 25th New York Cavalry Regiment (dismounted) and about 100 men from the 2nd Regiment District of Columbia Volunteers were ordered to the skirmish line in the trenches in front of Fort Stevens. A detachment of mixed cavalry from several regiments also arrived from Camp Stoneman at Giesboro Depot via the 7th Street Road. They rushed to the skirmish line as Confederate sharpshooters advanced to within 150 yards in front and 50 yards to the right of Fort Stevens. The reinforced skirmish line advanced under artillery support. They drove the Confederate line back some distance and established a new picket line by 1:30 p.m.[339]

About 3:00 p.m., Rodes' division was sent forward near the skirmish line. Cadwallader, who was at Fort Stevens, observed: "A regular line of battle was extended to the right and left, running across farms, through orchards and dooryards, and batteries planting their guns to open on our fortifications." Gordon ordered a battery of field pieces to unlimber in an open field on the right of Rodes' division and about 400 yards from Fort Stevens. At 4:00 p.m., a single artillery shot was fired from Fort Stevens at Mr. Carberry's house, which was filled with Confederates. The artillery round exploded, and the soldiers were forced to abandon their position. At the same time, the 9th Veteran Reserve Corp was ordered to relieve a portion of the 25th New York Cavalry Regiment (dismounted) from the skirmish line. After a brief engagement, the cavalrymen were relieved and the line was moved forward some distance.[340]

At Fort De Russy (located to the left of Fort Stevens) the artillerists provided support by shelling the Confederates as they moved down the 7th Street Road. Two shells struck the outbuildings of Mr. John Wilson, about a half-mile north of Silver Spring. Although these shots were no serious threat, they caused the Confederates to periodically move their camps. As the Confederate skirmishers advanced toward the forts, they took positions in and around a house, about a mile north of the fort. A number of shells were directed at the house so it would catch on fire. The skirmishers were forced to fall back toward Wilson's house, leaving one casualty behind. Another advance was made to the right of Fort De Russy, focused on the ravine of Rock Creek that was covered by two redoubts (temporary small enclosed

---

339 *OR*, 37, s. 1, pt. 1, p. 231, 246; "Dismounted Cavalry," *National Tribune*, August 9, 1900; "The Fight at Fort Stevens," *National Tribune*, January 22, 1914; Cannon, p. 15

340 Thomas, p. 226-227; I.G. Bradwell, "On To Washington," *Confederate Veteran*, Vol. XXXVI, March 1928, p. 95; Beavans, Diary, July 11, 1864, UNC; Old, Diary, July 11, 1864, LOC; *OR*, 37, s. 1, pt. 1, p. 231, 246, 344

defensive positions). One regiment from the 9th Veteran Reserve Corps was ordered to establish a line on a crest of a ridge and, with artillery from the fort, opened fire. Once again, the Confederates were forced to fall back.[341]

In the evening, Early held a council of war with Breckenridge, Rodes, Gordon and Ramseur at the home of Montgomery Blair. They determined to attack in force; but since the soldiers were exhausted and many lagged behind, the assault would have to wait until first light the next morning. During the night a message was received from Brigadier General Bradley Johnson—who was carrying out the Point Lookout operation—that two corps had arrived in Baltimore from the Petersburg area and were on their way to Washington. This information was not entirely accurate. Reinforcements were on the way, but they were not en route to Baltimore. With this information, Early decided to delay the attack the next morning until after he inspected the defenses.[342]

Public Destruction

As the Confederates deployed—primarily around Fort Stevens—they occupied a number of houses and surrounding structures to seek cover from Union small arms and artillery fire. In order to relieve the pressure, Union artillery from forts De Russy, Stevens and Slocum directed their fire at these structures. The homes or outbuildings of Messrs Rives, Bramer, Carberry, Abner Shoemaker, John Wilson, Richard Butt, William Bell, J.H. McChesney, William Morris and Francis Blair were either damaged or destroyed. Secretary of the Navy Gideon Welles, who visited Fort Stevens, observed:

> Two houses in the vicinity were in flames set on fire by our own people, because they obstructed the range of our guns and gave shelter to Rebel sharpshooters. Other houses and buildings had also been destroyed. A pretty grove nearly opposite the fort was being cut down.[343]

---

341 *OR*, 37, s. 1, pt. 1, p. 238, 241

342 Robert Grier Stephens, Jr. ed. and comp. *Intrepid Warrior Clement Anselm Evans Confederate General from Georgia: Life, Letters, and Diaries of the War Years* (Dayton, OH: Morningside, 1992), p. 427; Early, p. 392; Douglas, I Rode With Stonewall, p. 294-295; Bradley Johnson, "My Ride Around Baltimore In Eighteen Hundred and Sixty-Four," *Journal of the United States Cavalry Association,* Vol. II, (Fort Leavenworth, KS: 1889), p. 254-255

343 Gideon Welles, *Diary of Gideon Welles: Secretary of the Navy under Lincoln and Johnson,* Vol. II (NY: Norton, 1960), p. 72; *OR*, 37, s. 1, pt. 1, p. 232, 235, 241, 246, 247; "Rebel Advance on Washington," *The Philadelphia Inquirer*, July 14, 1864

Upon Breckinridge's arrival at "Silver Spring," the estate of Montgomery Blair, he ordered a guard placed over the house and property. No one was to enter the home or disturb the grounds. Breckinridge had befriended Blair prior to the conflict and he wished that Blair's residence be spared the brutality of war, but during his stay the wine cellar was much depleted of its contents. After the guards were recalled during the withdrawal, the house was burned and was a total loss. It is unclear who or what started the fire. It might have been set by Confederate soldiers during the retreat or Union artillery that had bombarded the area and set other homes on fire. "Falkland," home of Francis Blair (father of Montgomery), was unharmed; however, Early authorized Major Jedadiah Hotchkiss to take some maps from the library.[344]

Reinforcements Arrive

About noon on July 11 the prayers of the panic-stricken citizens of Washington were answered. Five ships from City Point, loaded with reinforcements from the 2nd Division, VI Corps, arrived at the 6th Street wharfs in Washington. Another ship containing about 600 soldiers from the XIX Corps also arrived from New Orleans at this time. Halleck immediately ordered Wright to move his troops to the east on the extreme left of the Union defense. They were to establish a camp between the Chain Bridge and the defenses of the Potomac, with orders to enter the works only if attacked. The XIX Corps was ordered to the east of Washington and took the old Bladensburg Road to Fort Saratoga.[345]

While en route to the Chain Bridge, Wright's order was countermanded and a new order issued to report to Crystal Spring, located about a half-mile south of Fort Stevens. Here the VI Corps troops established a camp on 14th Street Road at the crossing of Piney Branch Road. Wright arrived at Fort Stevens shortly after 4:00 p.m. and requested permission to send a brigade against the Confederate skirmish line that was currently engaged with Union forces, and "clean them out." This request was denied by Major General Augur on the grounds that the Union lines needed to first be better established.[346]

---

344 McMurran, Diary, July 11, 1864, LOV; Jones, *Southern Historical Society Papers*,
   Vol. 1, p. 379-380; Stephens, Jr., p. 427; Hotchkiss, Diary, July 11, 1864, LOC; *OR*,
   37, s. 1, pt. 2, p. 259; *OR*, 37, s. 1, pt. 1, p. 259; Douglas, p. 295
345 *OR*, 37, s. 1, pt. 2, p. 193, 207, 209, 231
346 *OR*, 37, s. 1, pt. 2, p. 208, 209; *OR*, 37, s. 1, pt. 1, p. 264, 265

By 5:00 p.m. the Confederates quite effectively pressured the skirmish line and pushed it back toward Fort Stevens. Orders were issued to relieve the skirmish line and drive the Confederates back. Seven companies from the 9th Veteran Reserve Corps, the remaining troops from the 25th New York Cavalry Regiment (dismounted) and 100 men from the 2nd Regiment District of Columbia Volunteers were relieved by 500 men from the 1st Brigade, 2nd Division, VI Corps. The 98th, 102nd and 139th Pennsylvania Infantry regiments successfully drove the Confederates back to a position 800 yards from the fort before 7:00 p.m. At dark about 400 men from the 93rd Pennsylvania and 62nd New York Infantry regiments were brought forward to strengthen the skirmish line, which was engaged throughout the night.[347]

On the left of Fort Stevens three companies from the 9th Veteran Reserve Corps and one company each from the 1st and 6th Veteran Reserve Corps were sent from the rifle pits to Fort De Russy and Battery Smead. From there they were deployed in front of the defensive positions and successfully advanced the skirmish line about 1,500 yards. It was decided to reinforce the skirmish line when, at 7:30 p.m., the Confederates were seen strengthening their line. As darkness fell, the remainder of the 6th Veteran Reserve Corps was sent to the right and center of the skirmish line, and six companies from the 22nd Veteran Reserve Corps were sent to the left.[348]

Attack on Fort Stevens

On the morning of July 12, Early awoke to see the fortifications before him had been reinforced during the night by the 1st and 2nd divisions, VI Corps. There was little likelihood of successfully taking Fort Stevens, and so the decision was made to withdraw across the Potomac River, back to Virginia. Sharpshooters and skirmishers would continue to engage the fortifications throughout the day, and under the cover of darkness the army would pull out. A courier was also sent to recall Johnson, who was on his way to attack the Union prison at Point Lookout. His new orders were to make his way to Silver Spring and report to the headquarters there.[349]

After a restless night the Union forts to the left of Fort Stevens were strengthened with troops. The right of the skirmish line in front

---

347 *OR*, 37, s. 1, pt. 1, p. 264, 273, 275-276; "The Fight at Fort Stevens," *National Tribune*, January 22, 1914
348 *OR*, 37, s. 1, pt. 1, p. 344
349 Johnson, "My Ride...," p. 257

of Fort De Russy was advanced at 6:00 a.m., about a quarter-mile. Once they dislodged some Confederates and took control of a hill, the center and left moved forward. An hour later the 24th Veteran Reserve Corps was moved from Fort Sumner on the extreme left near the Potomac River to reinforce Fort Kearny. At 1:00 p.m. the skirmish line held by the 6th Veteran Reserve Corps between forts De Russy and Stevens was replaced by the 1st Veteran Reserve Corps. An hour later the 6th Veteran Reserve Corps was ordered to occupy the rifle pits at Fort Reno, and 85 men were detailed to the picket line. At 5:00 p.m. the 25th New York Cavalry Regiment (dismounted) relieved the 1st Veteran Reserve Corps, which then occupied the rifle pits previously held by the 6th Veteran Reserve Corps.[350]

At 5:00 p.m. the 6th Veteran Reserve Corps Company H, commanded by Captain Clark, was ordered to confirm reports that Confederate artillery was positioned on the right of a barn in front of Fort De Russy. If the information was accurate, Clark was directed to burn the barn occupied by Confederate sharpshooters. Artillery from forts Reno and De Russy attempted to burn or knock down the structure as Clark's company advanced under artillery cover. As they neared, the Confederate sharpshooters engaged Clark's men. Outnumbered, Clark was forced to fall back, but only after he was able to confirm that the report was inaccurate. As Clark's company fell back, Confederate reinforcements moved toward the structure but were effectively shelled and forced to fall back to the Wilson property. Five men, including Clark, were wounded in the engagement.[351]

June 12th began tragically at Fort Stevens when the artillery was ordered to shell Confederate sharpshooters that occupied Carberry's house. The first shot malfunctioned and exploded after traveling just five yards, resulting in the death of one of the Union skirmishers. Artillery fire continued and was directed at the Carberry and Rives houses and at other locations where groups of Confederates had been found massing.[352]

At 8:00 a.m. Gordon's division formed a line of battle to the left of Rodes' division, which was in front of Fort Stevens. Although the decision had been made to withdraw during the evening, it was necessary to establish a strong battle line to repel any potential attack. Once in position, brigade commander Colonel Edmund Atkinson, who days earlier replaced the wounded Brigadier General Clement Evans

350 *OR*, 37, s. 1, pt. 1, p. 344-345
351 *OR*, 37, s. 1, pt. 1, p. 236, 242, 343, 345
352 *OR*, 37, s. 1, pt. 1, p. 246

of Gordon's division, recorded that the men, "lay in line during the whole day" and "nothing of importance transpired." Throughout the day the Union defenders anxiously waited for the Confederate attack that never came.[353]

McCook decided to relieve the pressure on the skirmish line at 5:00 p.m. Confederate sharpshooters about 1,100 yards out in the Carberry and Rives houses and on some hills had an advantage over the skirmish line. Colonel Daniel Bidwell, commander of the 3rd Brigade, 2nd Division, VI Corps, received orders to move his command undetected from Fort Stevens to the skirmish line. He used the ravine and woods to mask his movements and reached the skirmish line at about 6:00 p.m. The 1st Brigade (62nd New York, 93rd Pennsylvania, 98th Pennsylvania and 102nd Pennsylvania), commanded by Brigadier General Frank Wheaton, and three regiments (43rd New York, 49th New York and 7th Maine) from the 3rd Brigade received orders to carry out an assault. The remaining three regiments (77th New York, 122nd New York and 61st Pennsylvania) were held in support. The 3rd Brigade formed two lines behind the 1st Brigade and waited for the order to attack.[354]

When a signal was given, all the artillery from Fort Stevens was brought to bear on Carberry's house. They unleashed 23 rounds at the house and set fire to it. Their attention then shifted to Rives' house, which received eight rounds and was likewise set on fire. Beavans recorded in his diary: "The yanks shelled our line furiously" and "soon after they charged." After the 36th shot was fired, a signal was given from the fort to initiate the infantry attack. The skirmish line sprung forward but found the Confederate position too strong. The support regiments (77th New York, 122nd New York and 61st Pennsylvania) were ordered forward on the right, along with 150 men of the picket reserve from the 102nd Pennsylvania Infantry Regiment and a detachment of 80 Vermonters from the 2nd Brigade. They engaged the Confederate left causing that portion of the line to fall back, followed by the entire Confederate line.[355]

Confederate sharpshooters were reinforced, and a counter attack was launched from a ravine behind Carberry's home to take back the ground they had lost. The Union skirmish line was able to maintain

353 COL Edmund N. Atkinson, Evan's Brigade, Report, July 22, 1864, Box 2, James Eldridge Collection, HL
354 *OR*, 37, s. 1, pt. 1, p. 232, 276-277; *OR*, 37, s. 1, pt. 2, p. 230
355 *OR*, 37, s. 1, pt. 1, p. 246, 259, 276-277; Beavans, Diary, July 12, 1864, UNC; Gideon Welles, p. 75

its new position with artillery support from forts Stevens and Slocum and the engagement continued until the last shot fired about 10:00 p.m. At some point in the engagement a resupply of ammunition was requested. The 150th Ohio National Guard's Company K was assigned this task. A small detail took an old buggy loaded with ammunition to the front. All the men returned unharmed, "but that buggy was riddled with led," reported 1st Sergeant James Laird of the 150th Ohio. About an hour after the engagement ended the 2nd Brigade relieved the 1st Brigade, which returned to camp near Crystal Spring.[356]

Civilian troops from the Quartermaster Department were involved in this action. The unit suffered two casualties, both from Company B. Mr. John Rynders was wounded in the arm and another unnamed civilian was shot and killed. The individual that was killed was a former employee who had joined the new recruits as they marched to the front.[357]

The President

During the crisis Company K of the 150th Pennsylvania Infantry Regiment, which was assigned as President Abraham Lincoln's personal guard, was detached from its camp at the Soldiers' Home, the president's retreat. The company was sent to the vicinity of Fort Reno to assist with the defense of the capital. This did not deter the President from personally visiting various locations throughout the city. On July 11 and 12, he was found at the 6th Street wharfs greeting newly arrived soldiers, on the 7th Street Road and at Fort Stevens.[358]

On the afternoon of the 12th the President stood atop the walls of Fort Stevens and observed the military actions that developed in the fields before him. While he watched the battle from this position he inadvertently made himself the most prominent target of the entire war. Confederate sharpshooters took aim and, as Gideon Welles reported: "[O]ccasionally a bullet from some long range rifle passed above our heads" in the fort. Lincoln became the only United States president to come under enemy fire while in office. Luckily, there

356 *OR*, 37, s. 1, pt. 1, p. 232, 246, 247, 259, 273; *OR*, 37, s. 1, pt. 2, p. 257-258; Whitaker, Diary, July 12, 1864, HL; Joseph T. Durkin, ed. *Confederate Chaplain: A War Journal of Rev. James B. Sheeran, 14th Louisiana, C.S.A.* (Milwaukee: Bruce Publishing Co., 1960), p. 92; Cannon, p. 17
357 *OR*, 37, s. 1, pt. 1, p. 256, 259, 263
358 *OR*, 37, s. 1, pt. 2, p. 265, 278-279, 307; "Dismounted Cavalry," *National Tribune*, August 9, 1900; "The Fight at Fort Stevens," *National Tribune*, January 22, 1914; Cannon, p. 14

was only one casualty in the fort and a few in the trenches. Sometime before 6:00 p.m., while Lincoln and others were on the walls of the fortification, Captain C.C.V.A. Crawford, 102nd Pennsylvania Infantry Regiment, was wounded in the leg. Immediately after this incident all persons on the wall, including the president, were ordered down. Welles, who arrived after the President, noted, "One man had been shot in the fort a few minutes before we entered."[359]

LOC

President Abraham Lincoln

Major D.H. Darling, 7th Michigan Cavalry Regiment, commanded a cavalry outpost of about 500 men three miles south of Bladensburg, Md. Around 3:00 p.m. they were engaged on the Baltimore Pike where the road crosses Paint Creek. Johnson's cavalry brigade, which was carrying out the Point Lookout operation, attacked Darling's force. Outnumbered and outgunned, Darling fell back to Fort Totten, while Johnson continued on his way.[360]

The engagement brought to light the inadequate number of troops from Fort Lincoln to Fort Totten. The trenches and rifle pits were unmanned and the forts were lightly garrisoned. Only two companies of 100-day men and a few unarmed convalescents defended Fort Lincoln. Major General Quincy A. Gilmore requested troops for this area, and Meigs was ordered to send 2,000 men to Fort Saratoga. The 2nd Regiment District of Columbia Volunteers, which was held in reserve at Fort Slocum, and the 12th Veteran Reserve Corps were sent. It was also determined on the morning of the 12th that, excluding preparation of vessels and materials of war, all work be suspended and that sailors and employees of the Navy Department be armed and sent to Fort Lincoln. Under the command of Rear-Admiral Louis Goldsborough, between 1,000 and 1,500 sailors were marched to the fort and remained there until the 14th.[361]

359 Welles, p. 75-76; *OR*, 37, s. 1, pt. 1, p. 247; *OR*, 37, s. 1, pt. 2, p. 257
360 *OR*, 37, s. 1, pt. 2, p. 224, 233, 234-235, 236, 241; *OR*, 37, s. 1, pt. 1, p. 256-257; J. Kelley Bennette, 8th VA Cavalry, Diary, July 12, 1864, Collection 886, UNC
361 *OR*, 37, s. 1, pt. 2, p. 225, 231, 232, 233-234, 241, 303; *OR*, 37, s. 1, pt. 1, p. 259, 264

Back to Virginia

At about 7:00 p.m., the Confederate retreat began. Breckinridge's division, followed by the wagon trains, led the army back up the 7th Street Road, retracing the route they had taken from Rockville. Marching through the night, the division camped near Poolesville, Md. The headquarters fell back about 11:00 p.m., followed by Rodes' division about an hour later. They traveled as far as Dawsonville, Md., where they made camp about 9:00 a.m. on the 13th. Gordon's division marched until they reached Darnestown, Md. and camped about 1:00 p.m. Ramseur's division, which brought up the rear, marched all night and also camped at Darnestown about 2:00 p.m. During the night the skirmish line was reinforced with cavalrymen, who departed just before daylight at 5:00 a.m. About 9:00 p.m. Johnson's cavalry brigade began to arrive in Silver Springs. Johnson reported after midnight and was ordered to bring up the rear with Colonel William L. Jackson's cavalry brigade, which provided the rear guard.[362]

The army's progress was greatly impeded by marching at night. Positioning the wagon train in front also slowed their movement. Beavans described the march as "very disagreeable & unpleasant," adding that the slow progress of the wagons and low light conditions caused the army to move "short distances at intervals of a few minutes. We only made about a mile an hour" and by morning the army had not covered a distance greater than seven or eight miles.[363]

Early's headquarters established camp at Conrad's Ferry at 12:00 a.m. and forded the river on the morning of the 14th. Ramseur's division passed through Poolesville about 4:00 a.m. and reached White's Ford about 7:00 a.m. Prior to their arrival Breckinridge's division had begun crossing the ford at sunrise. They camped for about 2 or 3 hours before they were ordered to cross. A Union signal officer at Sugar Loaf Mountain reported that he could see a large body of troops and wagon train crossing at White's Ford. Union prisoner Private Nelson A. Fitts, 9th New York Heavy Artillery, stated that artillery, Union prisoners, wagon train and infantry all crossed at Edwards ferry

---

362 Hotchkiss, Diary, July 12, 1864, LOC; Old, Diary, July 12 &13, 1864, LOC; Jones, *Southern Historical Society Papers,* Vol. 1, p. 380; Beavans, Diary, July 12-13, 1864, UNC; Whitaker, Diary, July 12-13, 1864, HL; Atkinson, Report, July 22, 1864, HL; Swank, p. 82; William Williams Stingfellow, 69th NC, Diary, July 13, 1864, Collection 1091, North Carolina State Archives (NCSA); *OR*, 37, s. 1, pt. 2, p. 251, 259, 266, 415; Johnson, "My Ride...," p. 257

363 Beavans, Diary, July 13-14, 1864, UNC; Jones, *Southern Historical Society Papers,* Vol. 1, p. 380-381; Swank, p. 82

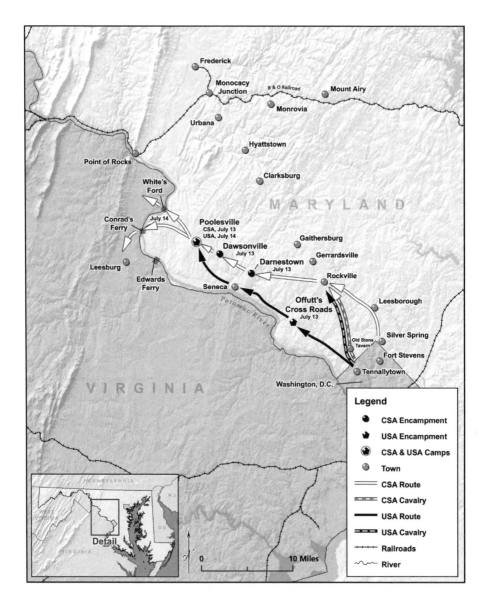

on the morning of the 14th. Fitts likely misidentified either White's Ford or Conrad's ferry as Edwards ferry. It is unclear where Gordon's and Rodes' divisions crossed.[364]

---

364 *OR*, 37, s. 1, pt. 1, p. 253; *OR*, 37, s. 1, pt. 2, p. 315, 316, 332, 344; Old, Diary, July 13-14, 1864, LOC; Swank, p. 83; Whitaker, Diary, July 14, 1864, HL; CPT Rufus J. Woolwine, 51st VA, Diary, July 14, 1864, Woolwine Papers, VHS

Aftermath

By the morning of July 13 skirmishing had ceased and as dawn enveloped the fields not a single Confederate soldier could be seen along the entire line. Two companies with cavalry on the flanks were sent out from Fort Stevens to reconnoiter the area and verify the absence of troops. As Early's army made its way to the Potomac River, Union forces in Washington took steps to determine where the Confederates had gone. Cavalry troops were sent toward Baltimore and Rockville to ascertain the route Early had taken. Meanwhile, Assistant Secretary of War Charles A. Dana sent a message to Grant:

> General Halleck will not give orders except as he receives them; the President will give none, and until you direct positively and explicitly what is to be done, everything will go on in the deplorable and fatal way in which it has gone on for the past week.

In the morning Wright received orders to be ready to move as soon as the Confederates could be located. As the troops waited, time was spent clearing obstructions and completing entrenchments. At Fort Slocum, which had not been heavily engaged, the troops immediately went to work clearing the timber and brush from the defenses. The fort was supplied with entrenching tools, axes and other supplies on the 12th that aided in accomplishing this task.[365]

As the Union army waited for the order to pursue Early, they began the grim task of recovering the dead and wounded from the battlefield. A Confederate hospital was found at Sligo Post Office in Silver Spring, where about 90 wounded soldiers and medical personnel were captured. All but 30 of these men were able to be moved to Lincoln Hospital in Washington, D.C. A number of wounded were also found on the grounds in front of Fort Stevens, in addition to those captured during the retreat. Confederates killed were buried in the area, but the largest concentration—17 men—would eventually be buried at Grace Episcopal Church. The largest concentration of Union killed—40 soldiers—would ultimately be laid to rest at Battle Ground Cemetery.[366]

There is very little specific information on casualties for either side. It is estimated that the Union took about 300, the majority of which came from the July 12 engagement. The Confederate numbers

---

365 *OR*, 37, s. 1, pt. 1, p. 232, 259; OR, 37, s. 1, pt. 2, p. 223, 259
366 *OR*, 37, s. 1, pt. 2, p. 232, 260, 263, 268; Benjamin F. Cooling III & Walton H. Owen II, *Mr. Lincoln's Forts: A Guide to the Civil War Defenses of Washington* (Lanham, MD: Scarecrow Press, 2010), p. 182, 184

are even more elusive. Union reports place Confederate casualties at roughly 200; however, this appears to be low. At least 300, if not more, seems more likely.[367]

Give Chase

Colonel Charles R. Lowell, Jr., and about 750 men from the 2nd Massachusetts Cavalry Regiment followed the Confederate rear guard to Rockville. At about noon, Lowell's advance guard of four companies, commanded by Lieutenant Colonel Casper Crowninshield, was sent west toward Darnestown, to observe the Confederate movements. Finding the rear guard, Crowninshield ordered an attack. His men charged and almost immediately found themselves attacked by a squad from General Bradley Johnson's cavalry brigade. Surprised and disorganized, Crowninshield's men fell back on Lowell's force at Rockville. Lowell dismounted his men, formed a line of battle and checked Johnson's pursuit after a spirited engagement. Johnson then engaged the rest of Lowells' brigade, which was forced to fall back to the south side of town. There they found Fry's detachment at the intersection of two roads. A strong dismounted skirmish line was established and held Johnson's troops. A short time later, Lowell discovered that Johnson had planned to flank his line and fell back two miles from Rockville.[368]

About 4:30 p.m. Wright was assigned as the principal commander of all the forces moving against Early's army. The pursuit began at 5:00 p.m. with the 1st and 2nd divisions, VI Corps and a portion of the XIX Corps passing Fort Reno by way of the Rockville Road. Taking River Road, they reached Offutt's Cross Roads about 6:30 p.m. and camped for the night. Major General Horatio Wright made the decision to delay the pursuit when his army of about 10,000 reached Poolesville on the evening of the 14th. Fearing that the size of the army was insufficient, Wright remained in camp until more troops of the XIX Corps caught up. Brigadier General William H. Emory arrived in Washington with 1,300 men from the XIX Corps on the 13th and another vessel with about 1,100 men was close by. The later vessel failed to navigate the river and ran aground down river. Additional ships continued to arrive with troops and make their way to Wright.[369]

---

367 *OR*, 37, s. 1, pt. 1, p. 232, 233, 237, 275
368 *OR*, 37, s. 1, pt. 1, p. 252, 260, 267-268, 280; Michael F. Fitzpatrick, "Jubal Early and the Californians," *Civil War Times*, May 1998, p. 54-61; Johnson, "My Ride...," p. 257
369 *OR*, 37, s. 1, pt. 1, p. 265-266, 267; *OR*, 37, s. 1, pt. 2, p. 258, 260, 261, 284, 285, 291, 350

While in camp on the 15th the army was summoned to witness an execution. Some time back a recent enlistee to the 67th New York Infantry killed and robbed a lieutenant and private. He deserted and escaped. While in Maryland this same soldier came into the Union lines as a Confederate deserter wishing to enlist in the Union army. He made one fatal mistake: He surrendered to pickets of the 67th New York. He was recognized and convicted as a deserter and spy. Surgeon Daniel Holt, 121st New York Infantry, who witnessed the hanging, stated that "he died of strangling. The neck was not broken, and at least fifteen [minutes] passed before he ceased to live." The next morning Wright moved his reinforced army toward White's Ford and crossed the Potomac River.[370]

With the threat to Washington alleviated, the civilian soldiers were relieved of duty on the evening of July 16. The following day, General Grant directed that the VI and XIX Corps pursue Early until it was certain that he was in full retreat toward Richmond, after which they were to return to Washington.[371]

Although the significance of Early's campaign has been forgotten over time, his retreat across the Potomac River into Virginia marked the end of the third and final major Confederate invasion of the north. The effort to capture Washington never fully developed, and in a sense mirrored Union Major General David Hunter's failed attempt to capture Lynchburg, Va., in June. Despite Early's failure to capture Washington, his campaign was still a success. Early accomplished his objectives by securing the Shenandoah Valley from Hunter, and in essence, removed that army from the campaign. Communication, railroad and canal operations and equipment were disrupted and destroyed. The army gathered horses, mules and other supplies. Early collected in excess of $220,000 in Union currency and captured roughly 600 Union soldiers. The national capital was threatened and panic spread throughout the northeast. As a result, Grant diverted troops to Washington (although not to the degree hoped for by Confederate General Robert E. Lee) and halted all offensive operations in Petersburg. If not for three factors, Early might have written a different chapter in American history. B&O Railroad President John Garrett's tireless effort to alert and aide the Union, Major General Lew Wallace's actions at the Battle of Monocacy and weather conditions all played a major role in saving the capital. Nine months later, the Civil War would end with a Union victory.

---

370 James M. Greiner, Janet L. Coryell and James R. Smither, eds. *A Surgeon's Civil War Letters & Diary of Daniel M. Holt, M.D.* (Kent, OH: Kent State University Press, 1994), p. 221-222; LT George Oscar French, 1st VT Heavy Artillery, July 15, 1864, Part 1, MSA 414, Civil War Letters 1864, VTHS; *OR*, 37, s. 1, pt. 1, p. 268
371 *OR*, 37, s. 1, pt. 1, p. 261; *OR*, 37, s. 1, pt. 2, p. 368

CONFEDERATE ORDER OF BATTLE

Army of the Valley District: Lt. Gen. Jubal A. Early

BRECKINRIDGE'S CORPS: Maj. Gen. John C. Breckinridge
GORDON'S DIVISION: Maj. Gen. John B. Gordon

Evans' Brigade: Brig. Gen. Clement A. Evans
13th Georgia Infantry Regiment: Colonel John H. Baker
26th Georgia Infantry Regiment: Colonel Edmund M. Atkinson
31st Georgia Infantry Regiment: Colonel John H. Lowe
38th Georgia Infantry Regiment: Major Thomas H. Bomar
60th Georgia Infantry Regiment: Captain Milton Russell
61st Georgia Infantry Regiment: Colonel John H. Lamar
12th Georgia Infantry Battalion: Captain J.W. Anderson

Consolidated Louisiana Brigade: Brig. Gen. Zebulon York
Hays' Brigade: Colonel William R. Peck
5th Louisiana Infantry Regiment: Major Alexander Hart
6th Louisiana Infantry Regiment: Lt. Colonel Joseph Hanlon
7th Louisiana Infantry Regiment: Lt. Colonel Thomas M. Terry
8th Louisiana Infantry Regiment: Captain Louis Prados
9th Louisiana Infantry Regiment: Lt. Colonel John J. Hodges

Stafford's Brigade: Colonel Eugene Waggaman
1st Louisiana Infantry Regiment: Captain Joseph Taylor
2nd Louisiana Infantry Regiment: Lt. Colonel Michael A. Grogan
10th Louisiana Infantry Regiment: Lt. Colonel Henry D. Monier
14th Louisiana Infantry Regiment: Lt. Colonel David Zable
15th Louisiana Infantry Regiment: Captain Henry J. Egan

Terry's Brigade: Brig. Gen. William Terry
2nd, 4th, 5th, 27th and 33rd Virginia
Consolidated Infantry Regiments: Colonel John H.S. Funk
21st, 25th, 42nd, 44th, 48th and 50th Virginia
Consolidated Infantry Regiments: Colonel Robert H. Dungan

10th, 23rd and 37th Virginia
Consolidated Infantry Regiments: Lt. Col. Samuel H. Saunders

<small>BRECKINRIDGE'S DIVISION:</small>   Brig. Gen. John Echols

Echol's Brigade   Colonel George Smith Patton
22nd Virginia Infantry Regiment: Lt. Col. John C. McDonald
25th Virginia Infantry Regiment: Captain William H. Fitchett
23rd Virginia Infantry Battalion: Lt. Col. Clarence Derrick
26th Virginia Infantry Battalion: Lt. Col. George M. Edgar

Wharton's Brigade: Brig. Gen. Gabriel C. Wharton
45th Virginia Infantry Regiment: Lt. Col. Edwin H. Harman
51st Virginia Infantry Regiment: Colonel Augustus Forsberg
30th Virginia Infantry Battalion: Major Peter Otey

Smith's Brigade: Colonel Thomas Smith
36th Virginia Infantry Regiment: Lt. Col. William Estill Fife
60th Virginia Infantry Regiment: Col. Buhring Hampden Jones
45th Virginia Infantry Battalion: Major Blake Lynch Woodson
Thomas' Legion: Major William W. Stringfield

Vaughn's Brigade: Brig. Gen. John C. Vaughn
Though a cavalry/mounted infantry unit, this brigade was dismounted when Early moved north into Maryland. Some elements of these units were left behind in the Shenandoah Valley.

1st Tennessee Cavalry Regiment: Colonel James E. Carter
39th Tennessee Mounted Infantry:*   Major Robert McFarland
43rd Tennessee Mounted Infantry: Captain Jasper N. Aiken
59th Tennessee Mounted Infantry: Colonel William L. Eakin
12th Tennessee Cavalry Battalion: Major George W. Day
16th Tennessee Cavalry Battalion: Lt. Col. John R. Neal
16th Georgia Cavalry Battalion: Lt. Col. Samuel J. Winn

*This regiment was first designated the 31st Tennessee Infantry Regiment.

<small>INDEPENDENT DIVISIONS:</small>

<small>RODES' DIVISION:</small>   Maj. Gen. Robert E. Rodes

Grimes Brigade: Brig. Gen. Bryan Grimes
2nd North Carolina Infantry Battalion: Colonel John P. Cobb
32nd North Carolina Infantry Reg: Colonel David G. Coward
43rd North Carolina Infantry Reg: Colonel Thomas S. Kenan

45th North Carolina Infantry Reg:	Colonel John R. Winston
53rd North Carolina Infantry Reg:	Colonel William A. Owens

Cook's Brigade: — Brig. Gen. Phillip Cook
4th Georgia Infantry Regiment:	Colonel William H. Willis
12th Georgia Infantry Regiment:	Captain James Everett
21st Georgia Infantry Regiment:	Colonel Thomas W. Hooper
44th Georgia Infantry Regiment:	Lt. Col. James W. Beck

Cox's Brigade: — Brig. Gen. William Cox
1st North Carolina Infantry Reg:	Lt. Col. Hamilton A. Brown
2nd North Carolina Infantry Reg:	Captain John P. Cobb
3rd North Carolina Infantry Reg:	Colonel S.D. Thurston
4th North Carolina Infantry Reg:	Colonel James H. Wood
14th North Carolina Infantry Reg:	Lt. Col. William A. Johnston
30th North Carolina Infantry Reg:	Colonel Francis M. Parker

Battle's Brigade: — Colonel Charles Pickens
3rd Alabama Infantry Regiment:	Colonel Charles Forsyth
5th Alabama Infantry Regiment:	Lt. Col. Edwin L. Hobson
6th Alabama Infantry Regiment:	Captain Rinaldo M. Greene
12th Alabama Infantry Regiment:	Colonel Samuel B. Pickens
61st Alabama Infantry Regiment:	Colonel William G. Swanson

RAMSEUR'S DIVISION: — Maj. Gen. Stephen D. Ramseur

Lilley's Brigade: — Brig. Gen. Robert D. Lilley
13th Virginia Infantry Regiment:	Major Charles T. Crittenden
31st Virginia Infantry Regiment:	Colonel John S. Hoffman
49th Virginia Infantry Regiment:	Captain William D. Moffett
52nd Virginia Infantry Regiment:	Colonel James H. Skinner
58th Virginia Infantry Regiment:	Colonel Francis H. Board

Johnston's Brigade — Brig. Gen. Robert D. Johnson
5th North Carolina Infantry Regiment:	Colonel John W. Lea
12th North Carolina Infantry Regiment:	Lt. Col. William S. Davis
20th North Carolina Infantry Regiment:	Colonel Thomas F. Toon
23rd North Carolina Infantry Regiment:	Colonel Charles C. Blacknall
1st N.C. Battalion Sharpshooters:	Major Reuben E. Wilson

Lewis' Brigade — Brig. Gen. William G. Lewis
6th North Carolina Infantry Regiment:	Lt. Col. Samuel M. Tate
21st North Carolina Infantry Regiment:	Major William J. Pfohl
54th North Carolina Infantry Regiment:	Lt. Col. Anderson Ellis
57th North Carolina Infantry Regiment:	Col. Archibald C. Goodwin

ARTILLERY:	Brig. Gen. Armistead Long

Nelson's Battalion: Lt. Col. William Nelson
Milledge's Georgia Battery: Captain John Milledge
Amherst Virginia Artillery: Captain Thomas J. Kirkpatrick
Fluvanna Virginia Artillery: Captain John L. Massie

Braxton's Battalion: Lt. Col. Carter Braxton
Allegheny Virginia Artillery: Captain John C. Carpenter
Stafford Virginia Artillery: Captain Raleigh L. Cooper
Lee Virginia Artillery: Captain William W. Hardwicke

McLauglin's Battalion: Lt. Col. J. Floyd King
The battalion was normally commanded by Major William McLauglin.

Lewisburg Virginia Artillery: Captain Thomas A. Bryan
Wise Legion Artillery: Captain William M. Lowry
Monroe Virginia Artillery: Major William McLauglin
This Battery was normally commanded by Capt. George B. Chapman.

CAVALRY:	Maj. Gen. Robert Ransom

McCausland's Brigade: Brig. Gen. John McCausland
14th Virginia Cavalry Regiment: Colonel James Cochran
16th Virginia Cavalry Regiment: Colonel Milton J. Ferguson
17th Virginia Cavalry Regiment: Lt. Col. W.C. Tavenner
22nd Virginia Cavalry Regiment: Colonel Henry S. Bowen

Johnson's Brigade: Brig. Gen. Bradley T. Johnson
8th Virginia Cavalry Regiment: Colonel James M. Corns
21st Virginia Cavalry Regiment: Colonel William E. Peters
34th Virginia Cavalry Battalion: Lt. Col. Vincent A. Witcher
36th Virginia Cavalry Battalion: Major James W. Sweeney
1st Maryland Cavalry Regiment: Captain Warner G. Welsh
2nd Maryland Cavalry Battalion: Major Harry W. Gilmor

Imboden's Brigade: Brig. Gen. John D. Imboden
18th Virginia Cavalry Regiment: Colonel George W. Imboden
23rd Virginia Cavalry Regiment: Colonel Robert White
62nd Virginia Mounted Infantry Regiment: Colonel George H. Smith

Jackson's Brigade: Colonel William L. Jackson
19th Virginia Cavalry Regiment: Lt. Col.William P. Thompson
20th Virginia Cavalry Regiment : Colonel William W. Arnett
46th Virginia Cavalry Battalion: Lt. Col. Joseph R. Kessler
47th Virginia Cavalry Battalion: Major William N. Harman

UNION ORDER OF BATTLE: HARPERS FERRY

RESERVE DIVISION: Major General Franz Sigel

Monocacy to Sleep Creek: Brig. Gen. Max Weber
Harpers Ferry and Maryland Heights Area:
5th New York Heavy Artillery
   (2nd and 3rd Battalions):   Colonel Samuel Graham
1st Penna. Light Artillery (Co. D):   Captain Andrew Rosney
11th West Virginia Infantry Regiment
   (Detachment):   Major James L. Simpson
17th Indiana Light Artillery Battery: Captain Milton L. Miner
1st West Va. Light Artillery (Co. A):   Captain George Furst
Kearneysville and Duffield's Areas:
1st Maryland Potomac Home Brigade: Lt. Col. Roger E. Cook
Martinsburg Area:
135th Ohio National Guard: Colonel Andrew Legg
152nd Ohio National Guard: Colonel David Putnam
160th Ohio National Guard: Colonel Cyrus Reasoner
161st Ohio National Guard: Colonel Oliver P. Taylor
32nd New York Independent
   Light Artillery Battery: Captain Charles Kusserow
1st West Va. Light Artillery (Co. F):   Captain George W. Graham
At Leetown:
10th West Virginia Infantry Regiment: Colonel Thomas M. Harris
23rd Illinois Infantry Regiment: Captain Samuel L. Simison
1st West Va. Light Artillery (Co. B):   Captain John V. Keeper
Location Not Identified:
Engineer Troops: Captain William P. Gaskill
Loudoun (Virginia) Rangers: Captain Daniel M. Keyes
Camp Distribution: Captain David S. Caldwell

West of Sleepy Creek: Brig. Gen. Benjamin F. Kelley
Sir John's Run Area:
153rd Ohio National Guard: Colonel Israel Stough
Cumberland Area:
152nd Ohio National Guard: Colonel David Putnam
6th West Virginia Cavalry Regiment: Lt. Col. Francis W. Thompson
1st West Va. Light Artillery (Co. E):   Lieutenant Francis M. Lowry
New Creek Area:
154th Ohio National Guard: Colonel Robert Stevenson

Patterson's Creek and South Branch Bridges:
6th West Virginia Infantry Regiment: Major John H. Showalter
Various Points Along B&O Railroad:
1st West Va. Light Artillery (Co. H):   Captain James H. Holmes
Location Not Identified:
2nd Maryland Potomac Home Brigade
   (Company F):   Captain Norval McKinley
   (Company K):   Captain Peter B. Petrie
1st West Virginia Cavalry Regiment
   (Company A):   Captain Harrison H. Hagan
16th Illinois Cavalry Regiment
   (Co. C, Schambeck's Ind. Cav.):   Captain Julius Jaehne
1st Illinois Light Artillery (Battery L):   Lieutenant John McAfee

1st Cavalry Division: Major General Julius Stahel
Martinsburg Area:
14th Pennsylvania Cavalry Regiment
   (Detachment):   Captain Ashbell F. Duncan
At Leetown:
1st New York Cavalry Regiment: Major Timothy Quinn
1st New York Veteran Cav. Reg.:   Lt. Col. John S. Platner
22nd Pennsylvania Cavalry Regiment
   (Detachment):   Colonel Jacob Higgins
15th New York Cavalry Regiment
   (Companies A, B, C and D):   Captain Oscar R. Colgrove
Shepardstown Area:
1st Maryland Potomac Home Brigade
   Cavalry Regiment: Major Robert S. Mooney
Pleasant Valley:
21st New York Cavalry Regiment: Lt. Col. Charles Fitz Simmon
Location Not Identified:
Engineer Troops: Lieutenant Levi Campbell, Jr.

UNION ORDER OF BATTLE: MONOCACY JUNCTION

MIDDLE DEPARTMENT AND
VIII ARMY CORPS: Major General Lew Wallace

1ˢᵗ Separate Brigade: Brig. Gen. Erastus B. Tyler
1ˢᵗ Maryland Potomac Home Brigade: Captain Charles J. Brown
3ʳᵈ Maryland Potomac Home Brigade: Colonel Charles Gilpin
11ᵗʰ Maryland Infantry Regiment: Colonel William T. Landstreet
144ᵗʰ Ohio National Guard (3 Co):   Colonel Allison L. Brown
149ᵗʰ Ohio National Guard (7 Co):   Colonel Allison L. Brown
Alexander's Baltimore Artillery: Capt. Frederick W. Alexander
8ᵗʰ New York Heavy Art. (10 Men):   Sergeant Peter S. Tower

Cavalry: Lt. Col. David R. Clendenin
8ᵗʰ Illinois Cavalry Regiment
(Co. B, C, I, K and M):   Lt. Col. David R. Clendenin
159ᵗʰ Ohio National Guard
(Mounted Infantry):   Captain Edward H. Leib
Mixed Cavalry: Major Charles A. Wells

3ᴿᴰ DIVISION, VI ARMY CORPS: Brig. Gen. James B. Ricketts
1ˢᵗ Brigade: Colonel William S. Truex
14ᵗʰ New Jersey Infantry Regiment: Lt. Col. Caldwell K. Hall
106ᵗʰ New York Infantry Regiment: Captain Edward M. Paine
151ˢᵗ New York Infantry Regiment: Colonel William Emerson
87ᵗʰ Pennsylvania Infantry Regiment: Lt. Col. James A. Stahle
10ᵗʰ Vermont Infantry Regiment: Colonel William W. Henry

2ⁿᵈ Brigade: Col. Matthew R. McClennan
The brigade was normally commanded by Colonel John F. Staunton.
9ᵗʰ New York Heavy Artillery
(1ˢᵗ & 3ʳᵈ Battalions):   Colonel William H. Seward

110th Ohio Infantry Regiment: Lt. Col. Otho H. Binkley
122nd Ohio Infantry Regiment
   (Co. B, C, E, I, K and part of F):   Lt. Charles J. Gibson
126th Ohio Infantry Regiment: Lt. Col. Aaron W. Ebright
138th Pennsylvania Infantry Reg.:*   Major Lewis A. May
*Matthew R. McClennan normally commanded this regiment.

The folowing units missed the battle and were found at Monrovia, Maryland.
6th Maryland Infantry Regiment: Captain John J. Bradshaw
67th Pennsylvania Infantry Regiment: Colonel John F. Staunton
122nd Ohio Infantry Regiment
   (Co. A, D, G, H and part of F):   Colonel William H. Ball

UNION ORDER OF BATTLE: NORTHERN DEFENSES OF WASHINGTON

(This is the order of battle on July11.
As the VI Corps arrived the troops shifted to different positions).

XII CORPS, DEPARTMENT OF WASHINGTON: Maj. Gen. Christopher Augur

NORTHERN DEFENSES OF WASHINGTON: Maj. Gen. Alexander McCook

Cavalry
8th Illinois Cavalry Regiment
    (Company D):   Captain Henry J. Hotopp
    (Company G):
    (Companies C and I):   Captain Albert Wells
7th Michigan Cavalry Regiment
    (Detachment):   Major Daniel H. Darling
2nd Massachusetts Cavalry Regiment
    (Detachment):   Colonel Charles R. Lowell, Jr.
Provisional Cavalry: Major William Fry

Hardin's Division: Brig. Gen. Martin D. Hardin
Fort Mansfield
24th U.S. Veteran Reserve Corps: Lt. Col. John F. Marsh

From Forts Kearny to Reno to Simmons
7th U.S. Veteran Reserve Corps: Colonel Edward P. Fyffe
9th New York Heavy Artillery (Battery):
1st U.S. Veteran Reserve Crops (Part):
2nd U.S. Artillery (Part of Battery I):
151st Ohio National Guard: Lt. Col. Richard T. Hughes
Fort Reno
151st Ohio National Guard (1 Company):

9th New York Heavy Artillery
(Company B):
2nd U.S. Artillery (Part of Battery I):   Lieutenant William P. Graves
150th Pennsylvania Infantry Regiment
(Company K):   Captain Thomas Getchell

Fort Kearny:
9th New York Heavy Artillery
(1 Company):   Lieutenant Charles W. Hough
151st Ohio National Guard (Co. K):   Captain Gilruth M. Webb
22nd U.S. Veteran Reserve Corps: Lt. Col. Allan Rutherford

Between Fort Kearny and Battery Smead
1st U.S. Veteran Reserve Corps: Lt. Col. Frederick E. Trotter

Battery Smead:
9th New York Heavy Artillery
(One Half of Battery E):
151st Ohio National Guard (Co. I):   Captain Joseph Chaney

Between Battery Smead and Fort De Russy:
19th U.S. Veteran Reserve Corps: Lt. Col. Oscar B. Dayton

Fort De Russy:
9th New York Heavy Artillery
(One Half of Battery L):   Lieutenant S. Augustus Howe
151st Ohio National Guard
(Companies C and G):   Major John L. Williams
1st Wisconsin Heavy Artillery
(Company A):   Captain Wallace M. Spear

Between Forts De Russy and Stevens:
1st Maine Light Artillery (2 guns):   Captain Albert W. Bradbury
147th Ohio National Guard: Colonel Benjamin F. Rosson
6th U.S. Veteran Reserve Corps: Lt. Col. Frederick S. Palmer
9th U.S. Veteran Reserve Corps: Lt. Col. Robert E. Johnston
157th Ohio National Guard: Colonel George W. McCook

Meigs' Division: Maj. Gen. Montgomery C. Meigs
Fort Stevens:
13th Michigan Independent
Light Artillery Battery: Lieutenant Charles Dupont

Provisional Brigade (Detachment):*
150th Ohio National Guard (Co. K):   Lt. Col. John N. Frazee
25th New York Cavalry Regiment
   (Detachment, Dismounted):

Between Forts Stevens and Slocum:
1st Ohio Independent Light Artillery
   (Battery L, 2 guns):   Captain Frank C. Gibbs
2nd District of Columbia Volunteers: Colonel Charles M. Alexander
12th U.S. Veteran Reserve Corps: Colonel Addison Farnsworth
Quartermaster Department Employees
   (3 Companies):

Fort Slocum:
14th Michigan Ind. Light Artillery: Captain Charles Heine
150th Ohio National Guard (Co. G):   Captain John Nevins
2nd Pennsylvania Heavy Artillery: Captain Joseph N. Abbey
Provisional Brigade (Detachment):*

Reserve Behind Fort Slocum:
Provisional Brigade:*

Between Forts Slocum and Totten:
Quartermaster Department Employees:
Provisional Brigade (Detachment):*   Colonel Francis Price

* The Provisional Brigade consisted of convalescents and troops from the hospitals and distribution camps.

Fort Totten:
150th Ohio National Guard: Colonel William Hayward

Gillmore's Division: Maj. Gen. Quincy A. Gillmore
Commanded Forts from Totten to Lincoln
The first troops of the XIX Corps that arrive were sent to Fort Lincoln.

VI ARMY CORPS: Maj. Gen. Horatio G. Wright

1st Division: Brig. Gen. David A. Russell
1st Brigade: Colonel William H. Penrose
4th New Jersey Infantry Regiment: Captain Ebenezer W. Davis
10th New Jersey Infantry Regiment: Lt. Col. William H. Tay
15th New Jersey Infantry Regiment: Lt. Col. Edward L. Campbell

2nd Brigade: Brig. Gen. Emory Upton
2nd Connecticut Heavy Artillery: Colonel Ranald S. Mackenzie

65th New York Infantry Regiment:	Colonel Joseph E. Hamblin
67th New York Infantry Regiment:	Lt. Col. Henry L. Van Ness
96th Pennsylvania Infantry Regiment:	Lt. Col. William H. Lessig
121st New York Infantry Regiment:	Major Henry M. Galpin
95th Pennsylvania Infantry Regiment:	Captain Francis J. Randall

3rd Brigade:	Colonel Olive Edwards
6th Maine Infantry Battalion:	Major George Fuller
37th Massachusetts Infantry Reg.:	Lt. Col. George L. Montague
23rd Pennsylvania Infantry Reg.:	Colonel John F. Glenn
49th Pennsylvania Infantry Reg.:	Major Amor W. Wakefield
82nd Pennsylvania Infantry Reg.:	Lt. Col. John M. Wetherill
119th Pennsylvania Infantry Reg.:	Lt. Col. Gideon Clark
2nd Rhode Island Infantry Reg.:	Major Henry C. Jenckes
5th Wisconsin Infantry Battalion:	Captain Charles W. Kempf

2nd Division:	Brig. Gen. George W. Getty
1st Brigade:	Brig. Gen. Frank Wheaton
62nd New York Infantry Regiment:	Captain Lewis J. Stewart
93rd Pennsylvania Infantry Regiment:	Lt. Col. John S. Long
98th Pennsylvania Infantry Regiment:	Lt. Col. John B. Kohler
102nd Pennsylvania Infantry Regiment:	Major Thomas McLaughlin
139th Pennsylvania Infantry Regiment:	Major Robert Munroe

2nd Brigade:	Brig. Gen. Lewis A. Grant
1st Vermont Heavy Artillery Regiment:	Colonel James M. Warner
2nd Vermont Infantry Regiment:**	Lt. Col. Amasa S. Tracy
3rd Vermont Infantry Regiment (5 Companies):**	Lt. Col. Stephen M. Pingree
4th Vermont Infantry Regiment:	Lt. Col. Stephen M. Pingree
5th Vermont Infantry Regiment:	Captain Friend H. Barney
6th Vermont Infantry Regiment:	Lt. Col. Oscar A. Hale

** These regiments were placed between Forts De Russy and Stevens.

3rd Brigade:	Colonel Daniel D. Bidwell
7th Maine Infantry Regiment:	Captain John W. Channing
43rd New York Infantry Regiment:	Captain Volkert V. Van Patten
49th New York Infantry Regiment:	Captain Erastus D. Holt
77th New York Infantry Regiment:	Lt. Col. Winsor B. French
122nd New York Infantry Regiment:	Major Jabez M. Brower
61st Pennsylvania Infantry Regiment:	Captain William H. Rodgers

Bibliography

Primary Source Material

Atkinson, COL Edmund N. Evan's Brigade. *Report*. July 22, 1864. Box 2. James Eldridge Collection. Huntington Library. San Marino, CA.

Baggs, George W. 36th OH. *Journal*. Charles Goddard Papers. Virginia Historical Society.

Battle, Cullen to John Campbell. July 14, 1864. Record Group 109. Register of Confederate Records. Telegrams Received by the Confederate Secretary of War. National Archives and Records Administration. Washington D.C.

Beavans, William. 43rd NC. *Diary*. No. 3244. Manuscript Department. University of North Carolina.

Bennette, J. Kelly. 8th VA Cavalry. *Diary*. Collection 886. University of North Carolina.

Beverige, Henry. 25th VA. *Diary*. Duke University Library.

Burrum, Absalom J. Thomas' Legion. *Diary*. Tennessee Historical Society.

Butler, William A. *Letter*. Company G 144th Ohio Volunteer Infantry. August 5, 1864. Civil War Newspapers: Wyandot County Correspondents. Center for Archival Collections. Bowling Green State University.

Chamberlayne, CPT Francis West. *Memoir*. Chamberlalyne Family Papers. Virginia Historical Society.

Clark, Will. *Letter*. July 11, 1864. 14th New Jersey File. Monocacy National Battlefield Archives.

Cordrey, SGT Francis. *Diary*. 126th Ohio File. Monocacy National Battlefield Archives.

Cowart, Enoch to Mary Ann Backus. August 10, 1864. Box 1. Folder 1. Cowart Family Papers. Monmouth County Historical Association Library & Archives. Freehold, NJ.

Davis, George E. 10th VT. Pension Record. National Archives and Record Administration. Washington D.C.

DeArmond, SGT Aaron L. 30th NC. *Diary*. Civil War Miscellaneous Collection. U.S. Army Military History Institute.

Douse, Hal. January 9, 2007, Email to Brett Spaulding, 10th Vermont File, Douse Folder, Monocacy National Battlefield Archives.

Dunbar, Ervin to George Douse. August 24, 1913. 10th Vermont File. Monocacy National Battlefield Archives.

Early, Jubal. *Letters*. Civil War Collection. Huntington Library. San Marino, CA.

Freeman, Daniel B., 10th VT, to Secretary of War. October 2, 1897. National Archives and Records Administration. Washington D. C.

French, LT George Oscar. 1st VT Heavy Artillery. July 15, 1864. Part 1. MSA 414. Civil War Letters 1864. Vermont Historical Society.

Fuller, Lewis. *Diary*. July 6, 1864. 106th New York File. Monocacy National Battlefield Archives.

Gilmor, MAJ Harry. *Report*. July 28, 1864. MS 1287. Harry Gilmor Papers. Maryland Historical Society.

Gordon, MG John to Robert E. Lee. February 6, 1868. Lee Headquarter Papers. Virginia Historical Society.

Gordon, MG John B. Report of Operations from June 28-July 9, 1864. Ni51. John Page Nicholson Collection. Huntington Library. San Marino, CA.

Halpine, LTC Charles G. *Diary*. Folder 191. Halpine Collection. Huntington Library. San Marino, CA.

Harper, COL George, to CPT Parker. AAG. July 31, 1864. Record Group 108. E112. National Archives and Records Administration. Washington D.C.

Hill, Robin Gustin, ed. A Civil War Diary kept by Josiah Lewis Hill from August 22, 1862 to July 1, 1865 and a History of the 110th Ohio Voluntary Infantry, (1986), 110th Ohio File, MNBA

Hoffman, G. Leonard to MG Lew Wallace. April 25, 1896. Lew Wallace Collection. Indiana Historical Society.

Hotchkiss, Jedediah. *Diary*. Manuscript Division. Library of Congress.

Hunter, MG David. Report of Operations June 8-July 14, 1864. Union Battle Reports. National Archives and Records Administration. Washington D.C.

Hyland, George. *Diary*. 8th Illinois Cavalry File. Monocacy National Battlefield Archives.

Johnson, Bradley T., to General John R. Kenly. July 10, 1864. Bradley T. Johnson Papers. Duke University Library.

Keifer, Joseph. *Official Report*. November 1, 1864. Box OV1. Joseph Warren Keifer Collection. Library of Congress

Keifer, COL Joseph W. *Official Report*. Box OV1. Joseph Warren Keifer Collection. Library of Congress.

King , LTC J. Floyd to MAJ J. Stoddard Johnston. July 22, 1864. Box 34. James Eldridge Collection. Huntington Library. San Marino, CA.

King, LTC Floyd to MAJ J. Stoddard Johnson. July 27, 1864. Thomas Butler King Papers. Southern Historical Society Collection. Univ. of North Carolina.

LaForge, Abiel T. *Diary*. 106th New York File. Monocacy National Battlefield Archives.

Long, Daniel. *Letters*. 151st New York File. Monocacy National Battlefield Archives.

McEntee, CPT J. to Colonel (Sharpe). July 1, 1864. Record Group 393. E3980. Army of the Potomac Miscellaneous Letters and Reports Received. National Archives and Records Administration. Washington D.C.

McClain, Samuel, 144th OH, to Lucinda. July 9, 1864. MS-640. Samuel McClain Papers. Center for Archival Collections. Bowling Green State Univ.

McMurran, SGM Joseph. 4th VA. *Diary*. Microfilm Reel Miscellaneous Nr 1316. Library of Virginia.

Meysenburg, MAJ Theodore A. Siegel's AAG. *Journal*. Duke Univ. Library.

Morrow, PVT Thomas E., 8th LA, to His Father. August 2, 1864. Special Collection. Tulane University Library.

Ord, MG Edward, to LG Ulysses Grant. July 12, 1864. Bradley T. Johnson Papers. Duke University Library.

Old, CPT William. Early's Adjutant. *Diary*. Manuscript Division. Library of Congress.

Randolph, CPT Buckner M. 49th VA. *Diary*. Randolph Sec. 10. Virginia Historical Society.

Read, LT James, 10th VT. *Diary*. James B. Ricketts Collection. Manassas National Battlefield Park Archives.

Read, LT James M., to His Father. July 19, 1864. 10th Vermont File. Monocacy National Battlefield Archives.

Roser, John, to His Wife Lucy. July 14, 1864. 110th Ohio File. Monocacy National Battlefield Archives.

Smith, Addison A. "The Story of The Life and Trials of A Confederate Soldier and The Great Loop He Made In Three Years, Including the Original Narrative and War Time Letters of Lieutenant Addison Austin Smith, Company G 17th Regiment of Virginia Cavalry, CSA." Unpublished Manuscript. Civil War Materials. Public Library. Jackson County, WV.

Snider, Joseph C. 31st VA. *Journal*. Accession #29147. Miscellaneous Nr 341. Library of Virginia.

Spaulding, Brett. 1/31/2007. Casualty List. Monocacy National Battlefield Archives.

St. Clair, Alexander, 16th VA Cavalry, to S.C. Graham. October 5, 1916. Tazewell County Historical Society Newsletter 1989. Virginia Historical Society.

Staunton, COL John F., 67th PA, to CPT A.J. Smith. 3rd Division AAG. August 8, 1864. COL Stanton Service Records. Record Group 94. National Archives and Records Administration. Washington D.C.

Staunton, COL John F., 67th PA. *Report*. August 8, 1864. National Archives and Records Administration. Washington D.C.

Staunton, COL John F., 67th PA, August 23, 1864. General Court Martial Proceedings. National Archives and Records Administration. Washington D.C.

Stingfellow, William Williams. 69th NC. *Diary*. Collection 1091. North Carolina State Archives.

Strather, COL David H., Hunter's Chief of Staff, Report of Operations May 21-August 9, 1864, Record Group 94, Serial 70, Box NR 72A, Union Battle Reports, National Archives and Records Administration. Washington D.C.

Stuart, Charles Thompson. "Autobiographical sketch of the war service of Charles Thompson Stuart, Lieutenant, Company H, 26th Regiment, Georgia Volunteers." Unpublished Manuscript. U.S. Army Military History Institute.

Terry, BG William. *Report*. July 22, 1864. Chicago Historical Society.

Toon, COL Thomas. 20th NC. *Diary*. Thomas Toon Papers. North Carolina State Archives.

Toon, COL Thomas. 20th NC, to CPT Halsey. August 1, 1864. Thomas Toon Papers. North Carolina State Archives.

Tynes, Achilles J. 8th VA Cavalry. *Letter*. June 22, 1864. Accession #27936. Library of Virginia.

Vredenburgh, MAJ Peter, 14th NJ, to His Mother. July 12, 1864. Collection 1. Folder 3. Peter Vredenburgh Papers. Monmouth County Historical Association Library & Archives. Freehold, NJ.

Waldrop, Richard W. 21st VA. *Diary*. Manuscript Department. University of North Carolina.

Walker, Aldace F. 11th VT, to His Father. July 11, 1864. Vermont Historical Society.

Wallace, MG Lew to Benson Lossing. July 24, 1864. Lew Wallace Papers. Indiana Historical Society.

Wallace, MG Lew to Senator Frye. April 13, 1896. Lew Wallace Collection. Indiana Historical Society.

Wesson, Silas D. 8th IL Cavalry. *Diary*. Civil War Times Illustrated Collection. U.S. Army Military History Institute.

Whitaker, CPT Cary. 43rd NC. *Diary*. BR 662. Brock Collection. Huntington Library. San Marino, CA.

Woolwine, CPT Rufus J. 51st VA. *Diary*. Woolwine Papers. Virginia Historical Society.

Wooley, LTC John to Col. Lew Wallace Collection. Indiana Historical Society.

York, BG Zebulon. *Report*. July 22, 1864. Ni 51. John Page Nicholson Collection. Huntington Library. San Marino, CA.

51st Virginia Record Book. Echols Division. 1864. Virginia Historical Society.

38th Annual Report of the President and Directors to the Stockholders of the Baltimore and Ohio Railroad Co., For the Year Ending September 30, 1864. Baltimore: J.B. Rose & Co.

Books

Abbott, Lemuel A. *Personal Recollections and Civil War Diary 1864*. Burlington, Vermont: Free Press, 1908.

Bain, William E. ed. *The B&O in the Civil War*. Denver, Colorado: Sage Books, 1966.

Beck, Brandon. *Third Alabama!: The Civil War Memoir of Brigadier General Cullen Andrews Battle*. Tuscaloosa, Alabama: The University of Alabama Press, 2000.

Benedict, George G. *Vermont in the Civil War: A History Of The Part Taken By The Vermont Soldiers And Sailors In The War For The Union 1861-5*, Vol. 2. Burlington, Vermont: The Free Press Association, 1888.

Buell, Augustus. *The Cannoneer: Recollections of Service in the Army of the Potomac*. Washington, D.C.: The National Tribune, 1890.

Cannon, James C. *Record of Service of Company K, 150th O.V.I. 1864*. Washington, D.C.: 1903.

Cooling, B. Franklin. *Monocacy: The Battle That Saved Washington*. Shippensburg, Pennsylvania: White Mane Publishing, 2000.

Cooling, Benjamin F. III and Walton H. Owen II. *Mr. Lincoln's Forts: A Guide to the Civil War Defenses of Washington*. Lanham, Maryland: Scarecrow Press, 2010.

Crow, Vernon. *Storm In The Mountains*. Cary, North Carolina: Cherokee, 1982.

Davis, George B., Leslie J. Perry and Joseph W. Kirkley. *The Official Military Atlas of the Civil War*. New York: Gramercy Books, 1983.

Donnelly, Ralph. *The Confederate States Marine Corps: The Rebel Leathernecks*. Shippensburg, Pennsylvania: White Mane, 1989.

Douglas, Henry Kyd. *I Rode With Stonewall*. New York: Van Rees Press, 1941.

Dowdey, Clifford and Louis H. Manarin. *The Wartime Papers of Robert E. Lee*. Boston: Dacapo Press, 1961.

Duncan, Richard R. *Lee's Endangered Left: The Civil War In Western Virginia Spring of 1864*. Louisiana State University Press, 1998.

Dunn, Wilbur R. *Full Measure of Devotion: The Eighth New York Volunteer Heavy Artillery* PART II. Kearney, Nebraska: Morris Publishing, 1997.

Durkin, Joseph T. ed. *Confederate Chaplain: A War Journal of Rev. James B. Sheeran, 14th Louisiana, C.S.A.* Milwaukee: Bruce Publishing Co., 1960.

Early, Jubal. *Narrative of the War Between the States*. Wilmington, North Carolina: Broadfoot, 1989.

Farrar, Samuel Clarke. *The Twenty-Second Pennsylvania Cavalry and the Ringgold Battalion 1861-1865*. Pittsburgh, Pennsylvania: The Twenty-Second Pennsylvania Ringgold Cavalry Association, 1911.

Freeman, Douglas Southall. *Lee's Lieutenants: A Study in Command*. New York: Simon and Shuster, 1998.

Gilmor, Harry. *Four Years In The Saddle*. New York: Harpers & Brothers, 1866.

Giunta, Mary A. ed. *A Civil War Soldier of Christ and Country: The Selected Correspondence of John Rodgers Meigs 1859-1864*. Urbana and Chicago: University of Illinois Press, 2006.

Goldsborough, Edward Y. *The Battle of Monocacy*. Frederick, Maryland: Historical Society 1898.

Gordon, General John B. *Reminiscences Of The Civil War*. New York: Charles Scribner's Sons, 1903.

Greiner, James M., Janet L. Coryell and James R. Smither. eds. *A Surgeon's Civil War Letters & Diary of Daniel M. Holt, M.D.* Kent, Ohio: Kent State University Press, 1994.

Hard, Abner. *History of the Eighth Cavalry Regiment Illinois Volunteers, During the Great Rebellion*. Aurora, Illinois, 1868.

Harris, Nathaniel E. *Autobiography: The Story of an Old Man's Life, with Reminiscences of Seventy-five Years*. Macon, Georgia: J.W. Burke, 1925.

Haynes, Edwin M. *A History of the Tenth Regiment Vermont Volunteers*. Lewiston, Maine: The Tenth Vermont Regimental Association, 1870.

Howell, Helena A. comp. *Chronicles of the One hundred fifty-first Regiment New York State Volunteer Infantry 1862-1865*. Albion, New York: A.M. Eddy, 911.

Johnson , Robert U. and Clarence C. Buel, eds. *Battles and Leaders of The Civil War*, Vol. IV. New York: The Century Co., 1887-1888.

Jones, Terry L. ed. *Campbell Brown's Civil War: With Ewell and the Army of Northern Virginia*. Louisiana University Press, 2001.

Judge, Joseph. *Season of Fire: The Confederate Strike on Washington*. Berryville, Virginia: Rockbridge, 1994.

Krick, Robert K. *Civil War Weather In Virginia*. Tuscaloosa: University of Alabama Press, 2007.

Lewis, Osceola. *History of the One hundred and Thirty-Eighth Regiment, Pennsylvania Volunteer Infantry*. Norristown, Pennsylvania: Iredell and Jenkins, 1866.

Martin, David G. *The Fluvanna Artillery*. Lynchburg, VA: H.E. Howard, Inc., 1992.

Martin, David G. ed. *The Monocacy Regiment: A Commemorative History of the Fourteenth New Jersey Infantry in the Civil War 1862-1865*. Highstown, New Jersey: Lonstreet House, 1987.

Mitchell, Joseph B. *Badge of Gallantry: Letters from Civil War Medal of Honor Winners*. New York: Macmillan, 1968.

Morris, George S. *Lynchburg in the Civil War*. Lynchburg Virginia: H.E. Howard, 1984.

Nichols, G. W. *A Soldier's Story of his Regiment (61st Georgia) and incidentally of the Lawton-Gordon-Evans brigade*. Jessup, Georgia: 1898.

Osborne, Charles C. *Jubal: The Life and Times of General Jubal A. Early, CSA*. Chapel Hill, North Carolina: Algonquin Books, 1992.

Pond, George E. *The Shenandoah Valley in 1864*. New York: Charles Scribner's Sons, 1883.

Pope, Thomas E. *The Weary Boys*. Ohio: The Kent State University Press, 2002.

Prowell, George R. *History of the Eighty-Seventh Regiment Pennsylvania Volunteers*. York, Pennsylvania: Press of the York Daily, 1903.

Quynn, William R. ed. *The Diary of Jacob Engelbrecht*. Frederick, Maryland: The Historical Society of Frederick County, 1976.

Roe, Alfred S. *The Ninth New York Heavy Artillery*. Worcester, Massachusetts, 1899.

Runge, William H. ed. *Four Years in The Confederate Artillery: The Diary of Henry Robinson Berkeley*. Chapel Hill: University of North Carolina Press, 1961.

Sheads, Scott and Daniel Toomey. *Baltimore During The Civil War*. Baltimore, Maryland: Toomey Press, 1997.

Shingleton, Royce Gordon. *John Taylor Wood: Sea Ghost of the Confederacy*. Athens, Georgia: University of Georgia Press, 1979.

Stephens, Robert Grier Jr. ed. and comp. *Intrepid Warrior Clement Anselm Evans Confederate General from Georgia: Life, Letters, and Diaries of the War Years*. Dayton, Ohio: Morningside, 1992.

Stotelmyer, Steven R. *The Bivouacs of the Dead*. Baltimore, Maryland: Toomey Press, 1997.

Swank, Walbrook D. ed. *Stonewall Jackson's Foot Cavalry: Company A, 13th Virginia Infantry*. Shippensburg, Pennsylvania: Burd Street Press, 2000.

Terrill, Newton. *Campaign of the Fourteenth Regiment New Jersey Volunteers*. New Brunswick: Daily Home News Press, 1884.

Tidwell, William A., James O. Hall and David Winfred Gaddy. *Come Retribution: The Confederate Secret Service and the Assassination of Lincoln*. Jackson, Mississippi: University Press of Mississippi, 1988.

Thomas, Benjamin P. ed. *Three Years with Grant As Recalled by War Correspondent Sylvanus Cadwallader*. New York: Alfred A. Knopf, 1955.

Toomey, Daniel C. *The Civil War In Maryland*. Baltimore, Maryland: Toomey Press, 2004.

U.S. Naval War Records Office. *Official Records of the Union and Confederate Navies in the War of the Rebellion*. Washington, 1894-1927, 30 Volumes.

U.S. War Department. *The War of the Rebellion: A Compilation of the Official Records of the Union and Confederate Armies*. Washington, 1880-1901, 128 Volumes.

Wallace, Lew. *Lew Wallace An Autobiography*, Vol. II. New York: Harpers & Brothers', 1906.

Welles, Gideon. *Diary of Gideon Welles: Secretary of the Navy under Lincoln and Johnson*, Vol. II. New York: Norton, 1960.

Wert, Jeffrey D. *Mosby's Rangers*. New York: Simon and Schuster, 1990.

Wild, Frederick W. *Memoirs and History of Capt. F. W. Alexander's Baltimore Battery of Light Artillery*. Loch Raven, Maryland: Press of the Maryland School for Boys, 1912.

Williams, Charles R. *The Life of Rutherford Birchard Hayes*. New York: Dacapo, 1971.

Williams, Thomas John Chew and Folger McKinsey. *History of Frederick County Maryland*, Vol. 1. Baltimore, Maryland: Regional, 1967; reprinted Genealogical, 2003.

Worthington, Glenn. *Fighting For Time*. Shippensburg, Pennsylvania: White Mane, 1985.

Articles and Essays

Bradwell, I.G. "Early's Demonstration Against Washington in 1864." *Confederate Veteran*. Vol. XXII. October 1914.

Bradwell, I.G. "On To Washington." *Confederate Veteran*. Vol. XXXVI. March 1928.

Bradwell, I.G. "In The Battle Of Monocacy, MD." *Confederate Veteran*. Vol. XXXVI. February 1928.

Bradwell, I.G. "Early's March To Washington In 1864." *Confederate Veteran*. Vol. XXVIII. May 1920.

Bradwell, I.G. "The Battle Of Monocacy, MD." *Confederate Veteran*. Vol. XXXVII. October 1929.

Brock, R.A. ed. *Southern Historical Society Papers* Vol. XXII. Richmond, Virginia: The Society, 1894; Reprint, New York: Kraus Reprint Company, 1977.

Brock, R.A. ed. *Southern Historical Society Papers* Vol. XXX. Richmond, Virginia: The Society, 1902; Reprint, New York: Kraus Reprint Company, 1977.

Brock, R.A. ed. *Southern Historical Society Papers* Vol. XXXVIII. Richmond, Virginia: The Society, 1910; Reprint, New York: Kraus Reprint Company, 1977.

Delaplaine, Edward. "General Early's Levy on Frederick." *Monocacy: July 9, 1864 The Battle That Saved Washington Centennial July 9, 1964*.

Duncan, Richard R. "Maryland's Reaction To Early's Raid In 1864: A Summer Of Bitterness." *Maryland Historical Magazine*. Fall 1969.

Fitzpatrick, Michael F. "Jubal Early and the Californians." *Civil War Times*. May 1998.

Hutcheson, James A. "Saved The Day At Monocacy." *Confederate Veteran*. Vol. XXIII. February 1915.

James, William H. "Blue and Gray: A Baltimore Volunteer of 1864." *Maryland Historical Magazine*. Vol. XXXVI, March 1941.

Johnson, Bradley. "My Ride Around Baltimore In Eighteen Hundred and Sixty-Four." *Journal of the United States Cavalry Association*. Vol. II. Fort Leavenworth, Kansas: 1889.

Jones, J. William. *Southern Historical Society Papers* Vol. 1. Richmond, Virginia: 1876.

Jones, J. William. *Southern Historical Society Papers* Vol. 9. January to December 1881. Millwood, New York: Kraus Reprint Company, 1977.

Neptune, Daisy C. "Flag of the Nighthawk Rangers." *Confederate Veteran* Vol. XL. 1932.

Moore, Frank. ed. *The Rebellion Record: A Diary of American Events* Vol. 10. New York: D. Van Nostrand, 1869.

Moore, Frank. ed. *The Rebellion Record: A Diary of American Events* Vol. 11. New York: D. Van Nostrand, 1869.

Thompson, Magnus S. "Plan To Release Our Men At Point Lookout." *Confederate Veteran*. Vol. XX. February 1912.

U.S. Army Center of Military History, Medal of Honor, Full Text of Civil War Citations; available from http://www.history.army.mil; Internet; accessed 23 January 2009

Wall, H.C. 23rd NC. p. 31-32. C.S.A. Archives. Army Units. Duke University Library.

Newspapers

Baltimore American

Baltimore Sun

Frederick News Post

Morgan County Herald

National Tribune

New York Daily Tribune

New York Times

Philadelphia Inquire

The Charleston Mercury

The Daily Journal

The Sunday Sun

The Valley Register

Index

About the Author

Brett W. Spaulding

Brett Spaulding is an Interpretive Park Ranger at Monocacy National Battlefield and a former U.S. Army Paratrooper. He graduated from The Pennsylvania State University, where he received a degree in Geography with a minor in History. He lives with his wife and two daughters in Maryland.